THE HIS...
THE COUNCILS ... ... CHURCH

VOLUME I: ANTE-NICENE COUNCILS

CHARLES JOSEPH HEFELE D. D.

THE HISTORY OF
THE COUNCILS OF THE CHURCH

VOLUME I: ANTE-NICENE COUNCILS

CHARLES JOSEPH HEFELE D. D.

TRANSLATED AND EDITED BY
WILLIAM R. CLARK

Editied and Re-typeset by
Paul A. Böer, Sr.

VERITATIS SPLENDOR PUBLICATIONS
et cognoscetis veritatem et veritas liberabit vos (Jn 8:32)
MMXVI

Cover Art

CATI DA IESI, Pasquale
The Council of Trent
1588
Fresco
Santa Maria in Trastevere, Rome

The text of this work is excerpted from:
Charles Joseph Hefele. *A History of the Councils of the Church. Volume I: Ante-Nicene Councils.* (Edinburgh: T & T Clark, 1871).

All texts are in the public domain.

Retypeset and republished in 2016 by Veritatis Splendor Publications.

Copyright © 2016. Veritatis Splendor Publications.

ALL RIGHTS RESERVED.

The typography of this publication is the property of Veritatis Splendor Publications and may not be reproduced, stored in a retrieval system, or transmitted in any form or by any means, in whole or in part, without written permission from the Publisher, except as permitted by United States and International copyright law.

Veritatis.splendor.publication@gmail.com

AD MAJOREM DEI GLORIAM

Table of Contents

A HISTORY OF THE
COUNCILS OF THE CHURCH:
VOLUMES 1 TO 5

CHARLES JOSEPH HEFELE D. D.

A HISTORY OF THE CHRISTIAN COUNCILS,
FROM THE ORIGINAL DOCUMENTS.

BY Charles Joseph Hefele, D. D., BISHOP OF
ROTTENBURG, FORMERLY PROFESSOR OF
THEOLOGY IN THE UNIVERSITY OF TÜBINGEN

Translated from the German, and Edited by
WILLIAM R. CLARK, M. A. OXON.,
PREBENDARY OF WELLS AND VICAR OF
TAUNTON.

EDINBURGH: T. & T. CLARK,
38, GEORGE STREET.
V1: 1871I. V2: 1876. V3: 1883. V4: 1895. V5: 1896.

BOOK I
ANTE-NICENE COUNCILS

PREFACE

"NO portion of Church History has been so much neglected in recent times as the History of the Councils. With the exception of a few monographs on particular synods, nothing of importance has appeared on this subject in our days. It is high time that this state of things should be altered, and altered not by a mere adaptation of old materials, but by a treatment of the subject suited to the wants of the present day. This has become less difficult, inasmuch as new documents have been brought to light, and we live in an age when many errors have been abandoned, many prejudices have been put on one side, great progress has been made in critical studies, and a deeper insight into the development of the Christian Church has undoubtedly been gained.

"I have been employed for a good many years in the composition of a History of the Councils of the Church, which should be of a comprehensive character, and founded upon original documents. I may affirm that I have spared no pains to secure accuracy, and have done my best to consult all the literature which bears upon the subject."

The hopes which Dr. Hefele thus expressed in his preface to the first volume of his History have been abundantly fulfilled. He has not only supplied an acknowledged want in his own country in a manner which leaves little to desire, but he has brought within the reach of all German scholars an amount of information in connection with the ancient councils which is to be found only in part even in those large collections of Hardouin and Mansi, which are seldom to be met with in private libraries. It is to be hoped that the interest manifested in that portion of his work which is translated in this volume may induce the publishers to carry it forward at least to the close of the fourth Œcumenical Council.

The Translator was at first in doubt as to the best form in which to present this History to the English public,—whether in the form of a paraphrase, in which case it must have been almost an original work, or as a simple translation. Various considerations induced him to adopt the latter course. There was little difficulty in doing so, as Dr. Hefele's German style, unlike that of many of his Protestant fellow-countrymen, is generally lucid and intelligible. The Editor, when he first undertook the work of preparing the History for English readers, intended to add a number of notes from writers who regard the subject from a different point of view. This he afterwards found to be unnecessary, and the additional notes are accordingly very few. Dr.

Hefele is so fair in the statement of facts, that every reader may very easily draw his conclusions for himself.

All possible care has been taken to make the references and quotations correct. It is almost certain, however, that slight mistakes may still be found in these pages; and the Editor will gratefully receive any corrections which may be forwarded to him, and make use of them should a second edition of the work be called for.

W. R. C.

INTRODUCTION

SEC. 1. Origin and Authority of Councils

THE two synonymous expressions, concilium and σύνοδος, signify primarily any kind of assembly, even a secular one; but in the more restricted sense of a Church assembly, i.e. of a regularly convoked meeting of the rulers of the Church for the discussion and decision of ecclesiastical business, the word concilium is found for the first time in Tertullian, and σύνοδος in the Apostolical Canons; while the Apostolical Constitutions designate even the ordinary meetings of Christians for divine service by the name of σύνοδος.

That the origin of councils is derived from the Apostolic Synod held at Jerusalem about the year 52, is undoubted; but theologians are not agreed as to whether they were instituted by divine or by human authority. The true answer to this question is as follows: They are an apostolical institution; but the apostles, when they instituted them, acted under the commission which they received from Christ, otherwise they could not have published the decisions of their synod with the words, "It seemed good to the Holy Ghost and to us." They must have been convinced that the Lord of the Church had promised and had granted His Spirit to the assemblies of the Church.

Later synods have acted and spoken in the same conviction, that the Holy Ghost governed the assemblies of the Church; and Cyprian in his time wrote, in the name of the Council over which he presided, A.D. 252, to Pope Cornelius: "It seemed good to us, under the guidance of the Holy Spirit" (Placuit nobis, Sancto Spiritu suggerente). To the same effect the Synod of Arles, A.D. 314, expressed itself: "It seemed good, therefore, in the presence of the Holy Spirit and His angels" (Placuit ergo, præsente Spiritu Sancto et angelis ejus: Hardouin, Collect. Concil. t. i. p. 262). And it was this conviction, which was so universal, that led the Emperor Constantine the Great to call the decree of the Synod of Arles a heavenly judgment (cæleste judicium); and he added, that the judgment of the priests ought to be so received as though the Lord Himself sat and judged (sacerdotum judicium ita debet haberi, ac si ipse DOMINUS residens judicet). Twenty years later he again publicly expressed the same belief, at the close of the first œcumenical council at Nicæa, in these words: "What seemed good to the three hundred holy bishops (that is, the members of the Nicene Synod) is no otherwise to be thought of than as the judgment of the only Son of God" (Quod trecentis sanctis episcopis visum est, non est aliud putandum, quam solius Filii Dei sententia). In perfect agreement with this are the testimonies of all the ancient Fathers, Greek as well as Latin, of Athanasius as of Augustine and Gregory the Great, the latter of whom goes so far as to compare the authority of the first four general councils with the importance of the four holy Gospels.

The earliest synods known to us were held about the middle of the second Christian century in Asia Minor: they were occasioned by the rise of Montanism. It is, however, not improbable that such assemblies were held earlier in the Greek Church, perhaps on account of the Gnostics, inasmuch as the Greeks from the earliest times had more inclination, and also greater need, for synods, than those of the Western Church.

SEC. 2. Different kinds of Synods

It has been customary, in dealing with ecclesiastical statistics, to divide the councils into four classes; but they may be more accurately divided into eight, since there have actually been ecclesiastical assemblies of the kinds described under the following numbers,—two, five, seven, and eight. Foremost of all stand,—

1. The Universal or Œcumenical Councils, at which the bishops and other privileged persons from all the ecclesiastical provinces of the world are summoned to be present under the presidency of the Pope or his legates, and are bound to attend, unless in case of reasonable hindrance; and whose

decisions are then received by the whole Church, and have the force of law for all the faithful. Hence it is clear that a council may possibly be intended to be œcumenical, and be summoned as such, and yet not receive the rank of an œcumenical synod,— as when its progress is stopped, or when it does not accomplish its object, or becomes divided, and the like; and for such reasons does not receive the approval of the whole Church, and particularly of the Pope. So it was with the so-called Latrocinium or Robber-Synod at Ephesus, A.D. 449. The bishops of all provinces were summoned, and the papal legates were present; but violence was used which prevented free discussion, so that error prevailed: and this Synod, instead of being recorded with honour, is marked with a brand on the page of history.

2. The second rank is given to General Councils or Synods of the Latin or Greek Church, at which were present the bishops and other privileged persons either of the whole Latin or of the whole Greek Church, and thus only the representatives of one-half of the whole Church. Thus, in the first instance, the Synod held at Constantinople, A.D. 381, was only a Greek or Eastern general council, at which were present all the four Patriarchs of the East,— those of Constantinople, of Alexandria, of Antioch, and of Jerusalem, with many other metropolitans and bishops. As, however, this Synod was

afterwards received by the West, it acquired the rank of an œcumenical council.

3. When the bishops of only one patriarchate or primacy (i.e. of a diocese, in the ancient sense of the word), or of only one kingdom or nation, assembled under the presidency of the patriarch, or primate, or first metropolitan, then we have respectively a national, or patriarchal, or primatial council, which frequently received the name of universal or plenary (universale or plenarium). The bishops of the Latin Church in Africa, for instance, metropolitans and suffragans, often assembled in synods of this kind under the Primate of Carthage; and in the same way the archbishops and bishops of all Spain under their primate, the Archbishop of Toledo. In still earlier times, the metropolitans and bishops of Syria assembled under the Archbishop of Antioch, their supreme metropolitan, afterwards called by the name of Patriarch.

4. A Provincial Synod is considerably smaller, and is formed by the metropolitan of an ecclesiastical province, with his suffragan bishops and other privileged persons.

5. Intermediate between the third and fourth classes are those synods, which are not uncommon in the history of the Church, in which the bishops of several contiguous ecclesiastical provinces united for the discussion of subjects of common interest.

They may be called the Councils of several United Provinces; and they rank lower than the national or primatial synod in this respect, that it is not the complete provinces of a nation or of a primacy which are represented in them.

6. By Diocesan Synods we understand those ecclesiastical assemblies which the bishop holds with his clergy, and over which he presides either personally or by his vicar-general.

7. Councils of a peculiar and even abnormal character, and known as σύνοδοι ἐνδημοῦσαι (Synods of Residents), were often held at Constantinople, when the Patriarch not unfrequently assembled around him bishops who happened to be staying (ἐνδημοῦντες) at Constantinople on private or other business, from provinces and patriarchates the most widely separated, for the discussion of important subjects, particularly for the decision of contests between the bishops themselves. We shall have occasion to adduce more on this subject when we come to discuss the ninth and twenty-eighth canons of Chalcedon.

8. Last of all, there appear in history not a few Mixed Councils (concilia mixta); assemblies in which the ecclesiastical and civil rulers of a kingdom meet together in order to take counsel on the affairs of Church and State. We come across them particularly in the beginning of the middle ages,—

not unfrequently in France, in Germany, in England, in Spain, and in Italy. Of this character are the fourth to the seventh Synods of Toledo, many synods held under Pepin, under Charles the Great [Charlemagne] and his successors, among others the Synod of Mainz, A.D. 852, and that held in the year 876 in the Palatium apud Ticinum, at which the election of Charles the Fat was approved by the bishops and princes of Italy. We shall further on meet with several English mixed councils, at which even abbesses were present. All such assemblies were naturally summoned by the King, who presided and brought forward the points which had to be discussed. The discussion was either carried on in common, or the clergy and the nobility separated, and formed different chambers,—a chamber of nobles, and a chamber of bishops,—the latter discussing only ecclesiastical questions. The decisions were often promulgated in the form of royal decrees.

Six grounds for the convocation of great councils, particularly œcumenical councils, are generally enumerated:

1. When a dangerous heresy or schism has arisen.

2. When two Popes oppose each other, and it is doubtful which is the true one.

3. When the question is, whether to decide upon some great and universal undertaking against the enemies of the Christian name.

4. When the Pope is suspected of heresy or of other serious faults.

5. When the cardinals have been unable or unwilling to undertake the election of a Pope.

6. When it is a question of the reformation of the Church, in its head and members.

Besides these, there may be many other kinds of reasons for the convocation of smaller synods; but all must have reference to the one supreme aim of all councils—"the promotion of the well-being of the Church through the mutual consultation of its pastors." In the ancient Church there were very many synods assembled, in order to resolve the contests of the bishops with one another, and to examine the charges brought against some of their number.

SEC. 3. By whom are Synods convoked?

If it is asked who convokes councils, there can be no controversy with regard to the greatest number of the eight kinds just specified. It is undoubted, that the ecclesiastical head of the diocese, the bishop, has to summon the diocesan synod; the ecclesiastical head of the province, the metropolitan, the provincial synod; the ecclesiastical head of a nation, a patriarchate, etc., the patriarch or primate, either at his own instance or at the wish of another, as of the sovereign, calls a national or primatial synod. It is equally clear, that when several provinces meet in a combined synod, the right of convocation belongs to the most distinguished among the metropolitans who meet. At the σύνοδος ἐνδημοῦσα, it was, of course, naturally exercised by the Bishop of Constantinople. Consequently, and from the very nature of the case, the summons to an œcumenical council must go forth from the œcumenical head of the Church, the Pope; except in the case, which is hardly an exception, in which, instead of the Pope, the temporal protector of the Church, the Emperor, with the previous or subsequent approval and consent of the Pope, summons a council of this kind. The case is similar with the other synods, particularly national synods. In the case of these, too, the temporal protector of the Church has occasionally issued the summons instead of the ecclesiastical ruler; and this not merely in ancient times in the Græco-Roman Church, but also later in the German and Roman States. Thus, e.g., Constantine the Great convoked the Synod of Arles in 314, and Theodosius the Great the Synod of Constantinople (already mentioned) in 381, in concert with the four Eastern patriarchs; Childebert, king of the Franks, a national synod at Orleans in the year 549; and Charles the

Great, in the year 794, the great Synod of Frankfurt. Even the Arian sovereign, Theodoric the Great, at the beginning of the sixth century, gave orders for the discontinuance of several orthodox synods at Rome. Further examples are noted by Hardouin.

Among those councils which were called by the emperors, the latter undertook many kinds of expenses, particularly the expense of travelling incurred by the numerous bishops, for whom they ordered houses and carriages to be put at their disposal at the public expense. This was done by Constantine the Great at the calling of the Synods of Arles and Nicæa. They also provided for the entertainment of the bishops during the sitting of those assemblies. At the later councils—those of Florence and Trent, for example—many of the expenses were borne by the Popes, the Christian princes, and the cities in which the synods were held.

Bellarmin endeavoured to prove, that it was formally recognised in the ancient Church that the calling of synods belonged to the hierarchical chiefs, and the summoning of œcumenical councils in particular to the Pope; but several of the passages which he adduces in proof are from the Pseudo-Isidore, and therefore destitute of all importance, while others rest upon an incorrect explanation of the words referred to. Thus, Bellarmin appeals above all to the legates of Leo I., who at the fourth Œcumenical

Council—that of Chalcedon in 451—had demanded the deposition of the Patriarch Dioscurus of Alexandria, because he had ventured to call an œcumenical council without permission from Rome. Their words are: σύνοδον ἐτόλμησε ποιῆσαι ἐπιτροπῆς δίχα τοῦ ἀποστολικοῦ θρόνου. In their obvious meaning, these words bear the sense indicated, and they are generally so explained. As, however, Pope Leo the Great had, by sending his legates, recognised and confirmed the summoning of the Latrocinium, or Robber-Synod—for it is to this that the reference is made—we are under the necessity of understanding that Dioscurus was accused at Chalcedon of thrusting the papal legates into the background, and taking the direction and presidency of the Council into his own hands. This is the way in which it is understood by the Ballerini and by Arendt. At the same time, it must not be overlooked that the general nature of the expression of which the papal legates made choice at Chalcedon, certainly involves the other side of the papal claim, and implies not only the right to preside over synods, but to convoke them.

Bellarmin appeals further to the seventh Œcumenical Council, which in its sixth session rejected the iconoclastic Synod of 754, and refused to recognise it as œcumenical, for this very reason, that the summons for its assembling did not go forth from the Pope. What the Synod does in fact say, however, is, that "this Synod had not the Roman Pope as its co-operator" (οὐκ ἔσχε συνεργὸν τὸν τῶν Ῥωμαίων πάπαν). There is nothing said in particular of the Pope's taking part or not in the summoning of the Synod.

On the other hand, it is perfectly certain that, according to Socrates, Julius I., even in his time, about the year 341, expressed the opinion that it was an ecclesiastical canon, μὴ δεῖν παρὰ γνώμην τοῦ ἐπισκόπου Ῥώμης κανονίζειν τὰς ἐκκλησίας; and there can be no doubt, if these words are impartially considered, that they mean that it was "not lawful to pass canons of universal obligation at synods without the consent of the Bishop of Rome." The question which is here to be decided, however, is this: Who, as a matter of fact, called or co-operated in calling the œcumenical synods? And the answer is: The first eight œcumenical synods were convoked by the Emperors, all later ones by the Popes; but even in the case of the early synods, there, is a certain participation of the Pope in convoking them, which in individual cases is more or less clearly seen.

1. The fact that the summons to the first Œcumenical Synod proceeded from the Emperor Constantine the Great, cannot be disputed. As, however, none of the letters have come down to us, we cannot tell whether they referred to any consultation with the Pope. On the other hand, it is

27

undeniable that the sixth Œcumenical Synod in 680 expressly asserted that the Synod of Nicæa was summoned by the, Emperor and Pope Sylvester (Κωνσταντῖνος ὁ ἀεισεβέστατος καὶ Σιλβεστρος ὁ ἀοίδιμος τὴν ἐν Νικαίᾳ μεγάλην τε καὶ περίβλεπτον συνέλεγον σύνοδον). The same is stated in the ancient Liber Pontificalis attributed to Pope Damasus; and if this authority be considered of slight value, the importance of the former must be admitted. Had the sixth Œcumenical Council been held in the West, or at Rome itself, its testimony might perhaps seem partial; but as it took place at Constantinople, and at a time when the bishops of that place had already appeared as rivals of the Bishop of Rome, and moreover the Greeks formed by far the greater number present at the Synod, their testimony for Rome must be regarded as of great importance. Hence even Rufinus, in his continuation of the Ecclesiastical History of Eusebius, says that the Emperor summoned the Synod of Nicæa at the suggestion of the priests (ex sententia sacerdotum); and certainly, if several bishops were consulted on the subject, among them must have been the chief of them all, the Bishop of Rome.

2. With regard to the second Œcumenical Synod, it is commonly asserted, that the bishops who composed it themselves declared that they were assembled at Constantinople in accordance with a

letter of Pope Damasus to the Emperor Theodosius the Great. But the document which has been relied upon as authority, refers not to the Synod of the year 381, the second œcumenical, but, as we shall show further on in the history of this Council, to the Synod of the year 382, which actually did meet in accordance with the wish of Pope Damasus and the Western Synod at Aquileia, but was not œcumenical. It is without effect, moreover, that Baronius appeals to the sixth Œcumenical Council to prove that Pope Damasus had a part in the calling of the second Œcumenical Synod. For what the Council says is this: "When Macedonius spread abroad a false doctrine respecting the Holy Spirit, Theodosius and Damasus immediately opposed him, and Gregory of Nazianzus and Nectarius (his successor in the See of Constantinople) assembled a synod in this royal city." This passage is obviously too vague and indefinite to afford grounds for concluding that Pope Damasus co-operated in the summoning of the Synod. Nay more, the words, "Gregory of Nazianzus and Nectarius assembled a synod," rather exclude than include the co-operation of Damasus. Besides, it should not be forgotten that the Synod in question, held A.D. 381, as we have already remarked, was not originally regarded as œcumenical, and obtained this rank at a later period on its being received by the West. It was summoned as a general council of the Greek or Eastern Church; and if the Pope had no share in convoking it, no inference can be drawn from this fact unfavourable to his claim to summon œcumenical synods.

3. The third Œcumenical Council at Ephesus, in the year 431, was summoned, as the Acts prove, by the Emperor Theodosius, in union with his Western colleague Valentinian III. It is clear, however, that the Pope Celestine I. concurred, from his letter to Theodosius, dated May 15, 431, in which he says that he cannot personally be present at the Synod, but will send his representatives. Still more distinct is his letter to the Council itself, dated May 8, 431, in which he sets before the assembled bishops their duty to protect the orthodox faith, expresses his expectation that they will agree to the sentence which he has already pronounced upon Nestorius, and adds that he has sent his legates, in order that they may give effect to this sentence at Ephesus. The members of the Synod themselves saw and acknowledged that there was here not merely an assent to the convocation of the Synod, but also directions for their guidance, inasmuch as they declare, in their most solemn act, the sentence of condemnation against Nestorius: "Compelled by the canons and by the letter of our most holy father and fellow-servant Celestine, Bishop of Rome, we have come to this sad sentence of condemnation upon Nestorius." They expressed the same when they said that "the letter of the Apostolic See (to Cyril,

which he had communicated to the Synod of Ephesus) had already set forth the sentence and rule to be followed (ψῆφον καὶ τύπον) in the case of Nestorius; and they, the assembled bishops, had, in accordance with this judgment, followed up this rule." It is herein clearly acknowledged that the Pope had not simply, like other bishops, so to speak, passively agreed to the convocation of the Synod by the Emperor, but had actively prescribed to the Synod rules for their guidance; and had thus, not in the literal sense, but in a sense higher and more real, called them to their work.

4. The manner in which the fourth Œcumenical Synod at Chalcedon, A.D. 451, met together, we learn from several letters of Pope Leo I., and of the Emperors Theodosius II. and Marcian. Immediately after the end of the unhappy Robber-Synod, Pope Leo requested the Emperor Theodosius II. (October 13, 449) to bring together a greater council, assembled from all parts of the world, which might best meet in Italy. He repeated this request at Christmas in the same year, and besought the Emperor of the West also, Valentinian III., together with his wife and mother, to support his request at the Byzantine Court. Leo renewed his petition on the 16th of July 450, but at the same time expressed the opinion that the Council would not be necessary, if the bishops without it would subscribe an orthodox confession of faith. About this time

Theodosius II. died, and was succeeded by his sister S. Pulcheria and her husband Marcian. Both of them intimated immediately to the Pope their disposition to call the Synod which had been desired, and Marcian in particular asked the Pope to write and inform him whether he would attend personally or by legates, so that the necessary invitations might be issued to the Eastern bishops. But Pope Leo now wished at least for a postponement of the Council. He went even so far as to say that it was no longer necessary; a change in his views which has often been made a ground of reproach to him, but which will be thoroughly discussed and justified at the proper place in this History of the Councils. We will only point out, at present, that what Leo had mentioned in his 69th letter, during the lifetime of Theodosius II., as a reason for dispensing with the Council, had actually taken place under Marcian and Pulcheria, inasmuch as nearly all the bishops who had taken part in the Robber-Synod had repented of their error, and in conjunction with their orthodox colleagues had signed the epistola dogmatica of Leo to Flavian, which was, in the highest sense, an orthodox confession of faith. Moreover, the incursions of the Huns in the West had made it then impossible for the Latin bishops to leave their homes in any great number, and to travel to the distant Chalcedon; whilst Leo naturally wished, in the interest of orthodoxy, that many of the Latins should be present at the Synod. Other motives contributed to the same desire; among these the fear, which the result proved to be well grounded, that the Synod might be used for the purpose of altering the hierarchical position of the Bishop of Constantinople. As, however, the Emperor Marcian had already convoked the Synod, the Pope gave his consent to its assembling, appointed legates, and wrote to the Synod describing their duties and business. And thus he could say with justice, in his later epistle, addressed to the bishops assembled at Chalcedon, that the Council was assembled "by the command of the Christian princes, and with the consent of the Apostolic See" (ex præcepto Christianorum principum et ex consensu apostolicæ sedis); as, on the other hand, the Emperor at an earlier period wrote to the Pope, "The Synod is to be held te auctore." The Pope's share in convoking the Council of Chalcedon was, moreover, so universally acknowledged, that, soon after, the Bishop of Mæsia said, in a letter to the Byzantine Emperor Leo: "Many bishops are assembled at Chalcedon by the order of Leo the Roman Pontiff, who is truly the head of the bishops" (per jussionem Leonis Romani Pontificis, qui vere caput episcoporum).

5. There can be no doubt that the fifth Œcumenical Synod in the year 553, like the first four, was convoked by the Emperor (Justinian I.); but it is also certain that it was not without consultation with the

Pope. Vigilius says himself that he had agreed with the Emperor Justinian, in the presence of the Archbishop Mennas of Constantinople and other ecclesiastical and civil rulers, that a great synod should be held, and that the controversy over the three chapters should rest until this synod should decide it. Vigilius expressed his desire for such a synod in a second letter ad universam ecclesiam, whilst he strongly disapproved of the Emperor's intention of putting an end to the controversy by an imperial edict, and was for that reason obliged to take to flight. When they had become reconciled, Vigilius again expressed his desire for the holding of a synod which should decide the controversy; and the deputies of the fifth Council afterwards declared that he had promised to be present at the Synod. What is certain is, that Vigilius had desired the postponement of the opening, in order to wait for the arrival of several Latin bishops; and in consequence, notwithstanding repeated and most respectful invitations, he took no part in the sessions of the Synod. The breach was widened when, on the 14th of May 553, the Pope published his Constitutum, declaring that he could not agree with the anathematizing of Theodore of Mopsuestia and Theodoret. At the suggestion of the Emperor, the Synod at its seventh session, May 26, 553, decided that the name of Vigilius should be struck out of the diptychs, which was done, so that the Pope and the Council were now in open antagonism. In his decree to Eutychius of Constantinople, however, dated December 8, 553, and in his second Constitutum of February 23, 554, Vigilius approved of the decrees of the fifth Synod, and pronounced the bishops who had put them forth—that is, the members of the Synod—to be his brethren and his fellow-priests.

6. The case of the sixth Œcumenical Synod, A.D. 680, is quite the same as that of the third. The Emperor Constantine Pogonatus convoked it, and requested the Pope to send legates to it. Pope Agatho, however, not only did this, which involves an assent to the imperial convocation of the Synod; but he sent to the Emperor, and thus also to the Council, a complete exposition of the orthodox faith, and thus prescribed to it a rule and directions for its proceedings; and the Synod acknowledged this, as the Synod of Ephesus had done, inasmuch as they say, in their letter to Agatho, "Through that letter from thee we have overcome the heresy … and have eradicated the guilty by the sentence previously brought concerning them through your sacred letter" (ex sententia per sacras vestras literas de iis prius lata).

7. The seventh Œcumenical Synod—the second of Nicæa, in the year 787—was suggested to the Empress Irene by the Patriarch Tarasius of Constantinople, who endeavoured to restore the reverence for images and union with Rome. The Empress and her son, the Emperor Constantine,

approved of this; but before the imperial letters of convocation were issued, they sent an ambassador to Pope Hadrian I. with a letter, in which they requested him to be present at the projected Œcumenical Synod, either personally or at least by his representatives. In the October of the following year, Hadrian I. sent an answer to the Emperor and Empress, as well as to the Patriarch, and promised to send his legates to the intended Synod, which he afterwards did, and thereby practically declared his consent to its convocation. Nay more, in his letter to Charles the Great, he goes so far as to say, "And thus they held that Synod according to our appointment" (et sic synodum istam secundum nostram ordtinationem); and thereby ascribes to himself a still closer participation in the holding of this Synod.

8. The last synod which was convoked by an emperor was the eighth œcumenical, which was held at Constantinople in the year 869. The Emperor Basil the Macedonian had dethroned his former colleague Michael III., or The Drunken, and deposed his creature, the schismatical Photius, from the patriarchal chair, replacing the unlawfully deposed Ignatius, and thereby restoring the union of the Greek and Latin Churches. As, however, Photius still had followers, the Emperor considered it necessary to arrange the ecclesiastical relations by means of a new œcumenical council, and for that

purpose sent an embassy to Pope Nicolas I., requesting him to send his representatives to the intended Council. In the meantime Nicolas died; but his successor, Hadrian II., not only received the imperial message, but sent the legates, as it had been wished, to the Council, and thereby gave his consent to the convocation of this Œcumenical Synod.

All the subsequent œcumenical synods were held in the West, and summoned directly by the Popes, from the first of Lateran, the ninth Œcumenical Synod, to the holy Synod of Trent, while smaller synods were still convoked by Kings and Emperors; and Pope Leo X. declared in the most decided way, at the eleventh session of the fifth Lateran Synod, with a polemical reference to the so-called propositions of Constance, that the Pope had the right to convoke, to transfer, and to dissolve œcumenical synods.

SEC. 4. Members of Councils

In considering the further question, who has a right to be a member of a synod, it is necessary first to distinguish between the diocesan and other synods. For whilst in the latter either the only members or at least the chief members are bishops, the diocesan synod, with the exception of the president, is made up of the other clergy; and whilst the privileged members of the other synods have a votum decisivum, a vote in determining the decrees of the synod, those of the diocesan synod have only a votum consultativum, a right to be present and speak, but not to vote on the decrees. Here the bishop alone decides, the others are only his counsellors, and the decision is pronounced in his name. The members of the diocesan synod are divided into three classes.

1. Those whom the bishop is bound to summon, and who are bound to appear. To this class belong deans, archpresbyters, vicarii foranei, the vicar-general, the parochial clergy by deputies; and, according to more recent law and custom, the canons of cathedral churches, the provost and canons of collegiate churches, and the abbates sæculares.

2. Those whom the bishop may, but need not summon, but who are bound to come when he summons them; for example, the prebendaries of cathedrals who are not canons.

3. Lastly, those who in general are not bound to appear, as the clerici simplices. But if the synod has for its special purpose to introduce an improvement in the morals of the clergy, or to impart to them the decisions of a provincial synod, these must also appear when they are summoned.

With respect to the members of other kinds of synods, ancient Church history gives us the following results:—

1. The earliest synods were those held in Asia Minor about the middle of the second century, on the occasion of Montanism. Eusebius does not say who were present at them; but the libellus synodicus informs us that one of these synods was held at Hierapolis by Bishop Apollinaris with twenty-six other bishops, and a second at Anchialus by Bishop Sotas and twelve other bishops.

2. The next synods in order were those which were held respecting the celebration of Easter, in the second half of the second century. With reference to these, Polycrates of Ephesus tells us that Pope Victor had requested him to convoke in a synod the bishops who were subordinate to him, that he did so, and that many bishops had assembled with him in synod. In the chapters of Eusebius in which these two classes of councils are spoken of, only bishops are mentioned as members of the Synod. And, in the same way, the libellus synodicus gives the number of bishops present at each council of this time, without referring to any other members.

3. The letters of convocation for an œcumenical synod were directed to the metropolitans, and to some of the more eminent bishops; and the metropolitans were charged to give notice to their

suffragans. So it was, e.g., at the convocation of the third Œcumenical Synod, for which an invitation was sent to Augustine, who was already dead. The invitation to appear at the synod was sometimes addressed to the bishops collectively, and sometimes it was simply required that the metropolitans should personally appear, and bring merely the most able of their suffragans with them. The latter was the case, e.g., in the summoning of the third and fourth Councils; to Nicæa, on the contrary, the bishops seem to have been invited without distinction. Sometimes those bishops who did not attend, or who arrived too late, were threatened with penalties, as well by. the Emperors, e.g. by Theodosius II., as by earlier and later ecclesiastical canons.

4. The chorepriscopi (χωρεπίσκοποι), or bishops of country places, seem to have been considered in ancient times as quite on a par with the other bishops, as far as their position in synods was concerned. We meet with them at the Councils of Neocæsarea in the year 314, of Nicæa in 325, of Ephesus in 431. On the other hand, among the 600 bishops of the fourth Œcumenical Council at Chalcedon in 451, there is no chorepiscopus present, for by this time the office had been abolished; but in the middle ages we again meet with chorepiscopi of a new kind at Western councils, particularly at those of the French Church, at

Langres in 830, at Mainz in 847, at Pontion in 876, at Lyons in 886, at Douzy in 871. Bishops without a diocese have a certain resemblance to these; and such we meet with at synods, as in the year 585 at Mâcon in France. It is disputed whether those who are merely titular bishops have a right to vote at a council; and it has generally been decided in this way, that there is no obligation to summon such, but when they are summoned they have a right to vote.

5. Towards the middle of the third century we find a departure from this ancient practice of having only bishops as members of synods, first in Africa, when Cyprian assembled, at those synods which he held with reference to the restoration of the lapsed, besides the bishops of his province and his clergy, confessores et laicos stantes, i.e. those laymen who lay under no ecclesiastical penance. So there were present at the Synod held by S. Cyprian on the subject of baptism by heretics, on the 1st of September (probably A.D. 256), besides eighty-seven bishops, very many priests and deacons, and maxima pars plebis. And the Roman clergy, in their letter to Cyprian on the subject, request that the bishops will take counsel in synods, in common with the priests, deacons, and laicis stantibus. It must not be overlooked, however, that Cyprian makes a difference between the membership of the bishops and of others. We learn from his thirteenth letter, that the bishops come together with the clergy, and

the laity are only present (præpositi cum clero convenientes, præsente etiam stantium plebe); from his sixty-sixth letter, that the priests, etc, were the assessors of the bishops (compresbyteri, qui nobis assidebant). In other places Cyprian speaks only of the bishops as members of the synod, and from other passages it comes out that the bishops had at these synods taken the advice and opinion of the laity as well as the clergy. It is never, however, in the least degree indicated that either the clergy or the laity had a votum decisivum; but the contrary is evident, namely, that in the Synod of Cyprian referred to, which was held September 1, 256, only bishops were voters.

6. Eusebius relates that a great number of bishops of Asia assembled in synod at Antioch in the year 264 or 265, on the subject of Paul of Samosata, and he adds that their priests and deacons came with them. In the following chapter Eusebius gives an account of the Synod at Antioch in 269, and makes special reference to the priest of Antioch, Malchion, who was present at the Synod, and by his logical ability compelled Paul of Samosata, who wanted to conceal his false doctrine, to explain himself clearly. In addition to this, Eusebius gives in the thirtieth chapter the circular letter which this Synod, after pronouncing the deposition of Paul, addressed to the rest of the Church. And this letter is sent forth not in, the name of the bishops only, but of the other

clergy who were present as well; and among these Malchion is named in the superscription, whilst the names of many of the bishops—and according to Athanasius there were seventy present—are wanting. We see, then, that priests and deacons were members of several synods; but we cannot determine from the original documents how far their rights extended, and whether they had more than a mere consultative voice in the acts of the synod. As far as analogy can guide us, it would appear they had no more.

7. In the two Arabian Synods which were held on the subject of Beryllus and the Hypnopsychites, Origen held a place similar to that which had been occupied by Malchion. The bishops summoned him to the Synod, so as to render his learning and ability serviceable to the Church; but it was the bishops themselves who held the Synod.

8. In many synods of the following centuries, besides the bishops, priests and deacons were present. So it was at Elvira, at Arles, at Carthage in 397, at Toledo in 400, etc. The bishops and priests had seats, but the deacons had to stand. The decrees of the ancient synods were for the most part signed only by the bishops. It was so at the Councils of Ancyra, of Neocæsarea—although in this case the subscriptions are somewhat doubtful; at the first and second Œcumenical Councils, those of Nicæa and Constantinople; at the Councils of

Antioch in 341, of Sardica, etc. Sometimes also the priests and deacons subscribed the decrees, and then either immediately after the name of their own bishop, as at Arles, or else after the names of all the bishops. It was, however, not so common for the priests and deacons to join in the subscription, and it did not occur in the fourth or fifth century: for we find that, even in the case of synods at which we know that priests and deacons were present, only bishops subscribed; as at Nicæa, at Carthage in 397, 389, 401, at Toledo in 400, and at the Œcumenical Councils of Ephesus. and Chalcedon.[1] At a later period we meet again, at some synods, with signatures of priests and deacons, as at Lyons in 830.[1] The difference between the rights of the priests and those of the bishops is made clear by the signatures of the Council of Constantinople under Flavian in 448. The deposition of Eutyches which was there pronounced was subscribed by the bishops with the formula, ὁρίσας ὑπέγραψα, definiens subscripsi, and afterwards by twenty-three archimandrites, or superiors of convents, merely with the word ὑπέγραψα without ὁρίσας.[1] At the Robber-Synod of Ephesus, on the contrary, along with other anomalies, we find the Archimandrite Barsumas of Syria signing, as a fully privileged member of the Synod, with the word ὁρίσας, and that because the Emperor Theodosius II. had summoned him expressly.

9. It is easily understood, and it is shown by the ancient acts of councils, that priests and deacons, when they were the representatives of their bishops, had a right to give, like them, a votum decisivum, and subscribed the acts of the synod with the formula ὁρίσας. And this is expressed at a much later period by the Synods of Rouen in 1581, and of Bordeaux in 1583,—by the latter with the limitation that only priests should be sent as the representatives of the bishops.

10. Other clergymen, deacons in particular, were employed at synods, as secretaries, notaries, and the like—at Ephesus and Chalcedon, for instance; and they had often no insignificant influence, particularly their head, the primicerius notariorum, although they had no vote. Some of these notaries were official, and were the servants of the synod; but besides these, each bishop could bring his own notary or secretary with him, and employ him to make notes and minutes of the sessions: for it was only at the Robber-Synod that the violent Dioscurus allowed no other notaries than his own, and those of some of his friends. From the nature of the case, there is nothing to prevent even laymen from being employed in such work; and we are informed distinctly by Æneas Sylvius that he performed such duties, as a layman, at the Synod of. Basle. It is, moreover, not at all improbable that the secretarii divini consistorii, who were present at some of the

ancient synods—at Chalcedon, for instance—were secretaries of the Imperial Council, and consequently laymen.

11. Besides the bishops, other ecclesiastics have always been brought in at councils, œcumenical as well as inferior, for the purpose of consultation, particularly doctors of theology and of canon law, as well as deputies of chapters and superiors of monasteries; and bishops were even requested to bring such assistants and counsellors with them to the synod. So it was at the Spanish Council at Tarragona in 516. But, at the same time, the fundamental principle is undoubted, that the vote for the decision of a question belonged to the bishops, as to those whom the Holy Ghost has appointed to rule the Church of God, and to all others only a consultative voice; and this was distinctly recognised by the Synods of Rouen in 1581, and Bordeaux in 1583 and 1684, partly in the most general way, in part specifically with reference to the deputies of chapters, titular and commendatory abbots. There has been a doubt with respect to abbots, whether they held a place similar to that of the bishops or not; and a different practice seems to have prevailed at different places and times. We have already seen that in the ancient Church the archimandrites had no vote, even when they were priests. On the other hand, a Synod at London, under the famous Dunstan Archbishop of

Canterbury, A.D. 1075, declares: "Besides the bishops and abbots, no one must address the Synod without the permission of the archbishop." The abbots are here plainly assigned a place of equality with the bishops as members of the Synod; and they subscribed the acts of this Synod like the bishops. In the same way the abbots subscribed at other synods, e.g. at Pontion in France, A.D. 876, at the Council held in the Palatium Ticinum, at Cavaillon, and elsewhere; but, on the other hand, at many other councils of the same time, as well as at those of an earlier and later period, the bishops alone, or their representatives, signed the decrees. So it was at Epaon in 517, at Lyons in 517, at Ilerda and Valencia in Spain in 524, at Arles in 524, at Carthage in 525, at Orange in 529, at Toledo in 531, at Orleans in 533; so also at Cavaillon in 875, at Beauvais in 875, at Ravenna in 877, at Tribur in 895. The archdeacons seem to have been regarded very much in the same way as the abbots, inasmuch as they appeared at synods not merely as the representatives of their bishops; but sometimes they signed the acts of the council, even when their bishop was personally present. So it was at the Synod of London already mentioned. At the end of the middle ages it was the common view that abbots and cardinal priests and cardinal deacons as well had a votum decisivum at the synods,—a fact which is expressly stated, as far as regards the abbots, by the historian of the Synod of Basle, Augustinus

Patricius, a Piccolomini of the fifteenth century. He adds, that only the Council of Basle allowed the anomaly, and conceded to other ecclesiastics the right of voting. But we must remark that, according to the statement of the famous Cardinal D'Ailly, even so early as at the Synod at Pisa in 1409, the doctors of divinity and of canon law had a votum decisivum; and that the Council of Constance extended this right, by adopting the division of the Council into nations. These were, however, anomalies; and after this stormy period had passed by, the ancient ecclesiastical order was restored, that only bishops, cardinals, and abbots should have the votum decisivum. A place of equality with the abbots was naturally assigned to the generals of those widespread orders, which had a central authority. This was done at the Council of Trent. With regard to the abbots, a distinction was made between those who possessed real jurisdiction, and those who were only titular or commendatory. To these last there was conceded no more than the votum consultativum; e.g. in the Synod at Rouen in 1581, and Bordeaux in 1583. The former went so far as to refuse to acknowledge any such right as belonging to the abbots; and a later synod at Bordeaux, in the year 1624, plainly declared that it was an error (erronea opinio) to affirm that any others besides bishops had a decisive voice in a provincial synod (præter episcopos quosdam alios habere vocem decisivam in concilio provinciali). In practice, however, abbots were still admitted, only with the distinction that the bishops were members of the synod "by divine right" (jure divino), and the abbots only "by ecclesiastical appointment" (institutione ecclesiastica).

12. We have already seen, that in the time of Cyprian, both in Africa and in Italy, laymen were allowed to be present at synods. This custom was continued to later times. Thus, e.g., the Spanish Synod at Tarragona, in 516, ordained that the bishops should bring to the Synod with them, besides the clergy, their faithful sons of the laity. Viventiolus Archbishop of Lyons, in the letter by which he summoned a synod at Epaon in 517, says: "Laicos permittimus interesse, ut quæ a solis pontificibus ordinanda sunt et populus possit agnoscere." [We permit the laity to be present, that the people may know those things which are ordained by the priests alone.] Moreover, the laity had the power of bringing forward their complaints with reference to the conduct of the clergy, inasmuch as they had a right to ask for priests of good character. The fourth Synod of Toledo, in 633, says expressly, that laymen also should be invited to the synods. So, in fact, we meet with distinguished laymen at the eighth Synod of Toledo in 653, and at the second of Orange in 529. In English synods we find even abbesses were present. Thus the Abbess Hilda was at the Collatio

Pharensis, or Synod of Whitby, in 664, where the question of Easter and of the tonsure, and other questions, were discussed; and the Abbess Ælfleda, the successor of Hilda, at the somewhat later Synod on the Nith in Northumberland. This presence of abbesses of the royal family is, however, exceptional, even when these assemblies were nothing else than concilia mixta, as Salmon, l.c., explains them to be. That, however, distinguished and well-instructed laymen should be introduced without delay into provincial synods, was expressly decided by the Congregatio interpret, concil. by a decree of April 22, 1598; and the Cæremoniale episcoporum refers to the same, when it speaks of the seats which were to be prepared at provincial synods for the laity who were present. Pignatelli recommends the bishops to be prudent in issuing such invitations to the laity; but we still find in 1736 a great many laymen of distinction present at the great Maronite Council which was held by Simon Assemani as papal legate. At many synods the laity present signed the acts; but at others, and these by far the most numerous, they did not sign. At the Maronite Council just mentioned, and at the second of Orange, they did sign. It is clear from the passage already adduced, referring to the Synod of Epaon, that these laymen were admitted only as witnesses and advisers, or as complainants. It is remarkable that the laity who were present at Orange signed with the very same formula as the bishops,—

namely, consentiens subscripsi; whilst in other cases the bishops made use of the words definiens subscripsi; and the priests, deacons, and laymen simply used the word subscripsi. As was natural, the position of the laity at the concilia mixta was different: from the very character of these, it followed that temporal princes appeared as fully qualified members, side by side with the prelates of the Church.

13. Among the laity whom we find at synods, the Emperors and Kings are prominent. After the Roman Emperors embraced Christianity, they, either personally or by their representatives and commissaries, attended the great synods, and particularly those which were œcumenical. Thus, Constantine the Great was personally present at the first Œcumenical Council; Theodosius II. sent his representatives to the third, and the Emperor Marcian sent his to the fourth; and besides, at a later period, he was personally present, with his wife Pulcheria, at the sixth session of this Council of Chalcedon. So the Emperor Constantine Pogonatus attended at the sixth Œcumenical Council; at the seventh, on the other hand, Irene and her son Constantine Porphyrogenitus were present only by deputies; whilst at the eighth the Emperor Basil the Macedonian took part, sometimes personally and sometimes by representatives. Only in the case of the second and fifth Œcumenical Synods we find

neither the Emperors nor their representatives present; but the Emperors (Theodosius the Great and Justinian) were at the time present in the city of Constantinople, where those councils were held, and in constant communication with the Synod.

It was, as we perceive, simply at the œcumenical synods that the Emperors were present. To this fact Pope Nicholas I. expressly appeals in his letter to the Emperor Michael, A.D. 865, and infers from it that all other synods ought to be held without the presence of the Emperor or his representatives. In agreement with this Pope, a few years later the eighth Œcumenical Council declared, that it was false to maintain that no synod should be held without the presence of the Emperor; that, on the contrary, the Emperors had been present only at the œcumenical councils; and, moreover, that it was not proper for temporal princes to be present at provincial synods, etc., for the condemnation of the clergy. They might have added, that so early as the fourth century the bishops complained loudly when Constantine the Great sent an imperial commissioner to the Synod of Tyre in 335.

In the West, on the contrary, the Kings were present even at national synods. Thus, Sisenand, the Spanish King of the West Goths, was present at the fourth Council of Toledo in the year 633, and King Chintilan at the fifth of Toledo in 638; Charles the Great at the Council of Frankfurt in 794, and two

Anglo-Saxon Kings at the Collatio Pharensis, already mentioned, in 664. We find royal commissaries at the eighth and ninth Synods of Toledo in 653 and 655. In later times the opinion gradually gained ground, that princes had a right to be present, either personally or by representatives, only at the œcumenical councils. Thus we find King Philip le Bel of France at the fifteenth Œcumenical Synod at Vienne in 1311, the Emperor Sigismund at the Council of Constance, and the representatives (oratores) of several princes at the last Œcumenical Synod at Trent. Pius IV. and Pius V. forbid the presence of a royal commissary at the Provincial Synod of Toledo; but the prohibition came too late. When, however, a second Provincial Synod was held at Toledo in 1582, in the presence of a royal commissary, Rome, i.e. the Congregatio Concilii, delayed the confirmation of the decrees until the name of the commissary was erased from the acts of the Synod. The Archbishop of Toledo, Cardinal Quiroga, maintained that such commissaries had been present at the ancient Spanish synods; but Rome held fast by the principle, that except in œcumenical synods, ubi agitur de fide, reformatione, et pace (which treated of faith, reformation, and peace), no commissaries of princes had a right to be present. At the later œcumenical synods, this presence of princes or of their representatives beyond all doubt had no other significance than to ensure protection to the synods, to increase their authority, and to bring before them the special wishes of the different states and countries. The celebrated Cardinal D'Ailly long ago expressed this judgment clearly; and, as a matter of fact, there was never conceded to a prince or his orator the right to vote, unless he was also a bishop. In reference to the most ancient œcumenical synods, it has even been maintained that the Emperors were their presidents; and this leads us to the further question of the presidency of the synods.

SEC. 5. The Presidency of Councils

As the presidency of a diocesan synod belongs to the bishop, of a provincial synod to the metropolitan, of a national to the primate or patriarch, so, in the nature of the case, the presidency of an œcumenical council belongs to the supreme ruler of the whole Church—to the Pope; and this is so clear, that the most violent partisans of the episcopal system, who assign to the Pope only a primacy of honour (primatus honoris), yet do not in the least impugn his right to preside at œcumenical synods. The Pope may, however, exercise this presidency in person, or he may be represented, as has frequently been the case, by his legates. Against this papal right of presidency at œcumenical synods the Reformers brought forward the objection, that the history of the Church showed clearly that the Emperors had presided at some of the first eight councils. There was, indeed, no difficulty in bringing forward proof in support of their assertion, since Pope Stephen V. himself writes that the Emperor Constantine presided at the first Council of Nicæa, and the ancient acts of the synods frequently refer to a presidency of the Emperor or his representatives. But all such objections, however dangerous they may at first seem to be to our position, lose their power when we come to consider more closely the state of things in connection with the ancient councils, and are willing to discuss the matter impartially.

Let us begin with the eighth Œcumenical Synod, as the last of those which here come into question— that is to say, the last of the Oriental Synods—and from this ascend back to the first

1. Pope Hadrian II. sent his legates to the eighth Œcumenical Synod, on the express written condition, addressed to the Emperor Basil, that they should preside. The legates, Donatus Bishop of Ostia, Stephen Bishop of Nepesina, and Marinus a deacon of Rome, read this letter before the Synod, without the slightest objection being brought forward. On the contrary, their names were always placed first in the minutes; the duration of the sessions was decided by them; and they gave permission for addresses, for the reading of the acts of the Synod, and for the introduction of other members of the Synod; and appointed the questions for discussion. In short, they appear in the first five

sessions without dispute as the presidents of the Synod. At the sixth and following sessions the Emperor Basil was present, with his sons Constantine and Leo; and he obtained the presidency, as the acts relate. But these acts clearly distinguish the Emperor and his sons from the Synod; for, after naming them, they add, "the holy and œcumenical Synod agreeing" (conveniente sancta ac universali synodo). Thus we perceive that the Emperor and his sons are not reckoned among the members of the Synod, whilst the papal legates are constantly placed first among the members. It is the legates, too, who in these later sessions decide the subjects which shall be brought forward: they also are the first who sign the acts of the Synod, and that expressly as presidents (præsidentes); whilst the Emperor gave a clear proof that he did not regard himself as the real president, by wishing to sign them after all the bishops. The papal legates, on the other hand, entreated him to place his own and his sons' names at the top; but he decidedly refused this, and at last consented to sign after the representatives of the Pope and the Oriental bishops, and before the other bishops. In perfect agreement with this, Pope Hadrian II., in his letter to the Emperor, commended him for having been present at this Synod, not as judge (judex), but as witness and protector (conscius et obsecundator). Still less than the Emperors themselves had the imperial commissaries who were present at synods a right of presidency, since their names were placed, in all minutes of the sessions, immediately after the representatives of the patriarchs, but before the other bishops, and they did not subscribe the acts at all. On the other hand, it may be said that the patriarchs of the East—Ignatius of Constantinople, and the representatives of the others—in some measure participated in the presidency, since they are always named along with the Roman legates, and are carefully distinguished from the other metropolitans and bishops. They form, together with the Roman legates, so to speak, the board of direction, deciding in common with them the order of the business, regulating with them the rule of admission to the synod. They subscribe, like the legates, before the Emperor, and are named in the minutes and in the separate sessions before the imperial commissaries. But, all this being granted, the papal legates still take undeniably the first place, inasmuch as they are always the first named, and first subscribe the acts of the Synod, and, what is particularly to be observed, at the last subscription make use of the formula, "presiding over this holy and œcumenical synod" (huic sanctæ et universali synodo præsidens); whilst Ignatius of Constantinople and the representatives of the other patriarchs claim no presidency, but subscribe simply with the words, "As receiving this holy and œcumenical synod, and agreeing with all things which it has decided, and which are written here,

and as defining them, I subscribe" (sanctam hanc et
universalem synodum suscipiens, et omnibus quæ
ab ea judicata et scripta sunt concordans, et
definiens subscripsi). Moreover, as we find a
remarkable difference between them and the papal
legates, so there is also, on the other side, a
considerable difference between their signature and
that of the other bishops. The latter, like the
Emperor, have simply used the words, suscipiens
subscripsi, without the addition of definiens, by
which the votum decisivum was usually indicated.

2. At all the sessions of the seventh Œcumenical
Synod, the papal legates, the Archpresbyter Peter
and the Abbot Peter, came first; after them Tarasius
Archbishop of Constantinople, and the
representatives of the other patriarchs; next to them
the other bishops; and, last of all, the imperial
commissaries. The decrees were signed in the
same order, only that the imperial commissaries
took no part in the subscription. The Empress Irene
and her son were present at the eighth and last
session of the Council as honorary presidents, and
signed the decrees of the first seven sessions,
which had been already signed by the bishops.
According to a Latin translation of the acts of this
Synod, it was only the papal legates, the Bishop of
Constantinople, and the representatives of the other
Eastern patriarchs, who on this occasion made use
of the word definiens in subscribing the decrees,

just as at the eighth Council; but the Greek version of the acts has the word ὁρίσας in connection with the signature of the other bishops. Besides, we must not omit to state that, notwithstanding the presidency of the papal legates, Tarasius Archbishop of Constantinople had the real management of the business at this Synod.

3. At the sixth Œcumenical Synod the Emperor Constantine Pogonatus was present in person, together with several high officials of the state. The minutes of the sessions name him as president, and give the names of his officials immediately after his own. They next proceed to the enumeration of the proper members of the Synod, with the formula, "the holy and œcumenical Synod being assembled" (συνελθούσης δέ καὶ τῆς ἁγίας καὶ οἰκουμενικῆς συνόδου),—thereby distinguishing, as in the case already mentioned, the Emperor and his officials from the Synod proper; and name as its first members the papal legates, the priests Theodore and George, and the deacon John. So these legates are the first to subscribe the acts of the Council; and the Emperor signed at the end, after all the bishops, and, as is expressly stated, to give more authority to the decrees of the Synods, and to confirm them with the formula, "We have read and consented" (legimus et consensimus). He thus made a distinction between himself and the Synod proper; whilst it cannot, however, be denied that the

Emperor and his plenipotentiaries often conducted the business of the Synod.

4. At the fifth Œcumenical Council, as has been already pointed out, neither the Emperor (Justinian) nor yet the Pope or his legate was present. It was Eutychius, the Archbishop of Constantinople, who presided.

5. The fourth Œcumenical Council is of more importance for the question now before us. So early as on the 24th of June 451, Pope Leo the Great wrote to the Emperor Marcian that he had named Paschasinus Bishop of Lilybæum as his legate (prædictum fratrem et coepiscopum meum vice mea synodo convenit præsidere). This legate, Paschasinus, in the name of himself and his colleagues (for Leo associated with him two other legates—the Bishop Lucentius and the Priest Boniface), at the third session of Chalcedon, issued the announcement that Pope Leo had commanded them, insignificant as they were, to preside in his place over this holy synod (nostram parvitatem huic sancto concilio pro se præsidere præcepit); and soon after, Pope Leo wrote to the bishops of Gaul, speaking of his legates, in the following terms: "My brothers who presided in my stead over the Eastern Synod" (Fratres mei, qui vice mea orientali synodo præsederunt). Pope Vigilius afterwards asserted the same, when, in a circular letter addressed to the whole Church, he says, "over which our

predecessor of holy memory, Pope Leo, presided by his legates and vicars" (cui sanctæ recordationis decessor noster papa Leo per legatos suos vicariosque præsedit). Of still greater importance is it that the Council of Chalcedon itself, in its synodal letter to Pope Leo, expressly says, ὧν (i.e. the assembled bishops) σὺ μὲν ὡς κεφαλὴ μελῶν ἡγεμόνευες ἐν τοῖς τὴν σὴν τάξιν ἐπέχουσι; that is to say, "Thou, by thy representatives, hast taken the lead among the members of the Synod, as the head among the members of the body" These testimonies—especially the last—are of so much weight, that they would seem to leave no room for doubt. And yet, on the other hand, it is a matter of fact that imperial commissaries had the place of honour at the Synod of Chalcedon, in the midst, before the rails of the altar; they are the first named in the minutes; they took the votes, arranged the order of the business, closed the sessions, and thus discharged those functions which belong to the president of an assembly. In the sixth session the Emperor Marcian was himself present, proposed the questions, and conducted the business. In these acts the Emperor and his commissaries also appear as the presidents, and the papal legates only as first among the voters. How, then, can we reconcile the contradiction which apparently exists between these facts and the statements already made? and how could the Council of Chalcedon say that, by sending his legates, the Pope had taken the lead among the members of the Synod? The solution of the difficulty is to be found in the same synodical letter written by the Pope to the Synod. It reads thus: "Faithful Emperors have used the presidency for the better preservation of order" (βασιλεῖς δὲ πιστοὶ πρὸς εὐκοσμίαν ἐξῆρχον). In fact, this presidency which was granted to the imperial commissaries referred only to the outward working—to the material conducting of the business of the synod. They were not connected with the internal work, and left the decisions of the synods without interference, gave no vote in the determination of questions concerning the faith, and repeatedly distinguished between themselves and the council. The acts of Chalcedon also show the same distinction. After having mentioned the imperial commissaries, they add these words, "the holy Synod assembled," etc. We may add also, that neither the Emperor nor his commissaries signed the acts of the Council of Chalcedon: it was the Pope's legate who always signed first, and repeatedly added to his name, even when the Emperor was present, the title of synodo præsidens

We are thus gradually able to explain the double relations existing between the papal legates and the imperial commissaries, quite analogous to that expressed in the words of Constantine the Great: "And I am a bishop. You are bishops for the interior business of the Church" (τῶν εἴσω τῆς ἐκκλησίας); "I

am the bishop chosen by God to conduct the
exterior business of the Church" (ἐγὼ δὲ τῶν ἐκτὸς
ὑπὸ Θεοῦ καθεσταμένος). The official conduct of
business, so to speak, the direction τῶν ἔξω as well
as the seat of honour, was reserved for the imperial
commissaries. The Pope's legates, although only
having the first place among the voters, had the
presidency, κατὰ τὰ εἴσω, of the synod, that is, of
the assembly of the bishops in specie; and when the
imperial commissaries were absent, as was the
case during the third session, they had also the
direction of the business.

6. The Emperor Theodosius II. nominated the
Comes Candidian as his representative at the third
Œcumenical Council, held at Ephesus in 431. In a
letter addressed to the assembled fathers, the
Emperor himself clearly determined the situation of
Candidian towards the Council. He says: "I have
sent Candidian to your Synod as Comes sacrorum
domesticorum; but he is to take no part in
discussions on doctrine, since it is not allowable to
any one, unless enrolled among the most holy
bishops, to intermeddle in ecclesiastical
discussions" (ἀθέμιτον γὰρ, τὸν μὴ τοῦ καταλόγου
τῶν ἁγιωτάτων ἐπισκόπων τυγχάνοντα τοῖς
ἐκκλησιαστικοῖς σκέμμασιν … ἐπιμίγνυσθαι).

The Emperor then positively indicates what were to
be the duties of Candidian: namely, that he was to
send away the laity and the monks, if they repaired

in too great numbers to Ephesus; he was to provide for the tranquillity of the city and the safety of the Synod; he was to take care that differences of opinion that might arise between the members of the Synod should not degenerate into passionate controversies, but that each might express his opinion without fear or hindrance, in order that, whether after quiet or noisy discussions upon each point, the bishops might arrive at a unanimous decision. Finally, he was to prevent any one from leaving the Synod without cause, and also to see that no other theological discussion should be entered into than that which had occasioned the assembling of the Synod, or that no private business should be brought up or discussed.

Pope Celestine I. on his side had appointed the two bishops Arcadius and Projectus, together with the priest Philippus, as his legates, and had instructed them to act according to the advice of Cyril, and to maintain the prerogatives of the Apostolic See. The Pope had before nominated Cyril as his representative in the Nestorian matter, and in his letter of 10th of August 430 he invested him with full apostolic power. It is known that from the beginning Candidian showed himself very partial to the friends of Nestorius, and tried to postpone the opening of the Council. When, however, Cyril held the first sitting on the 24th June 431, the Count was not present, and so his name does not appear in the minutes. On the contrary, at the head of the list of the bishops present is found the name of Cyril, with this significant observation, "that he took the place of Celestine, the most holy Archbishop of Rome." Cyril also directed the order of the business, either in person, as when he explained the chief object of the deliberations, or else through Peter, one of his priests, whom he made primicerius notariorum. Cyril was also the first to sign the acts of the first session, and the sentence of deposition pronounced against Nestorius.

In consequence of this deposition, Count Candidian became the open opponent of the Synod, and the protector of the party of Antioch, who held an unlawful council of their own under John of Antioch. Cyril notwithstanding fixed the 10th July 431 for the second session, and he presided; and the minutes mention him again as the representative of Rome. The other papal legates, who had not arrived in time for the first, were present at this second session; and they shared the presidency with Cyril, who continued to be called in the accounts the representative of the Pope. Cyril was the first to sign; after him came the legate Arcadius; then Juvenal of Jerusalem; next, the second legate Projectus; then came Flavian bishop of Philippi; and after him the third legate, the priest Philip. All the ancient documents are unanimous in affirming that Cyril presided over the Council in the name of Pope

Celestine. Evagrius says the same; so Pope Vigilius in the profession of faith which he signed; and Mansuetus Bishop of Milan, in his letter to the Emperor Constantine Pogonatus.1 In other documents Pope Celestine and Cyril are indiscriminately called presidents of the third Œcumenical Council; the acts of the fourth1 assert this several times, as well as the Emperor Marcian,1 and in the fifth century the Armenian bishops in their letter to the Emperor Leo.1

7. When we pass on to the second Œcumenical Council, it is perfectly well known and allowed that it was not presided over either by the Pope Damasus or his legate; for, as has been already said, this Council was not at first considered oecumenical, but only a general council of the Eastern Church. The first sessions were presided over by Meletius Archbishop of Antioch, who was the chief of all the bishops present, as the Archbishop of Alexandria had not arrived at the beginning. After the death of Meletius, which happened soon after the opening of the Council, it was not the Archbishop of Alexandria, but the Archbishop of Constantinople, Gregory of Nazianzus, who was the president, and after his resignation his successor Nectarius. This took place through the decision of the Council, which in its third session had assigned to the Bishop of new Rome— that is, Constantinople—the precedency immediately after the Bishop of old Rome.

8. The solution of the question respecting the presidency of the first Œcumenical Council is not without difficulty; and the greatest acumen has been displayed, and the most venturesome conjectures have been made, in order to prove that in the first Council, at any rate, the Pope was not the president. They have endeavoured to prove that the presidency belonged to the Emperor, who in a solemn discourse opened the series of the principal sessions, and took part in them, seated in the place of honour. But Eusebius, who was an eye-witness of the Council, and pays the greatest possible respect to the Emperor, says most explicitly: "After that (meaning after the opening discourse by the Emperor) the Emperor made way for the presidents of the Synod" (παρεδίδου τὸν λόγον τοῖς τῆς συνόδου προέδροις). These words prove that Constantine was simply the honorary president, as the Emperor Marcian was subsequently in the sixth session of the Council of Chalcedon; and, as a matter of course, he left to the ecclesiastical presidents the conducting of the theological discussions. In addition to the testimony of the eye-witness Eusebius, we have to the same effect the following documents:—(a.) The acts of the Council of Nicæa, as far as they exist, contain the signatures of the bishops, but not that of the Emperor. And if that is true which the Emperor Basil the Macedonian said at the eighth Œcumenical Council, that "Constantine the Great had signed at

Nicæa after all the bishops," this proves conclusively that Constantine did not consider himself as the president proper of the Council. (b.) Besides, the Emperor was not present in person at the commencement of the Synod. It must, however, have had its presidents before the Emperor arrived; and a short sentence in Eusebius alludes to these presidents: παρεδίδου ... τοῖς προέδροις; that is, "He left the management of the continuation with those who had before presided." (c.) When several complaints of the bishops against each other were presented to him, the Emperor had them all burnt, and declared that it was not becoming for him to give judgment upon priests. (d.) We will finally recall these words of the Emperor already quoted, that he was the bishop of the outward circumstances of the Church; words which entirely agree with the position in the Council of Nicæa which we have assigned to him.

Who was, then, really the president of the Synod? Some have tried to solve the question by considering as president that bishop who was seated first at the right hand of the Emperor, and saluted him with a discourse when he entered the Synod. But here arise two observations: first, from the Greek word προέδροις it would appear that there were several presidents; and besides, it is not positively known who addressed the discourse to the Emperor. According to the title of the eleventh chapter of the third book of the Life of Constantine by Eusebius, and according to Sozomen, it was Eusebius of Cæsarea, the historian, himself; but as he was not a bishop of any apostolic or patriarchal see, he could not possibly have had the office of president. We cannot say either with the Magdeburg Centuriators, that Eusebius was president because he was seated first on the right side; for the president sat in the middle, and not at one side; and those patriarchs who were present at the Council (we use this term although it had not begun to be employed at this period), or their representatives, were probably seated together in the middle, by the side of the Emperor, whilst Eusebius was only the first of the metropolitans seated on the right side. It is different with Eustathius Archbishop of Antioch, who, according to Theodoret, pronounced the speech in question which was addressed to the Emperor. He was one of the great patriarchs; and one of his successors, John Archbishop of Antioch, in a letter to Proclus, calls him the "first of the Nicene Fathers." The Chronicle of Nicephorus expresses itself in the same way about him. He cannot, however, be considered as the only president of the Council of Nicæa; for we must regard the expression of Eusebius, which is in the plural (τοῖς προέδροις); and, besides, it must not be forgotten that the Patriarch of Alexandria ranked higher than the Patriarch of Antioch. To which, thirdly, it must be added, that the Nicene Council itself, in its letter to the Church of Alexandria, says: "Your bishop will give you fuller explanation of the synodical decrees; for he has been a leader (κύριος) and participator (κοινωνός) in all that has been done." These words seem to give a reason for the theory of Schröckh and others, that Alexander and Eustathius were both presidents, and that they are intended by Eusebius when he speaks of the πρόεδροι. But apart from the fact that the word κύριος is here used only as an expression of politeness, and designates perhaps merely a very influential member of the Synod, and not the president, there is this against the theory of Schröckh, which is expressly asserted by Gelasius of Cyzicus, who wrote a history of the Council of Nicæa in the fifth century: "And Hosius was the representative of the Bishop of Rome; and he was present at the Council of Nicæa, with the two Roman priests Vitus and Vincentius." The importance of this testimony has been recognised by all; therefore every means has been tried to undermine it Gelasius, it is said, writes these words in the middle of a long passage which he borrowed from Eusebius; and he represents the matter as if he had taken these words also from the same historian. Now they are not to be found in Eusebius; therefore they have no historical value. But it must be remarked, that Gelasius does not copy servilely from Eusebius; but in different places he gives details which are not in that author, and which he had learned from other sources. Thus, after the passage concerning Hosius, he inserts some additional information about the Bishop of Byzantium. A little further on in the same chapter, he changes the number of two hundred and fifty bishops, given by Eusebius, into "three hundred and more," and that without giving the least indication that he is repeating literally the words of Eusebius. We are therefore brought to believe that Gelasius has acted in the same way as to Hosius in this passage, by introducing the information derived from another source into the passage taken from Eusebius, and not at all from having misunderstood Eusebius.

When Baronius and several other Catholic ecclesiastical historians assign to the papal legate Hosius the honour of the presidency, they are supported by several authorities for this opinion besides Gelasius. Thus, S. Athanasius, in his Apologia de fuga, thus expresses himself about Hosius: ποίας γὰρ οὐ καθηγήσατο; that is to say, "Of what synod was he not president?" Theodoret speaks just in the same way: Ποίας γὰρ οὐχ ἡγήσατο συνόδου. Socrates, in giving the list of the principal members of the Council of Nicæa, writes it in the following order: "Hosius, Bishop of Cordova; Vitus and Vincentius, priests of Rome; Alexander, Bishop of Alexandria; Eustathius, Bishop of Antioch; Macarius, Bishop of Jerusalem." We see that he follows the order of rank: he would therefore never have placed the Spanish bishop, Hosius, before the great patriarchs of the East, if he had not been the representative of the Pope.

An examination of the signatures of the Council of Nicæa leads us again to the same conclusion. It is true that there are many variations to be found in these signatures, if several manuscripts are consulted, and that these manuscripts are often faulty and defective, as Tillemont has conclusively shown; but in spite of these defects, it is a very significant fact, that in every copy, without one exception, Hosius and the two Roman priests sign the first, and after them Alexander Patriarch of Alexandria signs. On this subject the two lists of signatures given by Mansi may be consulted, as well as the two others given by Gelasius: in these latter Hosius expressly signs in the name of the Church of Rome, of the Churches of Italy, of Spain, and of the West; the two Roman priests appear only as his attendants. In Mansi's two lists, it is true, nothing indicates that Hosius acted in the Pope's name, whilst we are informed that the two Roman priests did so. But this is not so surprising as it might at first sight appear, for these Roman priests had no right to sign for themselves: it was therefore necessary for them to say in whose name they did so; whilst it was not necessary for Hosius, who as a bishop had a right of his own.

Schröckh says that Hosius had his distinguished position on account of his great influence with the Emperor; but this reasoning is very feeble. The bishops did not sign according as they were more or less in favour with Constantine. If such order had been followed, Eusebius of Cæsarea would have been among the first. It is highly important to remark the order in which the signatures of the Council were given. The study of the lists proves that they followed the order of provinces: the metropolitan signed first, and after him the suffragans; the metropolitan of another province followed, and then his suffragan bishops, etc. The enumeration of the provinces themselves was in no particular order: thus the province of Alexandria came first, then the Thebäid and Libya, then Palestine and Phœnicia; not till after that the province of Antioch, etc. At the head of each group of signatures was always written the name of the ecclesiastical province to which they belonged; and this is omitted only in the case of Hosius and the two Roman priests. They signed first, and without naming a diocese. It will perhaps be objected, that as the Synod was chiefly composed of Greek bishops, they allowed the Westerns to sign first out of consideration for them; but this supposition is inadmissible, for at the end of the lists of the signatures of the Council are found the names of the representatives of two ecclesiastical provinces of the Latin Church. Since Gaul and Africa are placed at the end, they would

73

certainly have been united to the province of Spain, if Hosius had represented that province only, and had not attended in a higher capacity. Together with the two Roman priests, he represented no particular church, but was the president of the whole Synod: therefore the name of no province was added to his signature,—a fresh proof that we must recognise in him and his two colleagues the πρόεδροι spoken of by Eusebius. The analogy of the other œcumenical councils also brings us to the same conclusion; particularly that of the Council of Ephesus, in which Cyril of Alexandria, an otherwise distinguished bishop, who held the office of papal legate, like Hosius at Nicæa, signed first, before all the other legates who came from Italy.

It would be superfluous, in the consideration of the question which is now occupying us, to speak of the œcumenical councils held subsequently to these eight first, since no one doubts that these more recent councils were presided over either by the Pope or his legates. We will therefore conclude the discussion of this point with the remark, that if in some national councils the Emperor or Kings were presidents, it was either an honorary presidency only, or else they were mixed councils assembled for State business as well as for that of the Church.

The Robber-Synod of Ephesus, which was held in 449, departed from the rule of all the œcumenical councils in the matter of the presidency; and it is well to mention this Synod, because at first it was regarded as an œcumenical council. We have before said that the presidency of it was refused to the Pope's legates; and by order of the Emperor Theodosius II., who had been deceived, it was bestowed upon Dioscurus of Alexandria. But the sensation produced by this unusual measure, and the reasons given at Chalcedon by the papal legates for declaring this Synod of Ephesus to be invalid, indisputably prove that we may here apply the well-known axiom, exceptio firmat regulam.

SEC. 6. Confirmation of the Decrees of the Councils

The decrees of the ancient œcumenical councils were confirmed by the Emperors and by the Popes; those of the later councils by the Popes alone. On the subject of the confirmation of the Emperors we have the following facts:—

1. Constantine the Great solemnly confirmed the Nicene Creed immediately after it had been drawn up by the Council, and he threatened such as would not subscribe it with exile. At the conclusion of the Synod he raised all the decrees of the assembly to the position of laws of the empire; declared them to be divinely inspired; and in several edicts still partially extant, he required that they should be most faithfully observed by all his subjects.

2. The second Œcumenical Council expressly asked for the confirmation of the Emperor Theodosius the Great, and he responded to the wishes of the assembly by an edict dated the 30th July 381.

3. The case of the third Œcumenical Council, which was held at Ephesus, was peculiar. The Emperor Theodosius II. had first been on the heretical side, but he was brought to acknowledge by degrees that the orthodox part of the bishops assembled at Ephesus formed the true Synod. However, he did not in a general way give his confirmation to the decrees of the Council, because he would not approve of the deposition and exclusion pronounced by the Council against the bishops of the party of Antioch. Subsequently, however, when Cyril and John of Antioch were reconciled, and when the party of Antioch itself had acknowledged the Council of Ephesus, the Emperor sanctioned this reconciliation by a special decree, threatened all who should disturb the peace; and by exiling Nestorius, and by commanding all the Nestorian writings to be burnt, he confirmed the principal decision given by the Council of Ephesus.

4. The Emperor Marcian consented to the doctrinal decrees of the fourth Œcumenical Council, held at Chalcedon, by publishing four edicts on the 7th February, 13th March, 6th and 28th July 452.

5. The close relations existing between the fifth Œcumenical Council and the Emperor Justinian are well known. This Council merely carried out and sanctioned what the Emperor had before thought necessary and decided; and it bowed so obsequiously to his wishes, that Pope Vigilius would have nothing to do with it. The Emperor Justinian sanctioned the decrees pronounced by the Council, by sending an official to the seventh session, and he afterwards used every endeavour to obtain the approbation of Pope Vigilius for this Council.

6. The Emperor Constantine Pogonatus confirmed the decrees of the sixth Council, first by signing them (ultimo loco, as we have seen); but he sanctioned them also by a very long edict which Hardouin has preserved.

7. In the last session of the seventh Œcumenical Council, the Empress Irene, with her son, signed the decrees made in the preceding sessions, and thus gave them the imperial sanction. It is not known whether she afterwards promulgated an especial decree to the same effect.

8. The Emperor Basil the Macedonian and his sons signed the acts of the eighth Œcumenical Council. His signature followed that of the patriarchs, and preceded that of the other bishops. In 870 he also published an especial edict, making known his approval of the decrees of the Council.

The papal confirmation of all these eight first œcumenical councils is not so clear and distinct:

1. The signatures of the Pope's legates, Hosius, Vitus, and Vincentius, subscribed to the acts of the Council before the other bishops, must be regarded as a sanction from the See of Rome to the decrees of Nicæa. Five documents, dating from the fifth century, mention, besides, a solemn approval of the acts of the Council of Nicæa, given by Pope Sylvester and a Roman synod of 275 bishops. It is granted that these documents are not authentic, as we shall show in the history of the Council of Nicæa; but we nevertheless consider it very probable that the Council of Nicæa was recognised and approved by an especial act of Pope Sylvester, and not merely by the signature of his legates, for the following reasons:—

It is undeniable, as we shall presently see, that

α. The fourth Œcumenical Council looked upon the papal confirmation as absolutely necessary for ensuring the validity of the decrees of the Council; and there is no good ground for maintaining that this was a new principle, and one which was not known and recognised at the time of the Nicene Council.

β. Again, in 485, a synod, composed of above forty bishops from different parts of Italy, was quite unanimous in asserting, in opposition to the Greeks, that the three hundred and eighteen bishops of Nicæa had their decisions confirmed by the authority of the holy Roman Church (confirmationem rerum atque auctoritatem sanctæ Romanæ Ecclesiæ detulerunt).

γ. Pope Julius I. in the same way declared, a few years after the close of the Council of Nicæa, that ecclesiastical decrees (the decisions of synods) ought not to be published without the consent of the Bishop of Rome, and that this is a rule and a law of the Church.

δ. Dionysius the Less also maintained that the decisions of the Council of Nicæa were sent to Rome for approval; and it is not improbable that it was the general opinion upon this point which contributed to produce those spurious documents which we possess.

2. When the Pope and the Western bishops heard the decrees of the Council of Constantinople, held in 381, subsesequently accepted as the second Œcumenical Council, they expressed in an Italian synod their disapproval of some of the steps taken, although they had not then received the acts of the Council. Soon after they had received the acts, Pope Damasus gave his sanction to the Council. This is the account given by Photius. This approval, however, must have related only to the Creed of Constantinople; for the canons of this Council were

rejected by Pope Leo the Great, and subsequently, towards the year 600, still more explicitly by Pope Gregory the Great. That the Creed of Constantinople had, however, the approbation of the Apostolic See, is shown by the fact that, in the fourth General Council held at Chalcedon, the papal legates did not raise the least opposition when this creed was quoted as an authority, whilst they protested most strongly when the canons of Constantinople were appealed to. It was, in fact, on account of the creed having been approved of by the Holy See, that afterwards, in the sixth century, Popes Vigilius, Pelagius II., and Gregory the Great, formally declared that this Council was œcumenical, although Gregory at the same time refused to acknowledge the canons it had promulgated.

3. The third Œcumenical Council was held in the time of Pope Celestine, and its decisions were signed by his legates, S. Cyril, Bishops Arcadius and Projectus, and the Priest Philip. Besides this sanction, in the following year Celestine's successor, Pope Sixtus III., sanctioned this Council of Ephesus in a more solemn manner, in several circular and private letters, some of which have reached us.

4. The decisions of the fourth Œcumenical Council, held at Chalcedon, were not only signed by the papal legates present at the Council, except the canons, and thus obtained a first sanction from the

Apostolic See; but the Council, at the conclusion of its sessions, sent all the acts of the Synod to the Pope, in order to obtain assent, approval, and confirmation for them, as is expressly set forth in the letter written by the Synod to the Pope with these acts. We there read: πᾶσαν ὑμῖν τῶν πεπραγμένων τὴν δύναμιν ἐγνωρίσαμιν εἰς σύστασιν ἡμετέραν καὶ τῶν παρ' ἡμῶν πεπραγμένων βεβαίωσίν τε καὶ συγκατάθεσιν (We acknowledge the whole force of the things which have been done, and the confirmation of all that we have accomplished, to be dependent upon your approval). The Emperor Marcian, like the Council, requested the Pope to sanction the decrees made at Constantinople in a special epistle, which he said would then be read in all the churches, that every one might know that the Pope approved of the Synod. Finally, the Archbishop of Constantinople, Anatolius, expressed himself in a similar way to the Pope. He says: "The whole force and confirmation of the acts has been reserved for the authority of your Holiness" (Gestorum vis omnis et confirmatio auctoritati Vestræ Beatitudinis fuerit reservata). However, Pope Leo confirmed only those articles of the Council of Chalcedon which concerned the faith: he expressly rejected the twenty-eighth canon, which granted inadmissible rights to the Bishop of Constantinople, without taking into account the sixth canon of Nicæa. Leo pronounced the same judgment in several letters addressed either to the

Emperor or to the Empress Pulcheria; and he charged his nuncio at Constantinople, Julian Bishop of Cos, to announce to the Emperor that the sanction of the Holy See to the Council of Chalcedon should be sent to all the bishops of the empire.

5. We have already seen that it was after a protracted refusal that Pope Vigilius finally sanctioned the decrees of the fifth Œcumenical Council. We have still two documents which refer to this question,—a decree sent to S. Eutychius Bishop of Constantinople, and the constitutum of February 23, 554.

6. The decisions of the sixth Œcumenical Council were signed and accepted not only by the Pope's legates; but, like the Council of Chalcedon, this Synod also desired a special sanction from the Pope, and asked for it in a letter written by the Synod to the Pope, whom they name Caput Ecclesiæ, and his see prima sedes Ecclesiæ œcumenicæ. The successor of Pope Agatho, Leo II., gave this sanction in letters addressed to the Emperor and to the bishops of Spain, which still exist. It is true that Baronius has endeavoured to prove these letters to be spurious, because they also mention the anathema pronounced against Pope Honorius; but their authenticity cannot be doubted on good grounds, and it has been successfully maintained by others, particularly by

Pagi, Dupin, Dom Ceillier, Bower, and Natalis
Alexander.

7. As the Pope had co-operated in the convocation
of the seventh Œcumenical Council, which was
presided over by his legates, so it was expressly
sanctioned by Hadrian I., as he says himself in a
letter to Charles the Great. His words are: Et ideo
ipsam suscepimus synodum. However, the Pope
would not immediately send his sanction of the
Council to the Emperor of Constantinople, who had
asked it of him, because the Emperor did not
accede to two demands of the See of Rome with
respect to the jurisdiction of the Patriarchal See, and
the restitution of the property of the Church.
Subsequently Pope Hadrian confirmed the sanction
which he gave to the second Council of Nicæa, by
having its acts translated into Latin, sending them to
the Western bishops, and defending them against
the attacks of the French bishops in the "Caroline
Books."

8. Finally, the eighth Œcumenical Council had not
merely that kind of sanction which is involved in the
signatures of the Pope's legates at the end of its
acts: it desired a more solemn and express
approbation, and Hadrian II. yielded to this desire;
and in his letter addressed to the Emperor, he
sanctioned the dogmatic part of the decisions of the
Synod, but noted his dissatisfaction with respect to
other points. The fact that the Pope confirmed this

Council is, moreover, made clear by his subsequently having a Latin translation of its acts made by the learned abbot and librarian Anastasius, and by the fact that Anastasius without hesitation calls it an Œcumenical Council in the preface addressed to the Pope at the commencement of his translation.

It would be superfluous to show that the Popes always confirmed the œcumenical councils of later times; for it is universally known that the influence of the Popes in all later Western councils has been greater, and that of the Emperor less, than in the first eight councils. Popes have often presided in person over these more recent councils, and then they could give their approbation orally. So it was in the ninth, the tenth, and the eleventh Œcumenical Councils: it was also the case in all the subsequent ones, except those of Basle and Trent; but the latter asked for and obtained an express confirmation from the Pope. Even in the middle ages several distinguished canonists demonstrated with much perspicuity that this papal approbation was necessary for the validity of œcumenical councils; and we shall see the reason for this statement: for the discussion of the celebrated question, "Is the Pope superior or inferior to an œcumenical council?" necessarily leads us to study more closely the relations which obtain between the Pope and the œcumenical council.

SEC. 7. Relation of the Pope to the Œcumenical Council

As every one knows, the Councils of Constance and Basle asserted the superiority of the œcumenical council to the Holy See; and the French theologians placed this proposition among the quatuor propositiones Cleri Gallicani—the so-called Gallican Liberties. Other theologians have affirmed the contrary, saying that the Pope is superior to an œcumenical council: for example, Roncaglia, in his learned reply to Natalis Alexander's dissertation; also, before Roncaglia, the pros and cons had been disputed at great length and with much animation. The Ultramontanes especially relied upon the fact that, at the fifth Council of Lateran, Pope Leo declared, without the least opposition in the Synod, that the authority of the Pope extended super omnia concilia. The Gallicans could only reply to this as follows: (a.) The Pope, it is true, had a document read in the Council which contained this sentence, and it passed without opposition; but the Council did not give any formal decision: it did not make a solemn decree of this proposition, (b.) The Pope only used this sentence argumentando, and not definiendo, in order to use it as a proof, but without giving it as a general proposition; and (c.) it is not certain that the fifth Lateran Council should be considered œcumenical. Many maintain that Pope Martin V. sanctioned the decree of the Council of

Constance establishing the superiority of the œcumenical council to the Pope, and Eugene IV. also sanctioned a similar decree from the Council of Basle. In point of fact, however, these two Popes sanctioned only a part of the decrees of the Councils of Basle and Constance. As for those of Basle, Eugene only sanctioned those which treated of three points, viz. the extinction of heresy, the pacification of Christendom, and the general reform of the Church in its head and in its members. When, therefore, Martin V. declared at the last session of the Council of Constance, that he approved and ratified all that had been decreed by the present holy Œcumenical Council of Constance in materiis fidei conciliariter (that is, by the whole Council, and not merely by individual nations), this approval had immediate reference only to the special matter of Falkenberg (see vol. vii. p. 368 of Hefele's Conciliengeschichte): he said nothing at all on the decrees respecting the superiority of an œcumenical council to the Pope; and if this Pope, in the bull of the 22d February 1418, required of every one the recognition of the Council of Constance as being œcumenical, and that all which it had decreed in favorem fidei et salutem animarum must be received and believed (vol. vii. p. 347), he evidently avoided giving it a complete and universal confirmation. His words, which we have quoted above, have a decidedly restrictive character. He indicated by them that he excluded some of the decrees of the Council from his approbation (evidently those referring to the superiority of the Council); but for the sake of peace, he did not choose to express himself more clearly. His successor, Eugenius IV., declared himself with greater distinctness in 1446, when he accepted the whole Council of Constance, and all its decrees, absque tamen præjudicio juris, dignitatis, et præeminentiæ sedis apostolicæ. There can be no question that by this he intended to exclude from his approbation the decrees of Constance respecting the superiority of an œcumenical synod to the Pope. Finally, it must not be forgotten that, on the 4th September 1439, Pope Eugene IV. and the Synod of Florence, in an especial constitution, Moses, solemnly rejected the proposition that the council is superior to the Pope,—a proposition which had just been renewed in the thirty-third session of the Council of Basle, and had been there made a dogma.

In confining themselves to this question, Is the Pope superior or inferior to a general council? the Gallicans and the Ultramontanes did not understand that they were keeping on the surface of a very deep question, that of the position of the Holy See in the economy of the Catholic Church. A much clearer and deeper insight into the question has more recently been shown; and the real question may be summed up in the following propositions:—An œcumenical council represents the whole Church: there must therefore be the same relation between the Pope and the council as exists between the Pope and the Church. Now, is the Pope above or below the Church? Neither the one nor the other. The Pope is in the Church; he necessarily belongs to it; he is its head and its centre. The Church, like the human body, is an organized whole; and just as the head is not superior or inferior to the body, but forms a part of it, and is the principal part of it, so the Pope, who is the head of the Church, is not superior or inferior to it: he is therefore neither above nor below the general council. The human organism is no longer a true body, but a lifeless trunk, when the head is cut off; so an assembly of bishops is no longer an œcumenical council when it is separated from the Pope. It is therefore a false statement of the question, to ask whether the Pope is above or below the general council. On the other side, we may rightly ask, Has an œcumenical council the right to depose the Pope? According to the Synods of Constance and Basle and the Gallicans, the Pope may be deposed for two principal reasons: (1) ob mores; (2) ob fidem, that is to say, ob hæresim. But, in reality, heresy alone can constitute a reason for deposition; for an heretical Pope has ceased to be a member of the Church: he therefore can be its president no longer. But a Pope who is guilty of ob mores, a sinful Pope, still belongs to the visible Church: he must be considered as the sinful and unrighteous head of a constitutional kingdom, who must be made as harmless as possible, but not deposed. If the question arises of several pretenders to the pontifical throne, and it is impossible to distinguish which is in the right, Bellarmin says that in this case it is the part of the council to examine the claims of the pretenders, and to depose those who cannot justify their claims. This is what was done by the Council of Constance. In proceeding to this deposition, however, the Council has not the authority of an œcumenical council: it cannot have that authority until the legitimate Pope enters into relation with it, and confirms it. The question is evidently only of the deposition of a pretender, who has not sufficient claim, and not that of a Pope legitimately elected. The Council of Constance would not have had any right to depose even John xxiii. if (a) the validity of this Pope's election had not been doubtful, (b) and if he had not been suspected of heresy. Besides, he abdicated, thus ratifying the deposition which had been pronounced.

We see from these considerations, of what value the sanction of the Pope is to the decrees of a council. Until the Pope has sanctioned these decrees, the assembly of bishops which formed them cannot pretend to the authority belonging to an œcumenical council, however great a number of bishops may compose it; for there cannot be an œcumenical council without union with the Pope.

SEC. 8. Infallibility of Œcumenical Councils

This sanction of the Pope is also necessary for ensuring infallibility to the decisions of the council. According to Catholic doctrine, this prerogative can be claimed only for the decisions of œcumenical councils, and only for their decisions in rebus fidei et morum, not for purely disciplinary decrees. This doctrine of the Catholic Church upon the infallibility of œcumenical councils in matters of faith and morality, proceeds from the conviction, drawn from Holy Scripture, that the Holy Spirit guides the Church of God (consequently also the Church assembled in an œcumenical council), and that He keeps it from all error; that Jesus Christ will be with His own until the end of the world; that the gates of hell (therefore the powers of error) will never prevail against the Church. The apostles evinced their conviction that the Holy Spirit is present in general councils, when they published their decrees with this formula, Visum est Spiritui sancto et nobis (it seemed good to the Holy Ghost and to us), at the Synod held at Jerusalem. The Church, sharing this conviction of the apostles, has always taught that the councils are infallible in rebus fidei et morum, and has considered all those who did not believe in this infallibility to be heretics, and separate from the Church. Constantine the Great called the decrees of the Synod of Nicæa a divine commandment (θείαν ἐντολήν). Athanasius, in his letter to the bishops of Africa, exclaimed: "What God hath spoken through the Council of Nicæa endureth for ever." S. Ambrose is so thoroughly convinced of the infallibility of the general council, that he writes: "Sequor tractatum Nicæni concilii a quo me nec mors nec gladius poterit separare" (I follow the guidance of the Nicene Council, from which neither death nor sword will be able to separate me). Pope Leo the Great, speaking of his explanation respecting the two natures in Jesus Christ, says expressly that it has already been corroborated by the "consensu irretractabili" of the Council of Chalcedon; and in another letter, "non posse inter catholicos reputari, qui resistunt Nicæno vel Chalcedonensi concilio" (that they cannot be counted among Catholics who resist the Council of Nicæa or Chalcedon). Pope Leo again says in this same letter, that the decrees of Chalcedon were given "instruente Spiritu sancto," and that they are rather divine than human decrees.

Bellarmin and other theologians quote a great number of other texts, drawn from the works of the Fathers, which prove that this belief in the infallibility of œcumenical councils has always been part of the Church's creed. We select from them this of Gregory the Great: "I venerate the four first œcumenical councils equally with the four Gospels" (sicut quatuor Evangelia). Bellarmin as well as Steph. Wiest have refuted every objection which can be brought against the infallibility of œcumenical councils.

The same infallibility must be accorded to councils which are not œcumenical, when their decrees have received the sanction of the Pope, and been accepted by the whole Church. The only formal difference, then, existing between these councils and those which are œcumenical is this, that all the bishops of the Church were not invited to take part in them.

SEC. 9. Appeal from the Pope to an Œcumenical Council

The question, whether one can appeal from the decision of a Pope to that of an œcumenical council, is highly important, and has often been ventilated. Pope Celestine I., as early as the fifth century, declared that such an appeal was inadmissible. It is true that, in the first centuries, questions were often considered by the councils which had before been decided by the Pope; but, as Peter de Marca has shown, that was not an appeal properly so called. He also shows that the Emperor Frederick II. was the first who formally appealed from the decision of a Pope to that of a general council. Pope Martin V., and subsequently Pope Pius II., were led again to prohibit these appeals, because they recurred too often, and especially on account of the exorbitant demands of the Council of Constance. Julius II. and Paul V. renewed these prohibitions in the sixteenth century. In 1717 a great sensation was caused by the appeal of many Jansenists to a general council against the Bull Unigenitus of Pope Clement XI. But in his brief Pastoralis officii the Pope threatened with excommunication every one who promoted the appeal, and did not sign the Bull Unigenitus; and also compelled the abandonment of the appeal, and the dispersion of the appealing party. Even the Protestant historian Mosheim wrote against this appeal, and plainly showed the contradiction there was between it and the Catholic principle of the unity of the Church; and indeed it must be confessed, that to appeal from the Pope to a council, an authority usually very difficult to constitute and to consult, is simply to cloak ecclesiastical insubordination by a mere formality.

SEC. 10. Number of the Œcumenical Councils

Bellarmin reckons eighteen œcumenical councils as universally acknowledged; but on the subject of the fifth Lateran Council, he says that it was doubted by many: "Au fuerit vere generale; ideo usque ad hanc diem quæstio superest, etiam inter catholicos." Some historians have also raised doubts as to the œcumenical character of the Council held at Vienne in 1311. There are therefore only the following sixteen councils which are recognised without any opposition as œcumenical:—

1. That of Nicæa in 325.

2. The first of Constantinople in 381.

3. That of Ephesus in 431.

4. That of Chalcedon in 451.

5. The second of Constantinople in 553.

6. The third of Constantinople in 680.

7. The second of Nicæa in 787.

8. The fourth of Constantinople in 869.

9. The first Lateran in 1123.

10. The second Lateran in 1139.

11. The third Lateran in 1179.

12. The fourth Lateran in 1215.

13. The first of Lyons in 1245.

14. The second of Lyons in 1274.

15.   That of Florence in 1439.

16.   That of Trent, from 1545 to 1563.

The œcumenical character of the following synods is contested:—

1.   That of Sardica, about 343–344.

2.   That in Trullo, or the Quinisext, in 692.

3.   That of Vienne in 1311.

4.   That of Pisa in 1409.

5.   That of Constance, from 1414 to 1418.

6.   That of Basle, from 1431 to 1439.

7.   The fifth Lateran, from 1512 to 1517.

We have elsewhere considered whether the Synod of Sardica can lay claim to the title of œcumenical, and we will again take up the question at the proper time. We may here recapitulate, in five short propositions, the result of our researches:—

a. The history of the Council of Sardica itself furnishes no reason for considering it to be œcumenical.

b. No ecclesiastical authority has declared it to be so.

c. We are not therefore obliged to consider it to be œcumenical; but we must also add,

d. That it was very early, and has been in all ages, highly esteemed by the orthodox Church.

e. Besides, it is of small importance to discuss its œcumenical character, for it gave no decree in rebus fidei, and therefore issued no decisions with the stamp of infallibility. As for disciplinary decrees, whatever council promulgates them, they are subject to modification in the course of time: they are not irreformable, as are the dogmatic decrees of œcumenical councils.

The Trullan Council, also called the Quinisext, is considered to be œcumenical by the Greeks only. The Latins could not possibly have accepted several of its decrees, which are drawn up in distinct opposition to the Roman Church: for instance, the thirteenth canon, directed against the celibacy observed in the West; the thirty-sixth canon, on the equal rank of the Bishops of Constantinople and of

Rome; and the fifty-fifth canon, which forbids the Saturday's fast.

The Council of Vienne is generally considered to be the fifteenth Œcumenical Council, and Bellarmin also accedes to this. The Jesuit Damberger, in his Synchronical History of the Middle Ages, expresses a different opinion. "Many historians," he says, "especially French historians, consider this Council to be one of the most famous, the most venerable, and the most important which has been held, and regard it as the fifteenth Œcumenical. The enemies of the Church will gladly accept such an opinion. It is true that Pope Clement v. wished to call an œcumenical council, and of this the Bull of Convocation speaks; but Boniface VIII. had also the same desire, and yet no one would give such a name to the assembly which he opened at Rome on the 13th October 1302. It is also true that, after the bishops of all countries have been summoned, the title and weight of an œcumenical council cannot be refused to a synod under the pretext that many bishops did not respond to the invitation; but the name demands at least that the assembly should be occupied with the common and universal concerns of the Church—that they should come to decisions which should then be promulgated for the obedience of the faithful. Now," says Damberger, "nothing of all this took place at the Council of Vienne." We reply, that this last statement is a mistake. The Council promulgated a whole series of decrees, which in great measure relate to the whole Church, and not merely to one province only—for example, those concerning the Templars; and these decrees were certainly published. Moreover, the fifth Lateran Council, which we admit to be œcumenical, spoke of that of Vienne, in its eighth session, as a generale. A different judgment must be given respecting the Council of Pisa, held in 1409. It was naturally from the beginning considered to be without weight or authority by the partisans of the two Popes whom it deposed, viz. Gregory XII. and Benedict XIII. The Carthusian Boniface Ferrer, brother to S. Vincent Ferrer, and legate of Benedict XIII. at this Synod, called it an heretical and diabolical assembly. But its character as œcumenical has also been questioned by those who took no part for either of the two antipopes—by Cardinal de Bar, and a little subsequently by S. Antonine Archbishop of Florence. We might add to these many friends of reform, like Nicholas of Clémonge and Theodoric of Brie, who were dissatisfied with it. Gerson, on the contrary, who about this time wrote his book De Auferibilitate Papæ, defended the decrees of the Council of Pisa. Almost all the Gallicans have tried, as he did, to give an œcumenical character to this Council, because it was the first to make use of the doctrine of the superiority of a general council to the Pope. But in order that a council should be œcumenical, it must be recognised as such by the whole of Christendom. Now, more than half the bishops of Christendom (episcopatus dispersus), as well as whole nations, have protested against its decisions, and would not receive them. For this reason, neither ecclesiastical authority nor the most trustworthy theologians have ever numbered it among the œcumenical councils. It must also be said that some Ultramontanes have had too little regard for this Council, in saying that the election made by it of Pope Alexander V. was valueless, and that Gregory XII. was still the legitimate Pope until his voluntary abdication in 1415.

The Gallicans were very anxious to prove the Council of Constance to be œcumenical. It is true that it was assembled in a regular manner; but, according to the principles we have explained above, it necessarily lost its œcumenical character as long as it was separated from the head of the Church. The sessions, however, which were held after the election of Pope Martin V., and with his consent and approbation—that is, sessions 42 to 45—must be considered as those of an œcumenical council. The same consideration must be given to the decrees of the earlier sessions, which concern the faith (res fidei), and were given conciliariter as they were approved by Pope Martin V. There was no special enumeration of them given by the Pope; but he evidently intended those condemning the heresies of Huss and Wickliffe. Natalis Alexander endeavours to show that this sanction also comprehended the fourth and fifth sessions, and their decrees establishing the superiority of councils over the Pope. But Roncaglia has refuted his opinion, and maintained the right view of the matter, which we have already asserted. As for those who entirely refuse an œcumenical character to the Council of Constance in all its parts, it suffices for their refutation to recall, besides the approbation of Martin V., what Pope Eugene IV. wrote on the 22d July 1446 to his legates in Germany: "Ad imitationem ss. PP. et prædecessorum nostrorum, sicut illi generalia concilia venerari consueverunt, sic generalia concilia Constantiense et Basileense ab ejus initio usque ad translationem per nos factam, absque tamen præjudicio juris, dignitatis et præ-eminentiæ S. Sedis apostolicæ ... cum omni reverentia et devotione suscipimus, complectimur et veneramur" [In imitation of the most holy Popes our predecessors, as they have been wont to venerate general councils, so do we receive with all reverence and devotion, embrace and venerate the General Councils of Constance and Basle, yet without prejudice to the right dignity and pre-eminence of the Holy Apostolic See]. The moderate Gallicans maintain that the Council of Basle was œcumenical until its translation to Ferrara, and that it then lost this character; for it would be impossible to consider as œcumenical the conciliabulum which remained behind at Basle, and was continued later at Lausanne under the antipope Felix V. Edmund Richer and the advanced Gallicans, on the contrary, consider the whole of the Council of Basle to be œcumenical, from its stormy beginning to its inglorious end. Other theologians, on the contrary, refuse this character to the Council of Basle in all its sessions. This is the opinion of Bellarmin, Roncaglia, and L. Holstenius. According to Gieseler, Bellarmin has given the title of œcumenical to the Council of Basle in another passage of his celebrated Disputationes. This is not so. Bellarmin says that the Council of Basle was legitimate at its opening, that is to say, so long as the papal legate and a great number of bishops were present; but subsequently, when it deposed the Pope, it was only a conciliabulum schismaticum, seditiosum, et nullius prorsus auctoritatis. It was by Bellarmin's advice that the acts of the Council of Basle were not included in the collection of œcumenical councils made at Rome in 1609.

Those who are absolutely opposed to the Council of Basle, and refuse the œcumenical character to all its sessions, give the following reasons:—

a. There was only a very small number of bishops (7–8) at the first sessions of this Synod, and therefore one cannot possibly consider it to be an œcumenical council.

b. Before its second session, this Council, promising no good results, was dissolved by Pope Eugene IV.

c. From this second session, according to the undeniable testimony of history, the assembly was ruled by passion; its members were embittered against each other; business was not carried on with becoming calmness, but in the midst of complete anarchy; the bishops' secretaries spoke and shouted in the sessions, as Æneas Sylvius and others testify.

d. Eugene IV. did certainly at a later period, after the fifteenth session, confirm all that had been done in the preceding; but this confirmation was extorted from him when he was ill, and by the threat that, if he did not consent to give it, he should lose the adherence of the princes and cardinals, and be deposed from the papal chair.

e. This confirmation has no value, even supposing that the Pope gave it in full consciousness, and with entire freedom; for it was only signed by him on condition that the members of the Council of Basle should repeal all the decrees which they had given against the authority of the Pope, which they never did.

f. The Pope simply allowed the Council to continue its sessions, and he withdrew his bull of dissolution again; but these concessions imply no sanction of what the Council had done in its preceding sessions, and the Pope took care to declare this himself.

It appears to us to be going too far to refuse an œcumenical character to the whole Council of Basle. The truth, according to our view, lies between this opinion and that of the moderate Gallicans in this way:

a. The Council of Basle was a true one from the first session to the twenty-fifth inclusive, that is, until its translation from Basle to Ferrara.

b. In these twenty-five sessions we must accept as valid only such decrees as treat, 1st, Of the extinction of heresy; 2d, Of the pacification of Christendom; 3d, Of the reformation of the Church in its head and in its members;—and always on condition that these decrees are not prejudicial to the papal power, and are approved by the Pope.

Our authority for the establishment of these two propositions is Pope Eugene IV. himself, who, in a bull read during the sixteenth session of the Council of Basle, sanctions those decrees of the preceding sessions which treat of these three points. In the letter already mentioned, which he wrote on the 22d July 1446 to his legates in Germany, he says: "As my predecessors have venerated the ancient councils (evidently meaning œcumenical councils),

103

so do I receive cum omni reverentia et devotione, etc., the General Councils of Constance and Basle, and this latter ab ejus initio usque ad translationem per nos factam, absque tamen præjudicio juris, dignitatis et præ-eminentiæ, S. Sedis apostolicæ ac potestatis sibi et in eadem canonice sedentibus concessæ."

But it is asked whether this acceptance be admissible, whether ecclesiastical authority had not already broken the staff over the whole Council of Basle. A passage in a bull published by Pope Leo X., in the eleventh session of the fifth Œcumenical Lateran Council, has been made use of for the support of this objection. It is as follows: "Cum ea omnia post translationem ejusdem Basileensis Concilii.... a Basileensi conciliabulo seu potius conventicula quæ præsertim post hujusmodi translationem concilium amplius appellari non merebatur, facta exstiterint ac propterea nullum robur habuerint." In this passage Pope Leo X. condemns what was resolved during the latter sessions of the Council of Basle, and which was taken into the pragmatic sanction of Bourges in 1438; and on this occasion he speaks of the Council of Basle in a very unfavourable manner. But apart from the fact that we might allege against this passage, which asserts the superiority of the Pope over a general council, what the Gallicans have already adduced against it, we will observe: (a.)

Even in this passage Pope Leo distinguishes between the Council of Basle, the assembly held before the translation, and the conciliabulum which began after the translation. (b.) It is true that he does not speak favourably of the Council itself, and the word præsertim seems to imply blame; but the Pope's language can be easily explained, if we reflect that he has in view the decrees which diminish the power of the Pope,—decrees which were afterwards inserted in the pragmatic sanction. He might therefore speak unfavourably of these decisions of the Council of Basle, as Pope Eugene IV. did, without rejecting the whole Synod of Basle.

It must also be understood in what sense Father Ulrich Mayr of Kaisersheim was condemned by Pope Clement XIV., viz. for maintaining that the twenty-five first sessions of the Council of Basle had the character and weight of sessions of an œcumenical council. The opinion of Mayr is very different from ours: we do not accept all the decrees of the twenty-five first sessions, but only those which can be accepted under the conditions enumerated above.

Some theologians, particularly Gallicans, since the time of Louis XIV., will not recognise the fifth Lateran Council as œcumenical, on account of the small number of its members; but the true reason for their hostility against this Council is that, in union with the Crown of France, it abolished the pragmatic sanction of Bourges, which asserted the liberties of the Gallican Church, and concluded. another concordat These attacks cannot, however, be taken into consideration: for the great majority of Catholic theologians consider this Council to be œcumenical; and even France, at an earlier period, recognised it as such. Here, then, we offer a corrected table of the œcumenical councils:—

    1.   That of Nicæa in 325.

    2.   The first of Constantinople in 381.

    3.   That of Ephesus in 431.

    4.   That of Chalcedon in 451.

    5.   The second of Constantinople in 553.

    6.   The third of Constantinople in 680.

    7.   The second of Nicæa in 787.

    8.   The fourth of Constantinople in 869.

    9.   The first of Lateran in 1123.

    10.   The second of Lateran in 1139.

11.   The third of Lateran in 1179.

12.   The fourth of Lateran in 1215.

13.   The first of Lyons in 1245.

14.   The second of Lyons in 1274.

15.   That of Vienne in 1311.

16. The Council of Constance, from 1414 to 1418; that is to say: (a.) The latter sessions presided over by Martin V. (sessions 41–45 inclusive); (b.) In the former sessions all the decrees sanctioned by Pope Martin V., that is, those concerning the faith, and which were given conciliariter.

17. The Council of Basle, from the year 1431; that is to say: (a.) The twenty-five first sessions, until the translation of the Council to Ferrara by Eugene IV.; (b.) In these twenty-five sessions the decrees concerning the extinction of heresy, the pacification of Christendom, and the general reformation of the Church in its head and in its members, and which, besides, do not strike at the authority of the apostolic chair; in a word, those decrees which were afterwards sanctioned by Pope Eugene IV.

17b. The assemblies held at Ferrara and at Florence (1438–42) cannot be considered as forming a separate œcumenical council. They were merely the continuation of the Council of Basle, which was transferred to Ferrara by Eugene IV. on the 8th January 1438, and from thence to Florence in January 1439.

18.   The fifth of Lateran, 1512–17.

19.   The Council of Trent, 1545–63.

SEC. 11. Customs observed in Œcumenical Councils with respect to Signatures, Precedence, Manner of Voting, etc.

In some countries—for instance, in Africa—the bishops held rank in the councils according to the period of their consecration; in other parts they ranked according to the episcopal see which they filled. The priests and deacons representing their absent bishop occupied the place belonging to that bishop in those councils which were held in the East; but in the West this custom was not generally followed. In the Spanish councils the priests always signed after the bishops. The Council of Arles (A.D. 314), in the signatures to which we cannot remark any order, decided that if a bishop brought several clerics with him (even in minor orders), they should give their signatures immediately after their bishop, and before the bishop who followed. The order of the signatures evidently indicates also the order of precedence. This Council of Arles gives an exception to this rule, for the Pope's legates—the two priests Claudian and Vitus—signed only after several bishops; whilst in all the other councils, and even in the Eastern, the legates always signed before all the other bishops and the patriarchs, even though they were but simple priests.

In the thirteenth century Pope Clement IV. ordained that, in order to distinguish the bishops from the exempt abbots in the synods, the latter should only have mitres bordered with gold, without pearls, without precious stones, or gold plates. The abbots who were not "exempt" were only to have white mitres, without borders.

The members of the councils ordinarily were seated in the form of a circle, in the centre of which was placed the book of the Holy Scriptures. There were added also sometimes the collections of the ecclesiastical canons, and the relics of the saints. Behind each bishop was generally seated the priest who accompanied him; the deacon used to sit lower, on one side, or before the bishop.

With respect to the ceremonies at the opening of the ancient Spanish councils, we have an order of the fourth Council of Toledo, which met in 633 (can. 4), which prescribed as follows: "Before sunset on the day appointed (May 18), all those who are in the church must come out; and all the doors must be shut, except the one by which the bishops enter, and at this door all the ostiarii (porters) will station themselves. The bishops will then come and take their places, according to the times of their ordination. When they have taken their places, the elected priests, and after them the deacons, will come in their turn to take their places. The priests sit behind the bishops; the deacons are in front; and all are seated in the form of a circle. Last of all, those laity are introduced whom the council by their election have judged worthy of the favour. The notaries who are necessary are also introduced.

"All keep silence. When the archdeacon says, 'Let us pray' (orate), all prostrate themselves upon the ground. After several moments, one of the oldest bishops rises and recites a prayer in a loud voice, during which all the rest remain on their knees. The prayer having been recited, all answer 'AMEN;' and they rise when the archdeacon says, 'Stand up' (crigite vos). While all keep silent, a deacon, clad in a white alb, brings into the midst the Book of the Canons, and reads the rules for the holding of councils. When this is ended, the metropolitan gives an address, and calls on those present to bring forward their complaints. If a priest, a deacon, or a layman has any complaint to make, he makes it known to the archdeacon of the metropolitan church; and the latter, in his turn, will bring it to the knowledge of the council. No bishop is to withdraw without the rest, and no one is to pronounce the council dissolved before all the business is ended." The Synod concluded with a ceremony similar to that of the opening; the metropolitan then proclaimed the time of celebrating Easter, and that of the meeting of the next synod, and some bishops were chosen to assist the metropolitan at Christmas and Easter.

Before the Council of Constance, they voted by numbers in all the councils; but at that Council, to neutralize the advantage the Italian prelates derived from their large number, the votes were given by nations. Five nations—Italy, France, Germany, England, and Spain—each had right to one vote; and within the nation they of course voted by numbers. Another arrangement was introduced into the Council. They divided, without distinctions of nationality, all who were present at the Synod into four great commissions—of the Faith, of the Peace, of the Reform of the Church, and of general business. Each commission had its own president, and they combined the commissions three times a week. When a commission had made a decree, it was communicated to the other three; and if it was approved by three commissions at the least, it was announced as a decree of the Synod by the president of the Council in a general session.

In the councils which followed that of Basle this manner of voting was abandoned; and when, at the commencement of the Council of Trent, the Pope's legates asked if they would vote by nations or by heads, the latter was the method which was recommended, as being the most conformable to the traditions of the Church. This is at least what Sarpi and Pallavicini relate. Sarpi adds, that several Fathers of the Council of Trent would have demanded to vote by nations; but this statement is refuted by Pallavicini, who proves that no one made that demand, and that the question asked by the legates was simply a prudential measure. The Council of Trent introduced a practice which was a departure from ancient custom. In the ancient councils the discussions upon the decrees to be promulgated took place during the sessions themselves; and the acts of these councils contain discussions of great length. In the Council of Trent, on the contrary, each matter was first carefully discussed in particular commissions; and when all was ready, and in fact decided upon, they presented the decree to the general session for confirmation. The acts of the Council of Trent, for this reason, contain no discussions, but only decrees, etc.

The decisions of the synods were regularly published in the name of the synod itself; but sometimes, when the Pope presided, the decrees were published in the form of papal decrees, with the addition of the formula: "with the approbation of the sacred œcumenical council" (sacra universali synodo approbante). This took place at the third, the fourth, and the fifth Lateran Councils, and in part also at the Council of Constance.

SEC. 12. Histories of the Councils

James Merlin, canon and chief penitentiary of the metropolitan church of Paris, was the first who had a collection of the acts of the councils published. This edition, naturally very incomplete, appeared at Paris in 1523, in one folio volume, in two parts. A second impression was published at Köln in 1530, enriched by two documents, the golden bull of Charles IV., and the bull of Pius II. in which he forbade an appeal from the Pope to an œcumenical council. The third edition, in octavo, published at Paris in 1536, had no additions. Like all the collections of the councils which have been made after it, with the exception of the Roman edition of 1609, the edition of Merlin contained, with the acts of the œcumenical councils, those of several provincial synods, as well as many papal decretals. It may be mentioned that this alone had the collection of the false Isidorian Decretals printed in a continuous form, whilst in the more recent collections they are distributed in chronological order, assigning to each council or each Pope the part attributed to him by the pseudo-Isidore.

In 1538 there appeared at Köln a second collection of the acts of the councils (two volumes folio), fuller than that of Merlin. It was published by the Belgian Franciscan, Peter Crabbe, who, to make it more complete, had searched in no less than five hundred libraries. The second edition, enlarged, dated 1551, is in three folio volumes. Lawrence Servius, the celebrated convert and Carthusian, published at Köln another and somewhat more complete collection of the councils in 1657, in four folio volumes; and the printer, Dominic Nicolini, put forth at Venice, in 1585, with the assistance of the Dominican Dominic Bollanus, a new impression, in five volumes folio.

Professor Severin Binius, canon of Köln, surpassed his predecessors by publishing another collection of the councils, in four volumes folio, in 1606. The text of the councils was enriched by historical and critical notes, taken for the most part from Baronius. The second editions, which were published in 1618 and 1636, are still better than the first. The latter was published at Paris by Charles Morel, in nine volumes, as the Roman collection of the acts of the councils could here be made use of. This Roman collection contained only the acts of the œcumenical councils. It consisted of four folio volumes, and was compiled between 1608 and 1612 under the authority of Pope Paul V. This work gave for the first time the original Greek text of many of the synodal acts, copied from the manuscripts of the Vatican and other MSS. The learned Jesuit Sirmond was the principal author of this collection; he wrote the interesting introduction which was prefixed to the whole work. At the beginning of the acts of each council there is a succinct but by no means worthless history of that council in Latin, which has been inserted into several other more modern collections,—in particular, into that of Mansi. We have already said that, by the advice of Bellarmin, the acts of the Synod of Basle were not admitted into this collection.

This Roman edition has served as a basis for all subsequent editions: these have added the acts of the national and provincial synods, besides the most important edicts and decrees of the Popes, all of them avoiding several faults and several singularities of the Roman editors. In these more recent editions the text has often also been improved by the study of various MSS., and has been enriched by many fragments and original documents which were wanting in the Roman edition.

The first collection which was made after the Roman collection is the Collectio Regia, which appeared at Paris in 1644 at the royal printing press, in thirty-seven folio volumes.

The printing and all the material part is magnificent, but the same praise cannot be awarded to the editing; for even those faults of the Roman edition which had been pointed out by Father Sirmond still remained uncorrected. In spite of the great number of its volumes, the royal edition is nearly one-fourth less complete than that of the Jesuit Philip Labbe

(Labbeus) of Bourges. Labbe died in 1667, whilst he was labouring on the ninth and tenth volumes of his collection; but Father Gabriel Cossart, a member of the same order, continued his work, which appeared at Paris in 1674. Stephen Baluze wished to add to this edition a supplement which would contain four volumes in folio, but only one volume has seen the light. Almost all the French savans quote from this edition of Labbe's with Baluze's supplement, making use of all these works, and consulting, besides, a very large number of MSS. John Hardouin, a Jesuit, gave a new Conciliorum Collectio regia maxima ad P. Labbei et P. Gabrielis Cossarti ... labores haud modica accessione facta, etc. Hardouin had been in 1685 entrusted with this work by the French clergy, on the condition that he submitted it for examination to Dr. Vitasse, professor of the Sorbonne, and to Le Merre, an advocate of the Parliament. Hardouin submitted only for a short time to this condition, and gained the protection of Louis XIV., who accepted the dedication of the work, and allowed it to be printed at the royal press. These different circumstances gave to the work a kind of official character, which contributed not a little to render it suspected by the Jansenists and Gallicans, as Hardouin in his dedication to Louis XIV. showed himself a very warm partisan of the Bull Unigenitus, and the bull itself was inserted in the last volume; besides which, the Index rerum betrayed an opposition to Gallican principles. He took care to point out especially (see, e.g., the art. on the authority of councils) the decisions of the Popes or of the councils which were opposed to the principles and maxims of the Gallican divines. Louis XIV. died at the moment when the printing of the work was almost finished; and as the Duke of Orleans, who then became regent, favoured the Jansenists, and showed himself hostile to the Bull Unigenitus, advantage was taken to complain to the Parliament of the publication of Hardouin's work. Parliament ordered Elias Dupin, Chas. Vitasse, Denys Léger, and Philip Anquetil to draw up a report on the subject; in consequence of which the sale of the work was prohibited, as being opposed to the principles of the State, and to those of the Gallican Church (1716). They destroyed all the copies they could seize, but happily some had already been sent from France. Later on, the Parliament was obliged to yield to the wishes loudly expressed in various quarters for the publication of the work. They authorized it, but on the condition that the Jesuits should add a volume of corrections, thinking they would by these means weaken the Ultramontanism of Hardouin. This volume appeared in 1722, printed at the royal press, under the title, Addition ordonnée par arrêt du Parlement, pour être jointe à la Collection des Conciles, etc. In the following year the Jesuits obtained the free publication of Hardouin's edition, without its being accompanied by the additional volume; and they gained their point so well, that that volume was even suppressed. Since then the Jansenists have republished it at Utrecht in 1730 and 1751, with this title, Avis des censeurs nommés par le Parlement de Paris pour examiner, etc.

Since Hardouin's edition has been widely circulated, it has become the favourite text-book of learned men among Catholics as well as Protestants. It is this which Benedict XIV. always quotes in his work, De synodo Diæcesana. It is composed of a rich collection of conciliar acts and other important documents, and extends as far as 1714, thus going much further than Mansi's celebrated edition. It is recommended on account of its very beautiful and correct although small type, and especially for the five very complete tables which it contains.

These tables contain: (1) a chronological table of all the Popes; (2) a table of all the councils; (3) an index episcoporum, et aliorum qui conciliis interfuerunt; (4) an index geographicus episcopatuum; (5) lastly, a very complete index rerum et verborum memorabilium. On account of these advantages, we have also used and quoted Hardouin's collection in our History of the Councils, along with the more complete work of Mansi. Salmon has analysed the details of Hardouin's collection, and has given a long list of its faults. As doctor of the Sorbonne, Salmon was not able to judge favourably of Hardouin's collection, to which he would rather have preferred that of Labbe and Cossart. He has, however, acknowledged the improvements and additions which distinguish Hardouin's work.

The collections which follow have been made since the publication of Salmon's work. The first is that of Nicholas Coleti, which appeared at Venice under the title, Sacrosancta concilia ad regiam editionem exacta. The Dominican Mansi, who became Archbishop of Lucca, his native town, compiled a supplement to Coleti's work. Several years afterwards, Mansi undertook a new collection of the acts of the councils, which should be more complete than all those which had hitherto appeared. He kept his word; and at the commencement of 1759, thirty-one volumes in folio of this edition appeared at Florence, with the title, Sacrorum conciliorum nova et amplissima collectio, in qua præter ea quæ Phil. Labbæus et Gabr. Cossartus et novissime Nicolaus Coleti in luccm edidere, ea omnia insuper suis in locis optime disposita exhibentur, quæ Jo. Dom. Mansi Lucensis, congregationis Matris Dei, evulgavit. Editio Novissima, ab eodem Patre Mansi, potissimum favorem etiam et opem præstante Em. Cardinali Dominico Passioneo, S. Sedis apostolicæ bibliothecario, aliisque item eruditissimis viris manus auxiliatrices ferentibus, curata, novorum conciliorum, novorumque documentorumque additionibus locupletata, ad MSS. codices Vaticanos

Lucenes aliosque recensita et perfecta. Accedunt etiam notæ et dissertationes quam plurimæ; quæ in cæteris editionibus desidcrantur. This edition was not completed, and the thirty-first volume reached only to the fifteenth century. It had consequently no indices, and its type, although larger and more modern than that of Hardouin's edition, is yet very inferior to the latter in accuracy. The order of the subjects in the latter volumes is sometimes not sufficiently methodical, and is at variance with the chronology.

By the side of these general collections there are other works, which contain only the acts of the councils held in particular countries. To these belong—

1. The Concilia Germaniæ, by Schannat and Harzheim, in eleven volumes folio (Cöln 1749–1790); Binterim, Pragmatische Geschichte der deutschen National- Provincial- und vorzüglichsten Diöcesan-concilien (Mainz 1835–1848), in seven volumes octavo, which reached as far as the end of the fifteenth century. We may, besides, consult, for the history of the German councils: (a) Lünig, Entwurf der in Deutschland von Anfang des Christenthums gehaltenen General- Provincial- und Partikularconcilien, in his Spicilegium des deutschen Reichsarchivs, P. i. p. 822; (b) Pfaff, Delineatio collectionis novæ conciliorum Germaniæ, reprinted in Fabricius, Biblioth. Græca, ed. Harless, t. xii p.

310 sqq.; (c) Joh. And. Schmid, Diss. de historiâ conciliorum Moguntinensium, Helmst. 1713; (d) De conciliis Moguntinis, in the work of Georg Christian Johannes, Scriptor. Mogunt. vol. iii. p. 281 sqq. Cf. Walch, Hist. der Kirchenvers. S. 53, and Salmon, l.c. p. 382 sqq.

2. Concilia antiqua Galliæ, by Father Sirmond (Paris 1629), in three volumes folio, and one volume folio,—a supplement added by his cousin De La Lande in 1666. Concilia novissima Galliæ a tempore concilii Tridentini celebrata, ed. Ludov. Odespun de la Mechinière, a priest of Tours (Paris 1646), one volume folio. Shortly before the Revolution, the Benedictines of the congregation of S. Maur undertook a complete collection of the councils of France; but one folio volume alone appeared (Paris 1789), with the title, Conciliorum Galliæ tam editorum quam ineditorum Collectio, temporum ordine digesta ab anno Christi 177 ad an. 1563, cum epistolis pontificum, principum constitutionibus et aliis ecclesiasticæ rei Gallicanæ monumentis. Opera et studio monachorum congregationis S. Mauri, t. i. ab anno 177 ad annum 591. Paris, sumptibus Petri Didot. In folio.

3. Garcias Loaisa was the first to publish a collection of the Spanish councils, at Madrid 1593, in one volume folio. That of Cardinal Joseph Saenz de Aguirre is much more complete: Collectio maxima Conciliorum omnium Hispaniæ et novi orbis

(Rome 1693), in four volumes folio. More recent is the Collectio canonum Ecclesiæ Hispanæ ex probatissimis et pervetustis Codicibus nunc primum in lucem edita a publica Matritensi bibliotheca (per FRANC. ANT. GONZALEZ, publ. Matr. bibl. præfectum), Matriti, ex typographia regia, 1808. In folio.

4. England and Ireland had two collections. The older is that of Henry Spelman: Concilia, decreta, leges, constitutiones in re Ecclesiarum orbis Britannici, London, t. i. 1639, t. ii. 1664; the third volume, although announced, never appeared. That of David Wilkins followed, which is better and more complete: Concilia Magna Britanniæ et Htberniœ, ed. DAV. WILKINS (London 1734), in four volumes folio.

5. Sacra concilia Ecclesiæ Romano-catholicæ in regno Unqariæ, a collection due to Father Charles Peterfy (Vienna 1742), in two volumes folio.

6. There does not exist a general collection of the Italian councils, but the councils of certain periods or of certain provinces have been in part collected. There is, e.g., a collection of the synods held at Milan, by S. Charles Borromeo (in his complete works); a Synodicon Beneventanensis Ecclesiæ, by Vinc. Mar. Orsini (Pope Benedict XIII.), Beneventum 1695, folio.

Among the numerous works on the history of the councils, the most useful to consult are:

1. John Cabassutius' Notitia Ecclesiastica historiarum conciliorum et canonum, Lyons 1680, folio. Very often reprinted.

2. Hermant, Histoire des Conciles, Rouen 1730, four volumes 8vo.

3. Labbe, Synopsis Historica Conciliorum, in vol. i. of his Collection of Councils.

4. Edm. Richer, Historia conciliorum generalium (Paris 1680), three volumes 4to. Reprinted in 8vo at Cöln.

5. Charles Ludovic Richard, Analysis conciliorum generalium et particularium. Translated from French into Latin by Dalmasus. Four volumes 8vo, Augsburg 1778.

6. Christ Wilh. Franz Walch, Entwurf einer vollständigen Historie der Kirchenversammlungen, Leipzig 1759.

7. Fabricius, Bibliotheca Græca, edit. Harless, t. xii. p. 422 sqq., in which is contained an alphabetical table of all the councils, and an estimate of the value of the principal collections.

8. Alletz, Concilien-Lexikon, translated from French into German by Father Maurus Disch, a Benedictine and professor at Augsburg, 1843.

9. Dictionnaire universel et complet des Conciles, tant généraux que particuliers, etc., rédigé par M. l'Abbé P——, prêtre du Diocèse de Paris, published by the Abbé Migne (Paris 1846), two volumes 4to.

In the great works on ecclesiastical history—for example, in the Nouvelle Bibliothèque des auteurs Ecclesiastiques, by El. Dupin, and the Historia Literaria of Cave, and particularly in the excellent Histoire des auteurs sacrés, by Remi Ceillier—we find matters relating to the history of the councils. Salmon, l.c. p. 387 sqq., and Walch in his Historie der Kirchenversammlungen, pp. 48–67, have pointed out a large number of works on the history of the councils. There are also very valuable dissertations on the same subject in.

1. Christian Lupus' Synodorum generalium ac provincialium decreta et canones, scholiis, notis ac historica actorum dissertatione illustrata, Louv. 1665, Bruxelles 1673, five volumes 4to.

2. Lud. Thomassin, Dissertationum in Concilia generalia et particularia, t. i. Paris 1667; reprinted in Rocaberti, Bibl. pontificia, t. xv.

3. Van Espen, Tractatus Historicus, exhibens scholia in omnes canones conciliorum, etc., in his complete works.

4. Barth. Caranza has written a very complete and useful abstract of the acts of the councils in his Summa Conciliorum, which has often been re-edited.

5. George Daniel Fuchs, deacon of Stuttgart, has, in his Bibliothek der Kirchenversammlungen (four volumes, Leipsic 1780–1784), given German translations and abstracts of the acts of the councils in the fourth and fifth centuries.

6. Francis Salmon, Doctor and Librarian of the Sorbonne, has published an Introduction to the Study of the Councils, in his Traité de l'Etude des Conciles et de leurs collections, Paris 1724, in 4to, which has often been reprinted.

CHAPTER I
COUNCILS OF THE FIRST TWO CENTURIES

THE first Christian Council, the type and model of all the others, was held at Jerusalem by the apostles between the years 50 and 52 A.D., in order to solve the question of the universal obligation of the ancient law. No other councils were probably held in the first century of the Christian era; or if they were, no trace of them remains in history. On the other hand, we have information of several councils in the second century. The authenticity of this information is not, it is true, equally established for all; and we can acknowledge as having really taken place only those of which Eusebius Pamphili, the father of Christian Church history, speaks, or other early and trustworthy historians. To these belong, first of all:—

SEC. 1. Synods relative to Montanism

Eusebius has given us, in his Church History, a fragment of a work composed by Apollinaris Bishop of Hierapolis in Phrygia, in which the following words occur: "The faithful of Asia, at many times and in many places (πολλάκις καὶ πολλαχῇ τῆς Ἀσίας), came together to consult on the subject of Montanus and his followers; and these new doctrines were examined, and declared strange and impious." This fragment unfortunately gives no other details, and does not point out the towns at which these synods were held; but the Libellus Synodicus of Pappus tells us that Apollinaris, the holy Bishop of Hierapolis in Asia, and twenty-six of his colleagues in the episcopate, held a provincial council at Hierapolis, and there tried and condemned Montanus and Maximilla the false prophets, and at the same time Theodotus the currier (the celebrated anti-Trinitarian). Further on he adds: "A holy and particular (μερική) synod, assembled under the very holy Bishop Sotas of Anchialus (in Thrace, on the Black Sea), and consisting of twelve other bishops, convicted of heresy the currier Theodotus, Montanus, and Maximilla, and condemned them."

The Libellus Synodicus, to which we are indebted for these details, it is true, can lay claim to no very early origin, as it was compiled by a Greek towards the close of the ninth century. But this Greek derived his statements from ancient authentic sources; and what he says of the two synods agrees so perfectly with the statement of Eusebius, that in this passage it is worthy of all confidence. We read in Eusebius' Church History (book v. cc. 16 and 19), that Apollinaris of Hierapolis, and Sotas of Anchialus, contemporaries of Montanus, zealously opposed his errors, and wrote and preached against him. Sotas even wished to exorcise the evil spirit from Priscilla, a companion of Montanus; but these hypocrites, adds Eusebius, did not consent to it.

The strong opposition which these two bishops made to Montanus makes it probable that they gave occasion to several of the numerous synods in which, according to the summaries of Eusebius, the Church rejected Montanism.

The date of these synods is nowhere exactly pointed out. The fragment which is given in Eusebius proves that they were held shortly after the commencement of the Montanist agitations; but the date of the rise of Montanism itself is uncertain. The Chronicle of Eusebius gives 172; S. Epiphanius 126 in one place, and 156 or 157 in another. He says, besides, that Maximilla died about A.D. 86. In this there is perhaps an error of a whole century. Blondel, relying on these passages, has shown that Montanus and his heresy arose about 140 or 141; and, more recently, Schwegler of Tübingen has expressed the same opinion. Pearson, Dodwell, and Neander, on the contrary, decide for 156 or 157; Tillemont and Walch for 171. As for our own opinion, we have adopted Blondel's opinion (the year 140), because the Shepherd of Hermas, which was certainly anterior to 151, and was written when Pius I. was Pope, seems already to oppose Montanism. In this case, the synods with which we are occupied must have taken place before 150 of the Christian era. The Libellus Synodicus gives a contrary decision to this, although it attributes to the same synods the condemnation of the currier

Theodotus, whose apostasy can only be fixed at the time of the persecution by M. Aurelius (160–180). In reality, Theodotus was excommunicated at Rome by Pope Victor towards the close of the second century (192–202). In allowing that sentence of condemnation had been pronounced against him before that time in certain synods of Asia Minor and of Thrace (he was living at Constantinople at the time of his apostasy), those synods which, according to the Libellus Synodicus, have also condemned Montanism could not have been held before M. Aurelius: they must therefore have been held under that Emperor. The supposition that Theodotus and Montanus were contemporary would oblige us to date these councils between A.D. 160 and 180; but to us it appears doubtful whether these two were contemporaries, and the conclusion that they were so seems to result from a confusion of the facts. In reality, the author of the ancient fragment given us by Eusebius speaks also of a Theodotus who was one of the first followers of Montanus, and shared his fate, i.e. was anathematized in the same synods with Montanus and Maximilla. He depicts him as a well-known man. The author of the Libellus Synodicus having read this passage, and finding that the ancient Synods of Hierapolis and Anchialus had condemned a Theodotus, easily identified the currier Theodotus with the Theodotus whom the author of the fragment declared to be celebrated in his time. If this is so, nothing will hinder our placing the rise of Montanism and the Synods of Hierapolis and Anchialus before A.D. 150.

SEC. 2. Synods concerning the Feast of Easter

The second series of councils in the second century was caused by the controversy regarding the time of celebrating Easter. It is not quite correct to regard the meeting of S. Polycarp of Smyrna, and Anicetus Bishop of Rome, towards the middle of the second century, as a synod properly so called; but it is certain that towards the close of the same century several synods were occasioned by the Easter controversy. Eusebius, in the passage referred to, only shows in a general way that these synods were held in the second half of the second century; but S. Jerome gives a more exact date, he says in his Chronicle, under the year 196: "Pope Victor wrote to the most eminent bishops of all countries, recommending them to call synods in their provinces, and to celebrate in them the feast of Easter on the day chosen by the Church of the West."

Eusebius here agrees with S. Jerome; for he has preserved to us a fragment of a letter written by Polycarp from Ephesus, in which this bishop says that Victor had required him to assemble the bishops who were subordinate to him: that he had done so, but that he and all the bishops present at this synod had pronounced for the practice of the

Quartodecimans or of S. John; that these bishops, the number of whom was considerable, had approved of the synodical letter which he had drawn up, and that he had no fear (on account of the threats of Victor), "because we must obey God rather than man." We see from this fragment, that at the moment when the synods convoked at the request of Victor in Palestine pronounced in favour of the Western practice in Palestine, Pontus, Gaul, and Osrhoëne, a great synod of bishops from Asia Minor, held at Ephesus, the see of Polycarp, had formally declared against this practice; and it is precisely from the synodical letter of this council that we have the fragment given above.

Bishop Victor then wished to exclude the bishops of Asia Minor from the communion of the Church; but other bishops turned him from his purpose. S. Irenæus, in particular, addressed a letter to him on this occasion, in the name of the bishops of Gaul, over whom he presided; a letter in which, it is true, he defended the Western custom of celebrating Easter, but in which also he prayed Victor not to excommunicate "a great number of churches, who were only guilty of observing an ancient custom," etc. This fragment has also been preserved to us by Eusebius; and we may consider it as a part of the synodical letter of the bishops of Gaul, since, as Eusebius makes him remark, Irenæus expressly declared "that he wrote in the name of his brethren of Gaul, over whom he presided." It may be asked if the synod here spoken of is the same as that mentioned by Eusebius in another place, and which we mentioned above. If it be the same, it must be admitted that, at the request of Victor, there was at first a synod of the Quartodecimans in Asia Minor, and that it was only later on, when the result was known, that other councils were also assembled, and especially in Gaul. It may be also that S. Irenæus presided over two successive councils in Gaul, and that in the first he declared himself for the Western practice regarding Easter, in the second against the threatening schism. This is the opinion of the latest biographer of S. Irenæus, the Abbé J. M. Prat. The Synodicon (Libellus Synodicus) only speaks of one synod in Gaul, presided over by Irenæus, on the subject of the Easter controversy; and he adds that this synod was composed of Irenæus and of thirteen other bishops.

The Libellus Synodicus also gives information about the other councils of which Eusebius speaks, concerning the question of Easter. Thus:

a. From the writing of the priests of Rome of which we have spoken, and which was signed by Pope Victor, the Libellus Synodicus concludes, as also does Valesius in his translation of the Eccles: Hist. of Eusebius, that there must have been a Roman synod at which, besides Victor, fourteen other bishops were present. This is opposed by Dom

Constant in his excellent edition of the Epistolæ Pontif. p. 94, and after him by Mosheim in his book De Rebus Christianorum ante Constant. M. p. 267, who remarks that Eusebius speaks of a letter from the Roman priests and Pope Victor, and not of a synod. But it has often happened, especially in the following centuries, that the decrees of the synods, and in particular of the Roman synods, have only been signed by the president, and have been promulgated by him under the form of an edict emanating from him alone. This is what is expressly said by a Roman synod held by Pope Felix II. in 485.

b. According to the Synodicon, two synods were held in Palestine, on the subject of the Easter controversy: the one at Jerusalem, presided over by Narcissus, and composed of fourteen bishops; and the other at Cæsarea, comprising twelve bishops, and presided over by Theophilus.

c. Fourteen bishops were present at the Asiatic Synod of Pontus, under the presidency of Bishop Palmas, whom the Synodicon calls Plasmas.

d. Eighteen bishops were present at that of Osrhoëne; the Libellus Synodicus does not mention who presided.

e. It speaks also of a synod held in Mesopotamia, on the subject of Easter, which also counted eighteen bishops (it is probably the same synod as that of Osrhoëne).

f. And, lastly, of a synod at Corinth, presided over by Bishop Bacchyllus; whilst Eusebius says expressly that Bacchyllus of Corinth did not publish any synodical letter on the subject of the celebration of Easter, but simply a private letter.

SEC. 3. Doubtful Synods of the Second Century

The anonymous author of the Prædestinatus speaks of three other synods of the second century. According to him,

a. In A.D. 125 a synod was held of all the bishops of Sicily, presided over by Eustathius of Libybæum and Theodorus of Palermo. This synod considered the cause of the Gnostic Heraclionites, and sent its acts to Pope Alexander, that he might decide further in the matter.

b. In 152 the heresy of the Colarbasians, another Gnostic sect, was anathematized by Theodotus Bishop of Pergamum in Mysia, and by seven other bishops assembled in synod.

c. In 160 an Eastern synod rejected the heresy of the Gnostic Cerdo.

The Libellus Synodicus mentions, besides:

a. A synod held at Rome, under Pope Telesphorus (127–139), against the currier Theodotus, the anti-Trinitarian.

b. A second synod at Rome, held under Pope Anicetus, upon the Easter question, at the time when Polycarp Bishop of Smyrna visited the Pope.

c. A third Roman synod under Victor, and which condemned Theodotus, Ebion, and Artemon.

d. A fourth Roman synod, also held under Victor, and which anathematized Sabellius and Noëtus.

e. Finally, a synod of the confessors of Gaul, who declared against Montanus and Maximilla in a letter addressed to the Asiatics.

These eight synods mentioned by the author of Prædestinatus and by the Libellus Synodicus are apparently imaginary: for, on one side, there is not a single ancient and original document which speaks of them; and on the other, the statements of these two unknown authors are either unlikely or contrary to chronology. We will instance, for example, the pretended Roman synod, presided over by Victor, which anathematized Sabellius. In admitting that the usual date, according to which Sabellius would have lived a full half-century later (about 250), may be inexact, as the Philosophoumena recently discovered have proved, yet it is clear from this document that Sabellius had not yet been excluded from the Church under Pope Zephyrinus (202–218), the successor of Victor, and that he was not excommunicated until the time of Pope Calixtus.

It is also impossible that Theodotus the currier should have been condemned by a Roman synod held under Telesphorus, since Theodotus lived towards the close of the second century. It is the same with the pretended Sicilian Council in 125. According to the information afforded to us by the ancients, especially S. Irenæus and Tertullian, Heracleon changed the system of Valentine. He could not then have flourished till after 125. As to Pope Alexander, to whom this synod is said to have rendered an account of its acts in 125, he died a martyr in 119.

It is also by mistake that we have been told of a synod in which Pope Anicetus and Polycarp both took part. The interview of these two bishops has been confounded with a synod: it is the same with the pretended Synod of Gaul, held against Montanus.

The author of the Libellus Synodicus has evidently misunderstood Eusebius, who says on this subject: "The news of what had taken place in Asia on the subject of Montanus (the synod) was known to the Christians of Gaul. The latter were at that time cruelly persecuted by Marcus Aurelius; many of them were in prison. They, however, gave their opinion from their prison on the matter of Montanus, and addressed letters to their brethren of Asia, and to Eleutherus Bishop of Rome." It will be seen that the question here is not of a synod, but of letters written by confessors (the Libellus Synodicus also mentions confessors).

Finally, a ninth council, which is said to have conveyed to the Bishop of Seleucia a patriarchal right over the whole of Assyria, Media, and Persia, is evidently an invention; and the mention of a Patriarchate on this occasion is a patent anachronism, as has been proved by Assemani in his Bibliothèque Orientale.

CHAPTER II
THE SYNODS OF THE THIRD CENTURY

SEC. 4. First Half of the Third Century

THE series of synods of the third century opens with that of Carthage, to which Agrippinus bishop of that city had called the bishops of Numidia and of proconsular Africa. S. Cyprian speaks of this Synod in his seventy-first and seventy-third letters, saying that all the bishops present declared baptism administered by heretics to be void; and he supports his own view on this subject by what had passed in this ancient Synod of Carthage. This Synod was probably the most ancient of Latin Africa; for Tertullian, who recalls the Greek synods as a glory, tells not of one single council being held in his country. According to Uhlhorn it was about 205, according to Hesselburg about 212, that the work of Tertullian, de Jejuniis,. was composed; therefore the Synod in question must have been held either after 205 or after 212. It has not been possible up to this time to verify this date more exactly. But the newly-discovered φιλοσφούμενα, falsely attributed to Origen, and which were probably written by Hippolytus, have given more exact dates; and Döllinger, relying upon this document, has placed the date of this Synod of Carthage between 218 and 222. The Philosophoumena relate, indeed, that the custom of re-baptizing—that is to say, of repeating the baptism of those who had been baptized by heretics—was introduced under the Bishop of Rome, Callistus (in some churches in communion with him). One can scarcely doubt but that this passage referred to Bishop Agrippinus and his Synod at Carthage; for S. Augustine and S. Vincent of Lérins say expressly that Agrippinus was the first who introduced the custom of re-baptism. The Synod of Carthage, then, took place in the time of Pope Callistus I., that is to say, between 218 and 222. This date agrees with the well-known fact that Tertullian was the first of all Christian writers who declared the baptism of heretics invalid; and it may be presumed that his book de Baptismo exerted a certain influence upon the conclusions of the Council of Carthage. It is not contradicted by the forty-sixth (forty-seventh) apostolic canon, which orders bishops, under pain of deposition, to re-baptize those who had been baptized by a heretic; for it is known that these so-called apostolic canons were composed some centuries later.

S. Cyprian speaks, in his sixty-sixth letter, of a synod held long before (jampridem) in Africa, and which had decided that a clergyman could not be chosen by a dying person as a guardian; but nothing shows that he understood by that, the synod presided over by Agrippinus, or a second African council.

The great Origen gave occasion for two synods at Alexandria. About the year 228, being called into

Achaia on account of the religious troubles reigning there, Origen passed through Palestine, and was ordained priest at Cæsarea by his friends Alexander Bishop of Jerusalem and Theoctistus Bishop of Cæsarea, although there were two reasons for his non-admission to holy orders: first, that he belonged to another diocese; and secondly, that he had castrated himself. It is not known what decided him or the bishops of Palestine to take this uncanonical step. Demetrius of Alexandria, diocesan bishop of Origen, was very angry with what had been done; and if we regard it from the ecclesiastical point of view, he was right. When Origen returned to Alexandria, Demetrius told him of his displeasure, and reproached him with his voluntary mutilation. But the principal grievance, without doubt, had reference to several false doctrines held by Origen: for he had then already written his book de Principiis and his Stromata, which contain those errors; and it is not necessary to attribute to the Bishop of Alexandria personal feelings of hatred and jealousy in order to understand that he should have ordered an inquiry into Origen's opinions under the circumstances. Origen hastened to leave Alexandria of his own accord, according to Eusebius; whilst Epiphanius says, erroneously, that Origen fled because, shortly before, he had shown much weakness during a persecution. His bitterest enemies have never cast a reproach of this nature at him. Demetrius, however, assembled a synod of

Egyptian bishops and priests of Alexandria in 231, who declared Origen unworthy to teach, and excluded him from the Church of Alexandria. Demetrius again presided over a second synod at Alexandria, without this time calling his priests, and Origen was declared to be deprived of the sacerdotal dignity. An encyclical letter published by Demetrius made these resolutions known in all the provinces.

According to S. Jerome and Rufinus, a Roman assembly, probably called under Pope Pontian, shortly after deliberated upon this judgment; and Origen after that sent to Pope Fabian (236–250) a profession of faith, to explain and retract his errors. Several writers have thought that the word senatus must not be understood in the sense of a synod, and that we are to consider it only as an assembly of the Roman clergy. Döllinger, on the contrary, presumes that Origen had taken part in the discussions of the priest Hippolytus with Pope Callistus and his successors (Origen had learned to know Hippolytus at Rome, and he partly agreed with his opinions), and that for this reason Pontian had held a synod against Origen.

A little before this period, and before the accession of Pope Fabian, a synod was certainly held at Iconium in Asia Minor, which must have been of great authority in the controversy which was soon to begin on the subject of the baptism of heretics. Like the Synod of Carthage, presided over by Agrippinus, that of Iconium declared every baptism conferred by a heretic to be invalid. The best information upon this Council has been furnished us by the letter which Bishop Firmilian of Cæsarea in Cappadocia, who showed himself so active in this controversy, addressed to S. Cyprian. It says: "Some having raised doubts upon the validity of baptism conferred by heretics, we decided long ago, in the Council held at Iconium in Phrygia, with the Bishops of Galatia, Cilicia, and the other neighbouring provinces, that the ancient practice against heretics should be maintained and held firm (not to regard baptism conferred by them)." Towards the end of the letter we read; "Among us, as more than one Church has never been recognised, so also have we never recognised as holy any but the baptism of that Church. Some having had doubts upon the validity of baptism conferred by those who receive new prophets (the Montanists), but who, however, appear to adore the same Father and the same Son as ourselves, we have assembled in great number at Iconium: we have very carefully examined the question (diligentissime tractavimus), and we have decided that all baptism administered outside the Church must be rejected." This letter then speaks of the Council of Iconium as of a fact already old; and it says also, that it was occasioned by the question of the validity of baptism administered by Montanists. Now, as Firmilian wrote this letter about the middle of the third century, it follows that the Council of Iconium, of which he often speaks as of an ancient assembly held long before (jampridem), took place about twenty years before the writing of his letter Dionysius Bishop of Alexandria, about the middle of the third century, also says: "It is not the Africans (Cyprian) who have introduced the custom of re-baptizing heretics: this measure had been taken long before Cyprian (πρὸ πολλοῦ), by other bishops at the Synod of Iconium and of Synnada."

In these two passages of his letter to S. Cyprian, Firmilian gives us a fresh means of fixing the date of the Synod of Iconium, saying formally several times: "We assembled ourselves at Iconium; we have examined the question; we have decreed," etc. It results from this, that he was himself present at this Synod. On the other side, the jampridem and other similar expressions justify us in placing this Synod in the first years of Firmilian's episcopate. Now we know from Eusebius that Firmilian flourished so early as in the time of the Emperor Alexander Severus (222–235) as Bishop of Cæsarea; so that we can, with Valesius and Pagi, place the celebration of the Synod of Iconium in the years 230–235. Baronius, by a very evident error, assigns it to the year 258.

According to all probability, we must refer to the Synod of Iconium a short passage of S. Augustine, in the third chapter of his third book against Cresconius, in which he speaks of a synod composed of fifty Eastern bishops.

Dionysius the Great, Bishop of Alexandria, speaks, we have seen, not only of the Synod of Iconium, but also of a Synod of Synnada, a town also situated in Phrygia. In this Synod, he says, the baptism by heretics was also rejected. We may conclude from his words that the two assemblies took place about the same time. We have no other information on this subject.

We know very little about the concilium Lambesitanum, which, says S. Cyprian, in his fifty-fifth letter to Pope Cornelius, had been held long before in the Lambesitana Colonia (in Numidia) by ninety bishops, and condemned a heretic named Privatus (probably Bishop of Lambese) as guilty of several grave offences." The Roman priests also mention this Privatus in their letter to S. Cyprian; but they do not give any further information concerning him.

A better known council was that which was held about the year 244, at Bostra in Arabia Petræa (now Bosrah and Bosserat), on account of the errors of Beryllus, bishop of this town. It is known that Beryllus belonged to the party of the Monarchians, generally called Patripassianists. This bishop held other erroneous opinions, which were peculiar to himself, and which it is now very difficult to distinguish.

The attempt made by the Arabian bishops to bring back Beryllus from his errors having failed, they called in Origen to their aid, who then lived at Cæsarea in Palestine. Origen came and conversed with Beryllus, first in private, then in presence of the bishops. The document containing the discussion was known to Eusebius and S. Jerome; but it was afterwards lost. Beryllus returned to the orthodox doctrine, and later expressed, it is said, his gratitude to Origen in a private letter.

Another controversy was raised in Arabia about the soul, as to whether it passed away (fell asleep) with the body, to rise (awake) at the resurrection of the body. At the request of one of the great Arabian synods, as Eusebius remarks, Origen had to argue against these Hypnopsychites, and he was as successful as in the affair of Beryllus. The Libellus Synodicus adds that fourteen bishops were present at the Synod, but it does not mention, any more than Eusebius, the place where it was held.

About the same period must also have been held two Asiatic synods, on the subject of the anti-Trinitarian (Patripassian) Noetus; S. Epiphanius is the only one to mention them, and he does so without giving any detail, and without saying where they took place. The assertion of the author of

Præddestinatus, that about this time a synod was
held in Achaia against the Valesians, who taught
voluntary mutilation, is still more doubtful, and very
probably false. The very existence of this sect is
doubtful.

We are on more solid historical ground when we
approach the tolerably numerous synods which
were celebrated, chiefly in Africa, about the middle
of the third century. The letters of S. Cyprian
especially acquaint us with them. He first speaks, in
his sixty-sixth letter, of an assembly of his
colleagues (the bishops of Africa), and of his fellow-
priests (the presbyters of Carthage), and so of a
Carthaginian Synod, which had to decide upon a
particular case of ecclesiastical discipline. A
Christian named Geminius Victor, of Furni in Africa,
had on the approach of death appointed a priest
named Geminius Faustinus as guardian to his
children. We have seen above, that an ancient
synod of Africa, perhaps that held under Agrippinus,
had forbidden that a priest should be a guardian,
because a clergyman ought not to occupy himself
with such temporal business. The Synod of
Carthage, held under S. Cyprian, renewed this
prohibition, and ordained, in the spirit of that ancient
council, that no prayers should be said or sacrifices
(oblationes) offered for the deceased Victor, as he
had no claim to the prayers of priests who had
endeavoured to take a priest from the holy altar. In

the letter of which we speak, S. Cyprian gave an account of this decision to the Christians of Furni. The Benedictines of Saint Maur presume that this letter was written before the outbreak of the persecution of Decius, which would place this Synod in the year 249.

SEC. 5. First Synods at Carthage and Rome on account of Novatianism and the "Lapsi" (251)

The schism of Felicissimus and the Novatian controversy soon afterwards occasioned several synods. When, in 248, S. Cyprian was elected Bishop of Carthage, there was a small party of malcontents there, composed of five priests, of whom he speaks himself in his fortieth letter. Soon after the commencement of the persecution of Decius (at the beginning of the year 250) the opposition to Cyprian became more violent, because in the interest of the discipline of the Church he would not always regard the letters of peace which some martyrs without sufficient consideration gave to the lapsi. He was accused of exaggerated severity against the fallen, and his own absence (from February 250 until the month of April or May 251) served to strengthen the party which was formed against him. An accident caused the schism to break out. Cyprian had from his retreat sent two bishops and two priests to Carthage, to distribute help to the faithful poor (many had been ruined by the persecution). The deacon Felicissimus opposed the envoys of Cyprian, perhaps because he considered, the care of the poor as an exclusive right of the deacons, and because he would not tolerate special commissioners from the bishop on such a business. This took place at the end of 250, or at the beginning of 251. Felicissimus had been ordained deacon by the priest Novatus unknown to Cyprian, and without his permission, probably during his retreat Now, besides the fact that such an ordination was contrary to all the canons of the Church, Felicissimus was personally unworthy of any ecclesiastical office, on account of his deceitfulness and his corrupt manners. Cyprian, being warned by his commissioners, excommunicated Felicissimus and some of his partisans on account of their disobedience; but the signal for revolt was given, and Felicissimus soon had with him those five priests who had been the old adversaries of Cyprian, as well as all those who accused the bishop of being too severe with regard to the lapsi, and of despising the letters of the martyrs. These contributed to give to the opposition quite another character. Till then it had only been composed of some disobedient priests; henceforth the party took for a war-cry the severity of the bishop with regard to the lapsi. Thus not only the lapsi, but also some confessors (confessores) who had been hurt by the little regard that Cyprian showed for the libelli pacis, swelled the ranks of the revolt. It is not known whether Novatus was in the number of the five priests who were the first movers of the party. By some it is asserted, by others denied. After, having in vain recalled the rebels to obedience, Cyprian returned to Carthage, a year after the festival of Easter in 251; and he wrote his book de Lapsis as a preparation for the Synod which he assembled soon afterwards, probably during the month of May 251. The Council was composed of a great number of bishops, and of some priests and deacons: he excommunicated Felicissimus and the five priests after having heard them, and at the same time set forth the principles to be followed with regard to the lapsi, after having carefully examined the passages of Scripture treating of this question. All the separate decrees upon this subject were collected into one book, which may be considered as the first penitential book which had appeared in the Church; but unfortunately it is lost. Cyprian makes us acquainted with the principal rules in his fifty-second letter: namely, that all hope must not be taken away from the lapsed, that, in excluding them from the Church, they may not be driven to abandon the faith, and to fall back again into a life of heathenism; that, notwithstanding, a long penance must be imposed upon them, and that they must be punished proportionally to their fault.1 It is evident, continues Cyprian, that one must act differently with those who have gone, so to speak, to meet apostasy, spontaneously taking part in the impious sacrifices, and those who have been, as it were, forced to this odious sacrilege after long struggles and cruel sufferings: so also with those who have carried. with them in their crime their wife, their children, their servants, their friends, making them also share their fall, and those who have only been the victims, who have sacrificed to the gods in order to serve their families and their houses; that there should no less be a difference between the sacrificati and the libellatici, that is to say, between those who had really sacrificed to the gods, and those who, without making a formal act of apostasy, had profited by the weakness of the Roman functionaries, had seduced them, and had made them give them false attestations; that the libellatici must be reconciled immediately, but that the sacrificati must submit to a long penance, and only be reconciled as the moment of their death approached; finally, that as for the bishops and priests, they must also be admitted to penance, but not again permitted to discharge any episcopal or sacerdotal function.

Jovinus and Maximus, two bishops of the party of Felicissimus, who had been reproved before by nine bishops for having sacrificed to the gods, and for having committed abominable sacrilege, appeared before the Synod of Carthage. The Synod renewed the sentence originally given against them; but in spite of this decree, they dared again to present themselves, with several of their partisans, at the Synod of Carthage, held the following year.

Cyprian and the bishops assembled around him decided to send their synodical decisions of 251 to Rome, to Pope Cornelius, to obtain his consent with regard to the measures taken against the lapsi. It was the more necessary to understand each other on the subject of these measures, as the Roman Church had also been troubled by the Novatian schism. Pope Cornelius assembled at Rome in the autumn—probably in the month of October 251—a synod composed of sixty bishops, without counting the priests and deacons. The Synod confirmed the decrees of that of Carthage, and excommunicated Novatian and his partisans. The two authors who have preserved these facts for us are Cyprian and Eusebius. It must be remarked that several editors of the acts of the councils, and several historians, misunderstanding the original documents, have turned the two Synods of Carthage and Rome (251) into four councils. The Libellus Synodicus also speaks of another council which must have been held the same year at Antioch, again on the subject of the Novatians; but one can hardly rely on the Libellus Synodicus when it is alone in relating a fact.

The Novatian schism could not be extirpated by these synods. The partisans of Felicissimus and of Novatian made great efforts to recover their position. The Novatians of Carthage even succeeded in putting at their head a bishop of their party named Maximus, and they sent many complaints to Rome on the subject of Cyprian's pretended severity, as, on the other side, the persecution which was threatening made fresh measures necessary with regard to the lapsi. Cyprian assembled a fresh council at Carthage on the Ides of May 252, which sixty-six bishops attended. It was probably at this council that two points were discussed which were brought forward by the African Bishop Fidus. Fidus complained at first that Therapius Bishop of Bulla (near Hippo) had received the priest Victor too soon into the communion of the Church, and without having first imposed upon him the penance he deserved. The Synod declared that it was evidently contrary to the former decisions of the councils, but that they would content themselves for this time with blaming Bishop Therapius, without declaring invalid the reconciliation of the priest Victor, which he had effected. In the second place, Fidus enunciated the opinion that infants should be baptized, not in the first days after their birth, but eight days after; to observe, with regard to baptism, the delay formerly prescribed for circumcision. The Synod unanimously condemned this opinion, declaring that they could not thus delay to confer grace on the new-born.

The next principal business of the Synod was that concerning the lapsi; and the fifty-fourth letter of S.

Cyprian gives us an account of what passed on this subject. The Synod, he says, on this subject decided that, considering the imminent persecution, they might immediately reconcile all those who showed signs of repentance, in order to prepare them for the battle by means of the holy sacraments: Idoneus esse non potest ad martyrium qui ab Ecclesia non armatur ad prælium. In addressing its synodical letter to Pope Cornelius (it is the fifty-fourth of S. Cyprian's letters), the Council says formally: Placuit nobis, sancto Spiritu suggerente. The heretic Privatus, of the colonia Lambesitana, probably bishop of that town, who, as we have seen, had been condemned, again appeared at the Council; but he was not admitted. Neither would they admit Bishops Jovinus and Maximus, partisans of Felicissimus, and condemned as he was; nor the false Bishop Felix, consecrated by Privatus after he became a heretic, who came with him. They then united themselves with the fallen bishop Repostus Saturnicensis, who had sacrificed during the persecution, and they gave the priest Fortunatus as bishop to the lax party at Carthage. He had been one of S. Cyprian's five original adversaries.

A short time after, a new synod assembled at Carthage on the subject of the Spanish bishops Martial and Basilides. Both had been deposed for serious faults, especially for having denied the faith.

Basilides had judged himself to be unworthy of the episcopal dignity, and declared himself satisfied if, after undergoing his penance, he might be received into lay communion. Martial had also confessed his fault; but after some time they both appealed to Rome, and by means of false accounts they succeeded in gaining over Pope Stephen, who demanded that Basilides should be replaced in his bishopric, although Sabinus had been already elected to succeed him. Several Spanish bishops seem to have supported the pretensions of Basilides and Martial, and placed themselves, it appears, on their side; but the Churches of Leon, of Asturia, and of Emerita, wrote on this subject to the African bishops, and sent two deputies to them— Bishops Sabinus and Felix, probably the elected successors of Basilides and Martial Felix Bishop of Saragossa supported them with a private letter. S. Cyprian then assembled a council composed of thirty-seven bishops; and we possess the synodical letter of the assembly, in his sixty-eighth epistle, in which the deposition of Martial and Basilides is confirmed, the election of their successors is declared to be legitimate and regular, the bishops who had spoken in favour of the deposed bishops are censured, and the people are instructed to enter into ecclesiastical communion with their successors.

SEC. 6. Synods relative to the Baptism of Heretics (255–256)

To these synods concerning the lapsi, succeeded three African councils on the subject of baptism by heretics. We have seen that three former councils— that of Carthage, presided over by Agrippinus; two of Asia Minor, that of Iconium, presided over by Firmilian, and that of Synnada, held at the same period—had declared that baptism conferred by heretics was invalid. This principle, and the consequent practice in Asia Minor, would appear to have occasioned, towards the end of the year 253, a conflict between Pope Stephen and the bishops of Asia Minor, Helenus of Tarsus and Firmilian of Cæsarea, sustained by all the bishops of Cilicia, of Cappadocia, and the neighbouring provinces; so that Stephen, according to Dionysius the Great, threatened these bishops with excommunication because they repeated the baptism conferred by heretics. Dionysius the Great mediated with the Pope in favour of the bishops of Asia Minor; and the letter which he wrote prevented their being excluded from the Church. The first sentence of this letter would even allow it to be supposed that peace was completely re-established, and that the bishops of Asia Minor had conformed to the demand of the Pope. However, later on, Firmilian is again found in opposition to Rome.

The Easterns then stirred up the controversy on the baptism of heretics before S. Cyprian; and when Eusebius says, πρῶτος τῶν τότε Κυπριανός, κ.τ.λ., this passage must be thus understood: Cyprian was the most important, and in this sense the first, of those who demanded the re-baptism of heretics.

Let us now turn our attention to Africa, and particularly to S. Cyprian. Some African bishops being of the opinion that those who abandoned heretical sects to enter the Church must not be re-baptized, eighteen bishops of Numidia, who held a different opinion, and rejected baptism by heretics, asked of the Synod of Carthage of 255 if it were necessary to re-baptize those who had been baptized by heretics or schismatics, when they entered the Church. At this Synod, presided over by S. Cyprian, there were twenty-one bishops present: the seventieth epistle of Cyprian is nothing but the answer of the Synod to the eighteen Numidian bishops. It declares "that their opinion about the baptism of heretics is perfectly right; for no one can be baptized out of the Church, seeing there is only one baptism which is in the Church," etc.

Shortly afterwards, Cyprian being again consulted on the same question by Quintus, bishop in Mauritania, who sent him the priest Lucian, sent in answer the synodical letter of the Council which had just separated; and besides, in a private letter joined to this official document, he stated his personal opinion on the validity of the baptism of heretics, and answered some objections.

All the bishops of Africa were probably not satisfied with these decisions; and some time after, about 256, Cyprian saw himself obliged to assemble a second and larger council at Carthage, at which no fewer than seventy-one bishops were present. S. Cyprian relates that they treated of a multitude of questions, but the chief point was the baptism of heretics. The synodical letter of this great assembly, addressed to Pope Stephen, forms S. Cyprian's seventieth letter. The Council also sent to the Pope the letter of the preceding Synod to the eighteen Numidian bishops, as well as the letter of S. Cyprian to Quintus, and reiterated the assertion "that whoso abandoned a sect ought to be re-baptized;" adding, "that it was not sufficient (parum est) to lay hands on such converts ad accipiendum Spiritum sanctum, if they did not also receive the baptism of the Church." The same Synod decided that those priests and deacons who had abandoned the catholic Church for any of the sects, as well as those who had been ordained by the sectarian false bishops, on re-entering the Church, could only be admitted into lay communion (communio laicalis). At the end of their letter, the Synod express the hope that these decisions would obtain Stephen's approval: they knew, besides, they said, that many do not like to renounce an opinion which has once been adopted; and more than one bishop, without breaking with his colleagues, will doubtless be tempted to persevere in the custom which he had embraced. Besides this, it is not the intention of the Synod to do violence to any one, or to prescribe a universal law, seeing that each bishop can cause his will to be paramount in the administration of his Church, and will have to render an account of it to God. "These words," Mattes has remarked, "betray either the desire which the bishops of Africa had to see Stephen produce that agreement by his authority, which did not yet exist, and which was not easy to establish; or else their apprehensions, because they knew that there was a practice at Rome which did not accord with the opinion of Cyprian." This last was, in fact, the case; for Pope Stephen was so little pleased with the decisions of the Council of Carthage, that he did not allow the deputies of the African bishops to appear before him, refused to communicate with them, forbade all the faithful to receive them into their houses, and did not hesitate to call S. Cyprian a false Christian, a false apostle, a deceitful workman (dolosus operarius). This is at least what Firmilian relates. Pope Stephen then pronounced very explicitly, in opposition to the Africans, for the validity of the baptism of heretics, and against the custom of repeating the baptism of those who had already received it from heretics. The letter which he wrote on this occasion to Cyprian has unfortunately been lost, and therefore his complete argument is unknown to us; but Cyprian and Firmilian have preserved some passages of the letter of Stephen in their writings, and it is these short fragments, with the comments of Cyprian and Firmilian, which must serve to make known to us with some certainty the view of Stephen on the baptism of heretics.

It is commonly admitted that S. Cyprian answered this violence of Stephen's by assembling the third Council of Carthage; but it is also possible that this assembly took place before the arrival of the letter from Rome. It was composed of eighty-seven bishops (two were represented by one proxy, Natalis Bishop of Oëa) from proconsular Africa, from Numidia, and from Mauritania, and of a great number of priests and of deacons. A multitude of the laity were also present at the Synod. The acts of this Synod, which still exist, inform us that it opened on the 1st September, but the year is not indicated. It is probable that it was in 256.

First was read the letter of the African Bishop Jubaianus to Cyprian on the baptism of heretics, and the answer of Cyprian; then a second letter from Jubaianus, in which he declared himself now brought to Cyprian's opinion. The Bishop of Carthage then asked each bishop present freely to express his opinion on the baptism of heretics: he declared that no one would be judged or excommunicated for differences of opinion; for, added he, no one in the assembly wished to consider himself as episcopus episcoporum, or thought to oblige his colleagues to yield to him, by inspiring them with a tyrannical fear (perhaps this was an allusion to Pope Stephen). Thereupon the bishops gave their votes in order, Cyprian the last, all declaring that baptism given by heretics was invalid, and that, in order to admit them into the Church, it was necessary to re-baptize those who had been baptized by heretics.

About the same time Cyprian sent the deacon Rogatian with a letter to Firmilian Bishop of Cæsarea, to tell him how the question about the baptism of heretics had been decided in Africa. He communicated to him at the same time, it appears, the acts and documents which treated of this business. Firmilian hastened to express, in a letter still extant, his full assent to Cyrian's principles. This letter of Firmilian's forms No. 75 of the collection of the letters of S. Cyprian: its contents are only, in general, an echo of what S. Cyprian had set forth in defence of his own opinion, and in opposition to Stephen; only in Firmilian is seen a much greater violence and passion against Stephen,—so much so, that Molkenbuhr, Roman Catholic Professor at Paderborn, has thought that a letter so disrespectful towards the Pope could not be genuine.

We are entirely ignorant of what then passed between Cyprian and Stephen, but it is certain that church communion was not interrupted between them. The persecution which soon afterwards broke out against the Christians under the Emperor Valerian, in 257, probably appeased the controversy. Pope Stephen died as a martyr during this persecution, in the month of August 257. His successor Xystus received from Dionysius the Great, who had already acted as mediator in this controversy on the baptism of heretics, three letters in which the author earnestly endeavoured to effect a reconciliation; the Roman priest Philemon also received one from Dionysius. These attempts were crowned with success; for Pontius, Cyprian's deacon and biographer, calls Pope Xystus bonus et pacificus sacerdos, and the name of this Pope was written in the diptychs of Africa. The eighty-second letter of Cyprian also proves that the union between Rome and Carthage was not interrupted, since Cyprian sent a deputation to Rome during the persecution, to obtain information respecting the welfare of the Roman Church, that of Pope Xystus, and in general about the progress of the persecution. Soon after, on the 14th September 258, Cyprian himself fell, in his turn, a victim to the persecution of Valerian.

It remains for us now, in order fully to understand the controversy on the baptism of heretics, to express with greater precision the opinions and assertions of Cyprian and Stephen.

1. We must ask, first of all, which of the two had Christian antiquity on his side.

a. Cyprian says, in his seventy-third letter: "The custom of baptizing heretics who enter the Church is no innovation amongst us: for it is now many years since, under the episcopate of Agrippinus of holy memory, a great number of bishops settled this question in a synod; and since then, up to our days, thousands of heretics have received baptism without difficulty." Cyprian, then, wishing to demonstrate the antiquity of his custom, could not place it earlier than Agrippinus, that is to say, than the commencement of the third century (about 220 years after Christ); and his own words, especially the "since then" (exinde), show that it was Agrippinus who introduced this custom into Africa.

b. In another passage of the same letter, Cyprian adds: "Those who forbid the baptism of heretics, having been conquered by our reasons (ratione), urge against us the custom of antiquity (qui ratione vincuntur, consuetudinem nobis opponunt)." If Cyprian had been able to deny that the practice of his adversaries was the most ancient, he would have said: "They are wrong if they appeal to antiquity (consuetudo); it is evidently for us." But Cyprian says nothing of the kind: he acknowledges that his adversaries have antiquity on their side, and he only tries to take its force from this fact, by asking, "Is antiquity, then, more precious than truth? (quasi consuetudo major sit veritate);" and by adding, "In spiritual things we must observe what the Holy Spirit has (afterwards) more fully revealed (id in spiritualibus sequendum, quod in melius fuerit a Spiritu sancto revelatum)." He acknowledges, therefore, in his practice a progress brought about by the successive revelations of the Holy Spirit.

c. In a third passage of this letter, S. Cyprian acknowledges, if possible more plainly, that it was not the ancient custom to re-baptize those who had been baptized by heretics. "This objection," he says, "may be made to me: What has become of those who in past times entered the Church from heresy, without having been baptized?" He acknowledges, then, that in the past, in præteritum, converts from heresy were not re-baptized. Cyprian makes answer to this question: "Divine mercy may well come to their aid; but because one has erred once, it is no reason for continuing to err (non tamen, quia aliquando erratum est, ideo semper errandum est)." That is to say, formerly converts were not re-baptized; but it was a mistake, and for the future the Holy Spirit has revealed what is best to be done (in melius a Spiritu sancto revelatum).

d. When Pope Stephen appealed to tradition, Cyprian did not answer by denying the fact: he acknowledges it; but he seeks to diminish the value of it, by calling this tradition a human tradition, and not legitimate (humana traditio, non legitima).

e. Firmilian also maintained that the tradition to which Stephen appealed was purely human, and he added that the Roman Church had also in other points swerved from the practice of the primitive Church—for example, in the celebration of Easter. This example, however, was not well chosen, since the Easter practice of the Roman Church dates back to the prince of the apostles.

f. Firmilian says, in another passage of this same letter, that it was anciently the custom also in the African Churches not to re-baptize the converts: "You Africans," he says, "can answer Stephen, that having found the truth, you have renounced the error of your (previous) custom (vos dicere Afri potestis, cognita veritate errorem vos consuetudinis reliquisse)." Nevertheless, Firmilian thought that it was otherwise in Asia Minor, and that the custom of re-baptizing converts was traced back to a very far-off period; but when he wishes to give the proof of it, he only finds this one: "We do not remember (!) when this practice began amongst us." He appeals, in the last place, to the Synod of Iconium, which we know was not held until about the year 230.

g. It is worthy of remark, that even in Africa all the bishops did not pronounce in favour of the necessity of a fresh baptism, which would certainly have been the case if the practice of Agrippinus and Cyprian had always prevailed in Africa.

h. A very important testimony in favour of Stephen, and one which proves that the ancient custom was not to re-baptize, is given by the anonymous author of the book de Rebaptismate, a contemporary and probably a colleague of Cyprian. This author says that the practice maintained by Stephen, that of simply laying hands on the converts without re-baptizing them, is consecrated by antiquity and by ecclesiastical tradition (vetustissima consuetudine ac traditione ecclesiastica), consecrated as an ancient, memorable, and solemn observance by all the saints, and all the faithful (prisca et memorabilis cunctorum emeritorum sanctorum et fidelium solemnissima observatio), which has in its favour the authority of all the churches (auctoritas omnium Ecclesiarum), but from which unhappily some have departed, from the mania for innovations.

i. S. Vincent of Lérins agrees with the author we have just quoted, when he says that Agrippinus of Carthage was the first who introduced the custom of re-baptizing, contra divinum canonem, contra universalis Ecclesiæ regulam, contra morem atque instituta majorum; but that Pope Stephen condemned the innovation and re-established the tradition, retenta est antiquitas, explosa novitas.

k. S. Augustine also believes that the custom of not re-baptizing heretics is an apostolical tradition (credo ex apostolica traditione venientem), and that it was Agrippinus who was the first to abolish this

165

very safe custom (saluberrima consuetudo), without succeeding in replacing it by a better custom, as Cyprian thought.

l. But the gravest testimony in this question is that of the Philosophoumena, in which Hippolytus, who wrote about 230, affirms that the custom of re-baptizing was only admitted under Pope Callistus, consequently between 218 and 222.

m. Before arriving at the conclusion to be deduced from all these proofs, it remains for us to examine some considerations which appear to point in an opposite direction.

(a.) In his book de Baptismo, which he wrote when he was still a Cátholic, and before this work in a Greek document, Tertullian shows that he did not believe in the validity of baptism conferred by heretics. But, on considering it attentively, we find that he was not speaking of all baptism by heretics, but only of the baptism of those who had another God and another Christ. Besides, we know that Tertullian is always inclined to rigorism, and he certainly is so on this point; and then, living at Carthage at the commencement of the third century, being consequently a contemporary of Agrippinus, perhaps even being one of his clergy, he naturally inclined to resolve this question as Agrippinus resolved it, and his book de Baptismo perhaps exerted an influence upon the resolutions of the

Synod of Carthage. Also Tertullian does not pretend that it was the primitive custom of the Church to re-baptize: his words rather indicate that he thought the contrary. He says, Sed circa hæreticos sane quid custodiendum sit, digne quis retractet; that is to say, "It would be useful if some one would study afresh (or examine more attentively) what ought to be done about heretics, that is to say, in relation to their baptism."

(β.) Dionysius the Great says, in a passage which Eusebius has preserved: "The Africans were not the first to introduce this practice (that of re-baptizing converts): it is more ancient; it was authorized by bishops who lived much earlier, and in populous Churches." However, as he only mentions the Synods of Iconium and of Synnada before the Africans, his expression much earlier can only refer to these assemblies, and he adduces no earlier testimony for the practice of Cyprian.

(γ.) Clement of Alexandria certainly speaks very disdainfully of baptism by heretics, and calls it a foreign water; he does not, however, say that they were in the habit of renewing this baptism.

(δ.) The Apostolical Canons 45 and 46 (or 46 and 47, according to another order) speak of the non-validity of baptism by heretics; but the question is to know what is the date of these two canons: perhaps they are contemporary with the Synods of Iconium and of Synnada, perhaps even more recent.

We are hardly able to doubt, then, that in the ancient Church, those who returned to the orthodox faith, after having been baptized by heretics, were not re-baptized, if they had received baptism in the name of the Trinity, or of JESUS.

2. Let us see now whether Pope Stephen considered as valid baptism conferred by all heretics, without any exception or condition. We know that the Synod of Arles in 314, as well as the Council of Trent, teaches that the baptism of heretics is valid only when it is administered in the name of the Father, of the Son, and of the Holy Ghost. Were the opinions and assertions of Stephen agreeable to this doctrine of the Church?

At first sight Stephen appears to have gone too far, and to have admitted all baptism by heretics, in whatever manner it was conferred. His chief proposition, as we read it in S. Cyprian, is expressed in these terms: Si quis ergo a quacunque hæresi venerit ad nos, nil innovetur nisi quod traditum est, ut manus illi imponatur in pœnitentiam. He seems, then, to declare valid all baptism by heretics, in whatever manner it might have been administered, with or without the formula of the Trinity. Cyprian argues, in a measure, as if he

Volume I: Ante-Nicence Councils

understood Stephen's proposition in this sense. However,

a. From several passages in the letters of S. Cyprian, we see that Pope Stephen did not thus understand it.

(α.) Thus (Epist. 73, p. 130) Cyprian says: "Those who forbid the baptism of heretics lay great stress upon this, that even those who had been baptized by Marcion were not re-baptized, because they had already been baptized in the name of Jesus Christ." Thus Cyprian acknowledges that Stephen, and those who think with him, attribute no value to the baptism of heretics, except it be administered in the name of Jesus Christ.

(β.) Cyprian acknowledges in the same letter (p. 133), that heretics baptize in nomine Christi.

(γ.) Again, in this letter, he twice repeats that his adversaries considered as sufficient baptism administered out of the Church, but administered in nomine Christi.

(δ.) Cyprian, in answering this particular question—if baptism by the Marcionites is valid—acknowledges that they baptize in the name of the Trinity; but he remarks that, under the name of the Father, of the Son, and of the Holy Ghost, they understand something different from what the Church

169

understands. This argument leads us to conclude that the adversaries of S. Cyprian considered baptism by the Marcionites to be valid, because they conferred it in the name of the Trinity.

b. Firmilian also gives testimony on the side of Stephen.

(α.) He relates, indeed, that about twenty-two years before he had baptized a woman in his own country who professed to be a prophetess, but who, in fact, was possessed by an evil spirit. Now, he asks, would Stephen and his partisans approve even of the baptism which she had received, because it had been administered with the formula of the Trinity (maxime cui nec symbolum Trinitatis defuit)?

(β.) In the same letter Firmilian sums up Stephen's opinion in these terms: In multum proficit nomen Christi ad fidem et baptismi sanctificationem, ut quicunque et ubicunque in nomine Christi baptizatus fuerit, consequatur statim gratiam Christi.

c. If, then, Cyprian and Firmilian affirm that Pope Stephen held baptism to be valid only when conferred in the name of Christ, we have no need to have recourse to the testimony either of S. Jerome, or of S. Augustine, or of S. Vincent of Lérins, who also affirm it.

d. The anonymous author of the book de Rebaptismate, who was a contemporary even of S. Cyprian, begins his work with these words: "There has been a dispute as to the manner in which it is right to act towards those who have been baptized by heretics, but still in the name of Jesus Christ: qui in hæresi quidem, sed in nomine Dei nostri Jesu Christi, sinttincti."

e. It may again be asked if Stephen expressly required that the three divine Persons should be named in the administration of baptism, and if he required it as a condition sine qua non, or if he considered baptism as valid when given only in the name of Jesus Christ. S. Cyprian seems to imply that the latter was the sentiment of Pope Stephen, but he does not positively say so anywhere; and if he had said it, nothing could have been legitimately concluded against Pope Stephen, for Cyprian likes to take the words of his adversaries in their worst sense. What we have gathered (a δ and b a) tends to prove that Pope Stephen regarded the formula of the Trinity as necessary. Holy Scripture had introduced the custom of calling by the short phrase, baptism in the name of Christ, all baptism which was conferred in virtue of faith in Jesus Christ, and conformably to His precepts, consequently in the name of the Holy Trinity, as is seen in the Acts of the Apostles and in the Epistle to the Romans. It is not, then, astonishing that Pope Stephen should have used an expression which was perfectly intelligible at that period.

f. In this discussion Pope Stephen seems to believe that all the heretics of his time used the true formula of baptism, consequently the same formula among themselves, and the same as the Church. He declares this opinion clearly in these words, adduced from his letter by Firmilian: Stephanus in sua epistola dixit: hæreticos quoque ipsos in baptismo convenire; and it was on this account, added the Pope, that the heretics did not re-baptize those who passed from one sect to another. To speak thus, was certainly to affirm that all the sects agreed in administering baptism with the formula prescribed by our Lord.

S. Cyprian also attributes to Pope Stephen words which can be explained very well if we study them with reference to those quoted by Firmilian. According to S. Cyprian, Stephen had said: "We must not re-baptize those who have been baptized by heretics, cum ipsi hæretici proprie alterutrum ad se venientes non baptizent;" that is to say, the different sects have not a special baptism of their own (proprie non baptizent): and it is for this reason that heretics do not re-baptize those who pass from one sect to another. Now if the different sects have not special baptism, if they baptize in the same way—conveniunt in baptismo—as Firmilian makes Pope Stephen affirm, they hold necessarily the universal and primitive mode of Christian baptism; consequently they use the formula of the Trinity.

It is difficult to say whether, in admitting this hypothesis, Stephen falls into an historical error: for, on one side, S. Irenæus accuses the Gnostics of having falsified the baptismal formula, and of having used different erroneous formulas; and consequently he contradicts Stephen; and, on the other side, S. Augustine appears to agree with him, saying: Facilius inveniuntur hæretici qui omnino non baptizent quam qui non illis verbis (in nomine Patris, etc.) baptizent.

g. We may be inclined to make an objection against Stephen on the subject of the Montanists. There is no doubt, in fact, that Stephen considered the baptism of these heretics to be valid, while the Church afterwards declared it to be of no value. But Stephen's opinion is not in this contrary to the doctrine of the Church; neither did the Council of Nicæa (can. 19) mention the Montanists among those whose baptism it rejected. It could not do so any more than Stephen; for it was not until long after the time of Stephen and of the Council of Nicæa that a degenerate sect of Montanists fell away into formal anti-Trinitarianism.

3. It remains for us to understand what, according to Stephen's opinion, was to be done with the converts after their reception into the Church. These are

Stephen's words on this subject: Si quis crgo a quacumque hæresi venerit ad nos, nil innovetur nisi quod traditum est, ut manus illi imponatur in pœnitentiam. There is a sense which is often given to this passage, as follows: "No innovation shall be made; only what is conformable to tradition shall be observed; hands shall be laid on the convert in sign of penitence." But this interpretation is contrary to grammatical rules. If Stephen had wished to speak in this sense, he would have said: Nihil innovetur, sed quod traditum est observetur, etc. Hence Mattes translates the words of Stephen thus: "Nothing shall be changed (as regards the convert) but what it is according to tradition to change; that is to say, that hands shall be laid upon him," etc.

Stephen adds, in pœnitentiam, that is, that "it is necessary that a penance should be imposed on the convert." According to the practice of the Church, a heretic who enters into the Church ought first to receive the sacrament of penance, then that of confirmation. One may ask, if Stephen required these two sacraments, or if he only required that of penance? Each of these sacraments comprehended the imposition of hands, as some words of Pope Vigilius clearly indicate; and consequently by the expression, manus illi imponatur, Stephen may understand the administration of the two sacraments. To say that there is only in pœnitentiam in the text, is not a very strong objection; for this text is only a fragment, and Cyprian has transmitted to us elsewhere other texts of Stephen's thus abridged. The manner in which the adversaries of Pope Stephen analysed his opinions shows that this Pope really required, besides penance, the confirmation of the converts. Thus, in his seventy-third letter, Cyprian accuses his adversaries of self-contradiction, saying: "If baptism out of the Church is valid, it is no longer necessary even to lay hands on the converts, ut Spiritum Sanctum consequatur et signetur;" that is to say: You contradict yourselves if you attribute a real value to baptism by heretics; you must also equally admit the validity of confirmation by heretics. Now you require that those who have been confirmed by heretics should be so again. S. Cyprian here forgets the great difference which exists between the value of baptism and of confirmation; but his words prove that Stephen wished that penance and confirmation should be bestowed upon converts.

The same conclusion is to be drawn from certain votes of the bishops assembled at the third Council of Carthage (256). Thus Secundinus Bishop of Carpi said: "The imposition of hands (without the repetition of baptism, as Stephen required) cannot bring down the Holy Spirit upon the converts, because they have not yet even been baptized." Nemesianus Bishop of Thubuni speaks still more clearly: "They (the adversaries) believe that by imposition of hands the Holy Spirit is imparted, whilst regeneration is possible only when one receives the two sacraments (baptism and confirmation) in the Church." These two testimonies prove that Stephen regarded confirmation as well as penance to be necessary for converts.

4. What precedes shows that we must consider as incorrect and unhistorical the widespread opinion, that both Stephen and Cyprian carried things to an extreme, and that the proper mean was adopted by the Church only as the result of their differences.

5. It is the part of Dogmatic Theology, rather than of a History of the Councils, to show why Cyprian was wrong, and why those who had been baptized by heretics should not be re-baptized. Some short explanation on this point will, however, not be out of place here.

S. Cyprian repeated essentially Tertullian's argument, yet without naming it, and thus summed it up: "As there is only one Christ, so there is only one Church: she only is the way of salvation; she only can administer the sacraments; out of her pale no sacrament can be validly administered." He adds: "Baptism forgives sins: now Christ left only to the apostles the power of forgiving sins; then heretics cannot be possessed of it, and consequently it is impossible for them to baptize." Finally, he concludes: "Baptism is a new birth; by it children are

born to God in Christ: now the Church only is the
bride of Christ; she only can, therefore, be the
means of this new birth."

In his controversy against the Donatists (who
revived Cyprian's doctrine on this point), S.
Augustine demonstrated with great completeness,
and his accustomed spiritual power, two hundred
and fifty years afterwards, that this line of argument
was unsound, and that the strongest grounds
existed for the Church's practice defended by
Stephen. The demonstration of S. Augustine is as
simple as powerful. He brought out these three
considerations:—

a. Sinners are separated spiritually from the Church,
as heretics are corporally. The former are as really
out of the Church as the latter: if heretics could not
legally baptize, sinners could not either; and thus
the validity of the sacrament would absolutely
depend upon the inward state of the minister.

b. We must distinguish between the grace of
baptism and the act of baptism: the minister acts,
but it is God who gives the grace; and He can give it
even by means of an unworthy minister.

c. The heretic is, without any doubt, out of the
Church; but the baptism which he confers is not an
alien baptism, for it is not his, it is Christ's baptism,
the baptism which He confers, and consequently a

true baptism, even when conferred out of the Church. In leaving the Church, the heretics have taken many things away with them, especially faith in Jesus Christ and baptism. These fragments of Church truth are the elements, still pure (and not what they have as heretics), which enable them by baptism to give birth to children of God.

After S. Augustine, S. Thomas Aquinas, S. Bonaventura, the editors of the Roman Catechism, and others, have discussed the question anew; and the principal propositions upon which the whole subject turns are the following:—

(α.) He who baptizes is a simple instrument, and Christ can use any instrument whatever, provided that he does what Christ (the Church) wills that he should do. This instrument only performs the act of baptism; the grace of baptism comes from God. Thus any man, even a heathen, can administer baptism, provided that he will do as the Church does; and this latitude with respect to the administrant of baptism is not without reason: it is founded upon this, that baptism is really necessary as a means of salvation.

(β.) Baptism, then, by a heretic will be valid, if it is administered in the name of the Father, and of the Son, and of the Holy Ghost, and with the intention of doing as the Church does (intentio faciendi, quod facit ecclesia).

(γ.) Should he who has thus been baptized, after remaining a long time in heresy, acknowledge his error and his separation from the Church, he ought, in order to be admitted into the Church, to submit to a penance (manus impositio ad pœnitentiam); but it is not necessary to re-baptize him.

(δ.) The sacraments are often compared to channels through which divine grace comes to us. Then, when any one is baptized in a heretical sect, but is baptized according to the rules, the channel of grace is truly applied to him, and there flows to him through this channel not only the remission of sins (remissio peccatorum), but also sanctification and the renewal of the inner man (sanctificatio et renovatio interioris hominis); that is to say, he receives the grace of baptism.

(ε.) It is otherwise with confirmation. From the time of the apostles, they only, and never the deacons, their fellow-workers, had the power of giving confirmation. Now, too, it is only the legitimate successors of the apostles, the bishops, who can administer this sacrament in the Church. If, therefore, any one has been confirmed whilst he was in heresy, he can have been so only by a schismatical or heretical bishop or priest; so that his confirmation must be invalid, and it is necessary that the imposition of hands should be repeated, ut Spiritum sanctum consequatur et signetur.

Doctor Mattes has brought out, with much depth, in the dissertation which we have already frequently quoted, the different reasons for believing that baptism and marriage may be administered by those who are not Christians.

SEC. 7. Synod of Narbonne (255–260)

The councils of Christian Africa have chiefly occupied our attention so far: we are now to direct attention to those of the other countries of the Roman Empire, and first to those of Gaul. It is known that, about the middle of the third century, seven missionary bishops were sent into Gaul by Pope Fabian, and that one of them was S. Paul, first bishop of Narbonne. The acts of his life which have reached us speak of a synod held at Narbonne on his account between 255 and 260. Two deacons, whom the holy bishop had often blamed for their incontinence, wished to revenge themselves on him in a diabolical manner. They secretly put a pair of women's slippers under his bed, and then showed them in proof of the bishop's impurity. Paul found himself obliged to assemble his colleagues in a synod, that they might judge of his innocence or culpability. While the bishops continued the inquiry for three days, an eagle came and placed itself upon the roof of the house where they were assembled. Nothing could drive it away, and during those three days a raven brought it food. On the third day Paul ordered public prayer that God would make known the truth. The deacons were then seized by an evil spirit, and so tormented, that they ended by confessing their perfidy and calumny. They could only be delivered through prayer, and they renewed their confession. Instead of judging Paul, the bishops threw themselves at his feet, and with all the people entreated his intercession with God. The eagle then took flight towards the East.

Such is the account given in the Acts. They are ancient, but full of fables, and, as Remi Ceillier and others have already shown, cannot constitute a serious historical document.

SEC. 8. Synods at Arsinöe and Rome (255–260)

We have, unlike the case last considered, the most thoroughly historical records of the assembly over which Dionysius the Great, Archbishop of Alexandria, presided at Arsinöe, and of which he speaks himself in Eusebius. Nepos, an Egyptian bishop, also a very venerable man, and author of some Christian canticles, had fallen into the error of the Millenarians, and had endeavoured to spread it. Dying some time after, he could not be judged; and his primate, Dionysius the Great, had to content himself with refuting the opinions which he had propagated. He did so in two books, περὶ ἐπαγγελιῶν. Besides this, about 255, Dionysius being near to Arsinöe, where the errors of Nepos had made great progress, assembled the priests (of

Nepos) and the teachers of the place, and prevailed upon them to submit their doctrine to a discussion which should take place before all their brethren, who would be present at it. In the debate they relied upon a work by Nepos, which the Millenarians much venerated. Dionysius disputed with them for three days; and both parties, says Dionysius himself, showed much moderation, calmness, and love of truth. The result was, that Coration, chief of the party of Nepos, promised to renounce his error, and the discussion terminated to the satisfaction of all.

Some years later, about 260, the same Dionysius the Great, from his manner of combating Sabellius, gave occasion for the holding of a Roman synod, of which we shall speak more at length in giving the history of the origin of Arianism.

SEC. 9. Three Synods at Antioch on account of Paul of Samosata (264–269)

Three synods at Antioch in Syria occupied themselves with the accusation and deposition of the bishop of that town, the well-known anti-Trinitarian, Paul of Samosata.

Sabellius had wished to strengthen the idea of unity in the doctrine of the Trinity, by suppressing the difference between the persons, and only admitting, instead of the persons, three different modes of action in the one person of God; consequently denying the personal difference between the Father and the Son, and identifying them both. In his doctrinal explanation of the mystery of the Trinity, Paul of Samosata took an opposite course: he separated the one from the other, the Father and the Son, far too much. He set off, as Sabellius did, from a confusion of the divine persons, and regarded the Logos as an impersonal virtue of God in no way distinct from the Father. In JESUS he saw only a man penetrated by the Logos, who, although miraculously born of a virgin, was yet only a man, and not the God-man. His inferior being was ἐκπαρθένου; his superior being, on the contrary, was penetrated by the Logos. The Logos had dwelt in the man Jesus, not in person, but in quality, as virtue or power (οὐκ οὐσιωδῶς ἀλλὰ κατὰ ποιότητα). Moreover, by an abiding penetration, He sanctified him, and rendered him worthy of a divine name. Paul of Samosata further taught, that as the Logos is not a person, so also the Holy Spirit is only a divine virtue, impersonal, belonging to the Father, and distinct from Him only in thought.

Thus, while Paul on one side approached Sabellianism, on the other side he inclined towards the Subordinatians of Alexandria. We will not discuss whether Jewish errors, of which Philastrius accuses him, were mixed with this monarchianism, as this is merely an accessory question. Theodoret says more accurately, that Paul sought, by his anti-

Trinitarian doctrines, to please his protectress and sovereign Zenobia, who was a Jewess, and consequently held anti-Trinitarian opinions.

The new error was so much the more dangerous, as the ecclesiastical and political position of its author was of great importance. He filled the highest see in the East. We know also, that in 264 or 265 a great number of bishops assembled at Antioch; particularly Firmilian of Cæsarea in Cappadocia, Gregory Thaumaturgus and his brother Athenodorus, the Archbishop Helenus of Tarsus in Cilicia, Nicomas of Iconium, Hymenæus of Jerusalem, Theotecnus of Cæsarea in Palestine (the friend of Origen), Maximus of Bostra, and many other bishops, priests, and deacons. Dionysius the Great of Alexandria had also been invited to the Synod; but his age and infirmities prevented him from going in person, and he died a short time after. He had wished at least to be able in writing to defend the doctrine of the Church against Paul of Samosata, as he had before defended it against Sabellius. According to Eusebius, he addressed a letter to the church at Antioch, in which he would not even salute the bishop. Without entirely confirming this statement furnished by Eusebius, Theodoret relates that in that letter Dionysius exhorted Paul to do what was right, whilst he encouraged the assembled bishops to redoubled zeal for orthodoxy. From these testimonies we may conclude that

Dionysius wrote three letters—one to Paul, another to the bishops in Synod, a third to the church at Antioch; but it is also true that one single letter might easily contain all that Eusebius and Theodoret attribute to Dionysius.

In a great number of sessions and discussions they sought to demonstrate the errors of Paul, and entreated him to return to orthodoxy; but the latter, cleverly dissembling his doctrine, protested that he had never professed such errors, and that he had always followed the apostolic dogmas. After these declarations, the bishops being satisfied, thanked God for this harmony, and separated.

But they found that they were soon obliged to assemble again at Antioch. Firmilian appears to have presided over this fresh assembly, as he had over the first: its exact date is not certainly known. The Synod explicitly condemned the new doctrine introduced by Paul. As, however, Paul promised to renounce and retract his errors (as he had absolutely rejected them as his in the first Synod), Firmilian and the bishops allowed themselves to be deceived a second time.

Paul did not keep his promise, and soon, says Theodoret, the report was spread that he professed his former errors as before. However, the bishops would not cut him off immediately from communion with the Church: they tried again to bring him back to the right way by a letter which they addressed to him; and it was only when this last attempt had failed that they assembled for the third time at Antioch, towards the close of the year 269. Bishop Firmilian died at Tarsus in going to this Synod. According to Athanasius, the number of assembled bishops reached seventy, and eighty according to Hilarius. The deacon Basil, who wrote in the fifth century, raises it even to a hundred and eighty. Firmilian being dead, Helenus presided over the assembly, as we are expressly assured by the Libellus Synodicus. Besides Helenus, Hymenæus of Jerusalem, Theotecnus of Cæsarea in Palestine, Maximus of Bostra, Nicomas of Iconium, and others, were present. Among the priests who were present at the Synod, Malchion was especially remarkable, who, after having taught rhetoric with much success at Antioch, had been ordained priest there on account of the purity of his manners and the ardour of his faith. He was chosen by the bishops assembled at Antioch as the opponent in discussion of Paul of Samosata, on account of his vast knowledge and his skill in logic. The notaries kept an account of all that was said. These documents still existed in the time of Eusebius and of Jerome; but we have only some short fragments preserved by two writers of the sixth century—Leontius of Byzantium and Peter the deacon.

In these disputations Paul of Samosata was convicted of error. The Council deposed him, excommunicated him, and chose in his place Domnus, son of his predecessor Demetrian Bishop of Antioch. Before dissolving itself, the Council sent to Dionysius Bishop of Rome, to Maximus of Alexandria, and to the bishops of all the provinces, an encyclical letter, which we still possess in greater part, in which was an account of the errors and manners of Paul of Samosata, as well as of the deliberations of the Council respecting him. It is there said, "that Paul, who was very poor at first, had acquired great riches by illegal proceedings, by extortions and frauds, professedly promising his protection in lawsuits, and then deceiving those who had paid him. Besides, he was extremely proud and arrogant: he had accepted worldly employments, and preferred to be called ducenarius rather than bishop; he always went out surrounded by a train of servants. He was reproached with having, out of vanity, read and dictated letters while walking; with having, by his pride, caused much evil to be said of Christians; with having had a raised throne made for him in the church; with acting in a theatrical manner—striking his thigh, spurning things with his foot, persecuting and scorning those who during his sermons did not join with the clappers of hands bribed to applaud him; with having spoken disparagingly of the greatest doctors of the Church, and with applause of himself; with having suppressed the Psalms in honour of Christ, under the pretext that they were of recent origin, to substitute for them at the feast of Easter hymns sung by women in his honour; with having caused himself to be praised in the sermons of his partisans, priests and chorepiscopi. The letter further declared that he had denied that the Son of God descended from heaven, but that he personally had allowed himself to be called an angel come from on high; that, besides, he had lived with the subintroducti, and had allowed the same to his clergy. If he could not be reproached with positive immorality, he had at least caused much scandal. Finally, he had fallen into the heresy of Artemon; and the Synod had thought it sufficient to proceed only on this last point. They had therefore excommunicated Paul, and elected Domnus in his place. The Synod prayed all the bishops to exchange the litteras communicatorias with Domnus, whilst Paul, if he wished, could write to Artemon. It is with this ironical observation that the great fragment of the synodical letter preserved by Eusebius terminates. It is thought that in Leontius of Byzantium are to be found some more fragments of this letter treating of Paul's doctrine. Much more important is an ancient tradition, that the Synod of Antioch must have rejected the expression ὁμοούσιος. This is, at least, what semi-Arians have maintained; whilst S. Athanasius says "that he had not the synodical letter of the Council of Antioch before his eyes, but that the semi-Arians had maintained, in their Synod of Ancyra of 358, that this letter denied that the Son was ὁμοούσιος τῷ πατρί." What the semi-Arians affirmed is also reported by Basil the Great and Hilary of Poitiers. Thus it is impossible to maintain the hypothesis of many learned men, viz. that the semi-Arians had falsified the fact, and that there was nothing true about the rejection of the expression ὁμοούσιος by the Synod of Antioch. The original documents do not, however, show us why this Synod of Antioch rejected the word ὁμοούσιος; and we are thrown upon conjectures for this point.

Athanasius says that Paul argued in this way: If Christ, from being a man, did not become God—that is to say, if He were not a man deified—then He is ὁμοούσιος with the Father; but then three substances (οὐσίαι) must be admitted—one first substance (the Father), and two more recent (the Son and the Spirit); that is to say, that the divine substance is separated into three parts.

In this case Paul must have used the word ὁμοούσιος in that false sense which afterwards many Arians attributed to the orthodox: in his mind ὁμοούσιος must have signified the possessor of a part of the divine substance, which is not the natural sense of the word. Then, as Paul abused this expression, it may be that for this reason the Synod of Antioch should absolutely forbid the use of the

189

word ὁμοούσιος. Perhaps Paul also maintained that the ὁμοούσιος: answered much better to his doctrine than to that of the orthodox: for he could easily name as ὁμοούσιος with the Father, the divine virtue which came down upon the man Jesus, since according to him this virtue was in no way distinct from the Father; and in this case, again, the Synod would have sufficient ground for rejecting this expression.

These explanations would be without any use if the two creeds which were formerly attributed to this Council of Antioch really proceeded from it. In these creeds the word ὁμοούσιος is not only adopted, but great stress is laid upon it. The two creeds also have expressions evidently imitated from the Nicene Creed,—a fact which shows that they could not have proceeded from the Synod of Antioch. If in 269 such a profession of faith in the mystery of the Holy Trinity had been written at Antioch, the Fathers of Nicæa would have had much easier work to do, or rather Arianism would not have been possible.

We have already said that the synodical letter of the Council of Antioch was addressed to Dionysius Bishop of Rome. The Synod did not know that this Pope died in the month of December 269: thus the letter was given to his successor, Felix I., who wrote immediately to Bishop Maximus and the clergy of Alexandria to define the orthodox faith of the Church with greater clearness against the errors of Paul of Samosata.

Paul continued to live in the episcopal palace, notwithstanding his deposition, being probably supported by Zenobia; and he thus obliged the orthodox to appeal to the Emperor Aurelian after this prince had conquered Zenobia and taken Antioch in 272. The Emperor decided that "he should occupy the episcopal house at Antioch who was in connection with the bishops of Italy and the see of Rome." Paul was then obliged to leave his palace with disgrace, as Eusebius relates.

We have up to this time spoken of three Synods of Antioch, all of them held with reference to Paul of Samosata; but a certain number of historians will admit only two, as we think, wrongly. The synodical letter of the last Council of Antioch says distinctly that Firmilian went twice on this account to Antioch, and that on his third journey to be present at a new synod, consequently at a third, he died. As the synodical letter is the most trustworthy source which can be quoted in this case, we ought to prefer its testimony to Theodoret's account, who mentions only two Synods of Antioch. As for Eusebius, whose authority has been quoted, it is true that he first mentions only one synod, then in the following chapter another Synod of Antioch; but this other he does not call the second—he calls it the last. What he says in the twenty-seventh chapter shows that he united into one only the first and second Synods. "The bishops," he says, "assembled often, and at different periods." But even if Eusebius had spoken of only two synods, his testimony would evidently be of less value than the synodical letter.

It is with these Synods of Antioch that the councils of the third century terminate. The Libellus Synodicus certainly mentions another synod held in Mesopotamia; but it was only a religious conference between Archelaus Bishop of Carchara (or, more correctly, Caschara) in Mesopotamia, and the heretic Manes. As for the pretended Eastern Synod in the year 300, in which the patriarchs of Rome, of Constantinople (an evident anachronism), of Antioch, and of Alexandria, are said to have granted to the Bishop of Seleucia the dignity of patriarch of the whole of Persia, it is a pure invention.

CHAPTER III
THE SYNODS OF THE FIRST TWENTY YEARS
OF THE FOURTH CENTURY

SEC. 10. Pretended Synod of Sinuessa (303)

IF the document which tells us of a Synod of
Sinuessa (situated between Rome and Capua)
could have any pretension to authenticity, this
Synod must have taken place about the beginning
of the fourth century, in 303. It says: The Emperor
Diocletian had pressed Marcellinus Bishop of Rome
to sacrifice to the gods. At first stedfast, the bishop
had finally allowed himself to be dragged into the
temple of Vesta and of Isis, and there offered
incense to the idols. He was followed by three
priests and two deacons, who fled the moment he
entered the temple, and spread the report that they
had seen Marcellinus sacrificing to the gods. A
Synod assembled, and Marcellinus denied the fact.
The inquiry was continued in a crypt near Sinuessa,
on account of the persecution. There were
assembled many priests, no fewer than three
hundred bishops; a number quite impossible for that
country, and in a time of persecution. They first of all
condemned the three priests and the two deacons
for having abandoned their bishop. As for the latter,
although sixty-two witnesses had sworn against
him, the Synod would not pronounce judgment: it
simply demanded that he should confess his fault,
and judge himself; or, if he was not guilty, that he

should pronounce his own acquittal. On the morrow fresh witness arose against Marcellinus. He denied again. The third day the three hundred bishops assembled, once more condemned the three priests and the two deacons, called up the witnesses again, and charged Marcellinus in God's name to speak the truth. He then threw himself on the ground, and covering his head with ashes, loudly and repeatedly acknowledged his sin, adding that he had allowed himself to be bribed by gold. The bishops, in pronouncing judgment, formally added: Marcellinus has condemned himself, for the occupant of the highest see cannot be judged by any one (prima sedes non judicatur a quoquam). The consequence of this Synod was, that Diocletian caused many bishops who were present at it to be put to death, even Pope Marcellinus himself, on the 23d of August 303.

This account is so filled with improbabilities and evidently false dates, that in modern times Roman Catholics and Protestants have unanimously rejected the authenticity of it. Before that, some Roman Catholics were not unwilling to appeal to this document, on account of the proposition, prima sedes non judicatur a quoquam. The Roman breviary itself has admitted the account of Marcellinus' weakness, and of the sacrifice offered by him. But it is beyond all doubt that this document is an amplification of the falsehood spread by the

Donatists about the year 400. They maintain that during Diocletian's persecution Marcellinus had delivered up the Holy Scriptures, and sacrificed to the idols,—a falsehood which Augustine and Theodoret had already refuted.

SEC. 11. Synod of Cirta (305)

If the Donatists have invented the Synod of Sinuessa, which never took place, they have, on the other hand, contested the existence of a Council which was certainly held in 305 at Cirta in Numidia. This Synod took place on the occasion of the installation of a new bishop of this town. Secundus Bishop of Tigisium, the oldest of the eleven bishops present, presided over the assembly. A short time before, an edict of Diocletian had enacted that the sacred writings should be given up; and a multitude of Christians, and even bishops, had proved weak, and had obeyed the edict. Most of the bishops present at Cirta were accused of this fall; so that the president could say to almost all of them, when questioning them according to their rank, Dicitur te tradidisse. They acknowledged themselves to be guilty, adding, one that God had preserved him from sacrificing to the idols (which would have been doubtless a much greater fall); another, that instead of the sacred books he had given up books of medicine; a third, that he had been forced by violence, and so forth. All implored grace and pardon. The president then demanded of Purpurius

Bishop of Limata, if it was true that he had killed two of his nephews. The latter answered, "Do you think you can terrify me like the others? What did you do then yourself, when the curator commanded you to give up the Holy Scriptures?" This was to reproach him with the crime for which he was prosecuting the others; and the president's own nephew, Secundus the younger, addressed his uncle in these words: "Do you hear what he says of you? He is ready to leave the Synod, and to create a schism: he will have with him all those whom you wish to punish, and I know that they have reasons for condemning you." The president asked counsel from some of the bishops: they persuaded him to decide that "each one should render an account to God of his conduct in this matter (whether he had given up the Holy Scriptures or not)." All were of the same opinion, and shouted, Deo gratias!

This is what is told us in the fragment of the synodical acts preserved by S. Augustine in the third book of his work against the Donatist Cresconius. We also learn from this fragment, that the Synod was held in a private house belonging to Urbanus Donatus, during the eighth consulate of Diocletian and the seventh of Maximian, that is to say, in 303. Optatus of Mileve, on the other hand, gives to this Donatus the surname of Carisius, and tells us that they chose a private house because the churches of the town had not yet been restored since the persecution. As for the chronological question, S. Augustine says in another place, that the copy of the synodical acts, which was carefully examined on occasion of the religious conference of Carthage with the Donatists, was thus dated: post consulatum Diocletiani novies et Maximiani octies, tertio nonas Martis, that is to say, March 5, 305. That is, in fact, the exact date, as Valesius has proved in his notes upon the eighth book of the History of the Church by Eusebius, ch. 2. Natalis Alexander has also written a special dissertation upon this subject in his History of the Church.

When the affair respecting the bishops who had yielded up the Holy Scriptures had been decided, they proceeded to the election of the new Bishop of Cirta. The bishops nominated the deacon Silvanus, although, as is proved by a fragment of the acts preserved by S. Augustine, he had delivered up the sacred books in 303, together with his bishop Paul. This Silvanus and some others among the bishops assembled at Cirta, after having been so indulgent towards themselves, afterwards became the chiefs of the rigorous and exaggerated party of the Donatists, who saw traditores everywhere, even where there were none.

SEC. 12. Synod of Alexandria (306)

Almost at the same period, perhaps a year later, a synod was held at Alexandria, under the presidency of Peter, then archbishop of that place. The Bishop of Lycopolis, Meletius, author of the Meletian schism, was, as S. Athanasius tells us, deposed by this Synod for different offences; and among others, for having sacrificed to idols. These last words show that this Synod took place after the explosion of Diocletian's persecution, consequently after 303. S. Athanasius further adds, in his Epistola ad episcopos: "The Meletians were declared schismatics more than fifty-five years ago." This letter having been written in 356 or in 361, the latter date would give the year 306 as that of the Synod; and this is the date which we adopt For on the other hypothesis (reckoning from the year 356) we should be brought to 301, when the persecution of Diocletian had not begun.

To the beginning of the fourth century belongs the

SEC. 13. Synod of Elvira (305 or 306)

This Synod has been, more than any other, an occasion for many learned researches and controversies. The principal work on the subject is that by the Spaniard Ferdinand de Mendoza, in 1593; it comprises three books, the title of which is, de confirmando concilio Illiberitano ad Clementem VIII. The best text of the acts of this Council is found in the Collectio canonum Ecclesiæ Hispanæ, by Franc. Ant. Gonzalez, librarian (Madrid 1808, in folio). It was compiled from nine ancient Spanish manuscripts. Bruns has reproduced it in his Biblioth eccles.

Pliny the elder speaks of two towns named Illiberis: the one in Gallia Narbonensis, which is now called Collioure, in Roussillon (now French); the other in the south of Spain, in the province Bœtica, now Andalusia. As it is a Spanish council, there can be no question but that it was the latter town, as Illiberis in Narbonne had been demolished long before the time of Constantine the Great. Mendoza relates, that in his day the remains of walls bearing the name of Elbira might still be seen on a mountain not far from Granada; and the gate of Granada, situated in this direction, is called the gate of Elbira. There is also another Eliberis, but it dates only from the conquest of the Goths. Illiberris, with a double l and a double r, is the true one, according to Mendoza.

The synodical acts, whose genuineness could be doubted only by hypercriticism, mention nineteen bishops as present at the Council. According to a Codex Pithöanus of its acts, their number must have reached forty-three. The nineteen are: Felix of Acci (Cadiz), who, probably as being the eldest, was nominated president of the Synod; Hosius of Corduba, afterwards so famous in the Arian controversy as Bishop of Cordova; Sabinus of Hispalis (Seville), Camerismus of Tucci, Sinaginis of Epagra (or Bigerra), Secundinus of Castulo, Pardus of Mentesa, Flavian of Eliberis, Cantonius of Urci,

Liberius of Emerita, Valerius of Cæsaraugusta (Saragossa), Decentius of Legio (Leon), Melantius of Toledo, Januarius of Fibularia (perhaps Salaria in Hispania Tarraconensis), Vincent of Ossonoba, Quintianus of Elbora, Successus of Eliocroca, Eutychian of Basti (Baza), and Patricius of Malacca, There were therefore bishops from the most different parts of Spain; so that we may consider this assembly as a synod representing 'the whole of Spain. The acts also mention twenty-four priests, and say that they were seated at the Synod like the bishops, whilst the deacons and the laity stood up. The decrees proceeded only from the bishops; for the synodical acts always employed this formula: EPISCOPI universi dixerunt.

1. As for the date of this Synod, the acts tell us that it was celebrated, which means opened, at the Ides of May; that is, on the 15th May. The inscriptions on the acts also give the following particulars: Constantii temporibus editum, eodem tempore quo et Nicæna synodus habita est. Some of the acts add: era 362.

Of course it refers to the Spanish era, which began to be. used in Spain in the fifth century: it counted from the thirty-eighth year before Christ, so that the year 362 of the Spanish era corresponds to 324 of our reckoning. This date of 324 answers to that of the Council of Nicæa (325), also mentioned in the inscription on the synodical acts; but the tempore

Constantii does not agree with it, at least unless we should read Constantini. But there are very strong objections against this chronological reading.

a. Most of the ancient manuscripts of these synodical acts do not bear any date: one would therefore be led to conclude that this had been added at a later time.

b. Bishop Hosius of Corduba, named among the bishops present at the Synod, was not in Spain in 324: he passed the whole of that year either at the Emperor's court (in Nicomedia) or at Alexandria. Constantine the Great, with whom he was, after the defeat of Licinius, consequently in the autumn of 323 or in the spring of 324, sent him to that place in order to try to settle the Arian strife. Hosius not being able to succeed, in his mission, returned to the Emperor as counsellor on ecclesiastical matters, and immediately afterwards he took part in the first Œcumenical Council of Nicæa, in 325.

c. A long time previous to 323 and 324 Hosius had left Spain, and he generally resided with the Emperor. It is known that after the close of the Council of Arles, in 314, the Donatists appealed from the judgment of the Council to the Emperor Constantine the Great. The sentence given by the Emperor in 316 having been against them, they spread the report that it was Hosius of Cordova who had influenced the Emperor in his judgment.

Augustine, in relating this fact, adds that Hosius had, on the contrary, suggested to the Emperor more moderate measures than the Donatists deserved. Hosius was then at the imperial court, at the latest, in 316: a decree which Constantine addressed to Cecilian Bishop of Carthage in 313, and in which he mentions Osius, would even lead us to conclude that the Spanish bishop was with Constantine in 313.

d. We must also notice, that the purport of several canons of Elvira cannot agree with this date of 324.

(α.) Several of these canons appear, indeed, to have been compiled during or soon after a violent persecution, in which several Christians had apostatized. We say during, or soon after; but it is more likely that it was soon after: for during a persecution, bishops from the most distant provinces of Spain, from the north and the south, could hardly assemble in the same place. Now the last persecution of the Spanish Christians by the Emperors was that of Diocletian and of Maximianus Herculeus, from 303 to 305.

(β.) The decisions of Elvira about the lapsi are much more rigorous than those of Nicæa: thus the first canon of Elvira forbids that the holy communion should be administered to the lapsi, even in articulo mortis. This severity evidently indicates a date prior to that of the Synod of Nicæa. Such severity during a persecution, or immediately after, could be explained, but not so twenty years later.

2. It was indeed this severity of the canons of Elvira with regard to the lapsi which suggested to the oratorian Morinus the hypothesis which he propounds in his book de Pœnitentia, viz. that the Synod of Elvira must have assembled before the origin of the Novatian schism, about 250; otherwise the Fathers of Elvira, by their first canon, must have taken the side of the Novatians. But the severity of the Novatians is very different from that of the Synod of Elvira. The Novatians pretended that the Church had not the right to admit to the communion a Christian who had apostatized: the Fathers of Elvira acknowledged this right; they wished only that in certain cases, for reasons of discipline, she should suspend the exercise of this right, and delay the admission, non desperatione veniæ, sed rigors disciplinæ. We must add, that about 250 Hosius and the other bishops present at the Council of Elvira were not yet born, or at least they were not at any rate among the clergy.

3. The hypothesis of the Magdeburg Centuriators, which places the Synod of Elvira in the year 700, is still more unfortunate. To give such dates, is to make Hosius and his colleagues of Elvira into true Methuselahs of the new covenant.

4. Following the Fasti of Onuphrius, Hardouin has adopted the date 313, giving especially as his reason, that the canons of the Council of Arles in 314 have much in common with those of Elvira. But this is extremely feeble reasoning; for they might easily profit by the canons of Elvira at Arles, even if they were framed ten or twenty years previously. Besides, Hosius, as we have seen above, appears to have left his native country, Spain, in 313.

5. Baluze has propounded another theory. At the Council of Sardica (eleventh canon in Greek, fourteenth canon in Latin), Hosius proposed a law (on the subject of the Sunday festival), which had been before proposed in a former council (superiore concilio). This is an allusion to the twenty-first canon of the Council of Elvira. Baluze remarks, that since Hosius calls the Council of Elvira superius concilium, this Council must have taken place before the Council of Nicæa, which, with Hosius, when the Council of Sardica was held, was only the concilium postremum. The reasoning of Baluze can be maintained up to this point; but afterwards, from some other indications, he wishes to conclude that the Synod of Elvira took place after those of Ancyra and of Neocæsarea; consequently between 314 and 325. This latter part of his proof is very feeble; and besides, he has entirely forgotten that Hosius was not in Spain between 314 and 325.

6. Mansi thinks that the Synod of Elvira took place in 309. It is said in the acts, he remarks, that the Council was held in the Ides of May. Now in 309 these Ides fell on a Sunday; and at this period they began to hold synods on a Sunday, as the example of Nicæa shows. This last observation is not exact. The Council of Nicæa requires, in the fifth canon, that two synods should be celebrated annually,— one during Lent, the other in the autumn; but there is nowhere any mention of Sunday. The apostolic canons, No. 36 (38), give the same meaning: "The first synod shall be held in the fourth week after Pentecost; the second on the 12th of the month Hyperberataios." Here also, then, there is no mention of Sunday; the 12th of the month Hyperberataios might fall upon any day of the week. In the statutes of the Synod of Antioch in 341, Sunday is not prescribed more than any other day.

7. The calculation of Mendoza, of Natalis Alexander, of Tillemont, of d'Aguirre, of Rémi Ceillier, etc., appears to us more defensible: they all proceed upon the fact that Valerius Bishop of Saragossa, who, we know from the acts, was present at the Synod, was persecuted in 304, with his deacon Vincent, by the Roman prætor Dacian. The deacon was put to death, and Valerius exiled; afterwards he also was martyred, if we may believe an ancient tradition. They concluded from this, that the Council of Elvira could not have taken place before 304, that

is to say, before the arrest of Bishop Valerius; and they only disagreed upon the point whether the Council took place at the commencement of the year 300 or 301: d'Aguirre even mentions the commencement of 303. The difficulty is, that they place the Council of Elvira before the outbreak of the persecution; whilst, as has been said before, several of the canons were evidently written just after a persecution, and consequently could not have been promulgated between 300 and 304.

8. The opinion, then, which appears to us the most probable in this question, is the following: In May 305 Diocletian and Maximianus Herculeus had abdicated; and Constantius, celebrated for his benevolence towards the Christians, became sovereign ruler of Spain. The persecution, therefore, having ceased, the Spanish bishops could assemble at Elvira to deliberate, first, respecting the treatment of the lapsi, which was the chief subject of the canons which they formed, and also to seek for means against the invasion of moral corruption.

But it will be said, Was not Valerius of Saragossa dead in 305? I do not think so. To prove it, Rémi Ceillier appeals to Prudentius; but the latter does not say a word of the martyrdom of Valerius, either in his poem upon all the martyrs of Saragossa in general, or in his poem upon Vincent in particular. If Valerius had really been martyred, he would certainly not have failed to say so. Then, if Valerius was living at the time of the abdication of Diocletian and Maximian, he was undoubtedly recalled from exile by Constantius; and he could thus take part in the Synod of Elvira, which we therefore place in the autumn of 305, or in 306. Baronius, Binius in Mansi, and others, accept 305, but on other grounds than ours, whilst Pagi leaves the question undecided. The eighty-one canons of the Synod of Elvira are the following:—

CAN. 1. De his qui post baptismum idolis immolaverunt

Placuit inter nos: Qui post fidem baptismi salutaris adulta ætate ad templum idoli idolaturus accesserit, et fecerit, quod est crimen capitale, quia est summi sceleris, placuit nee in finem eum communionem accipere.

"If an adult who has been baptized has entered an idol's temple, and has committed a capital crime, he cannot be received into communion, even at the end of his life."

Several interpreters of this canon, among others Dr. Herbst, who has explained the canons of Elvira in the Tübinger Quartalschrift, have erroneously thought that we must understand here by communio, not eucharistic communion, but only communion with the Church, or sacramental absolution. This is a mistake: the word communio does not mean only communion with the Church, but sacramental communion as well. If any one is excluded from the Church, and if they cannot receive sacramental absolution, neither can they receive the holy Eucharist.

CAN. 2. De sacerdotibus gentilium qui post baptismum immolaverunt

Flamines, qui post fidem lavacri et regenerationis sacrificaverunt, eo quod geminaverint scelera accedente homicidio, vel triplicaverint facinus cohærente mœchia, placuit eos nec in finem accipere communionem.

CAN. 3. De eisdem si idolis munus tantum dederunt

Item flamines qui non immolaverint, sed munus tantum dederint, eo quod se a funestis abstinuerint sacrificiis, placuit in finem eis præstare communionem, acta tamen legitima pœnitentia. Item ipsi si post pœnitentiam fuerint mœchati placuit ulterius his non esse dandam communionem, ne illusisse de dominica communione videantur.

CAN. 4. De eisdem si catechumeni adhuc immolant quando baptizentur

Item flamines si fuerint catechumeni et se a sacrificiis abstinuerint, post triennii tempora placuit ad baptismum admitti debere.

The office of a flamen in the provinces of the Roman Empire consisted either in offering sacrifices to the gods, or in preparing the public games. It was hereditary in many families; and as it entailed many expenses, he who was legally bound to fill it could not give it up, even if he became a Christian, as is proved by the Code of Justinian, and S. Jerome's work De Vita Hilarionis. It followed from this, that the members of these families of flamines kept their office even when they were catechumens or had been baptized; but they tried to give up the duties which it imposed, especially the sacrifices. They consented still to continue to prepare the public games. In the time of a persecution, the people generally wished to oblige them to offer sacrifices also. This Synod decided on what must be done with these flamines in the different cases which might arise.

a. If they had been baptized, and if they had consented to fulfil all their duties, they had by that act alone (α) sacrificed to idols; (β) they had taken part in murders, by preparing for the games (in the games of gladiators), and in acts of immorality (in the obscene acts of certain plays). Their sin was therefore double and triple. Then they must be refused the communion as long as they lived.

b. If they had been baptized, but if, without sacrificing, they had only given the games, they might be received into communion at the close of their life, provided that they should have first submitted to a suitable penance. But if, after having begun to do penance (that is the sense, and not after the accomplishment of the penance), they should again be led into any act of immorality (that is to say, if as flamines they should allow themselves to organize obscene plays), they should never more receive the communion.

c. If a flamen was only a catechumen, and if, without sacrificing, he had fulfilled his duties (perhaps also given the games), he might be baptized after three years of trial.

CAN. 5. Si domina per zelum ancillam occiderit

Si qua fœmina furore zeli accensa flagris verberaverit ancillam suam, ita ut intra tertium diem animam cum cruciatu effundat, eo quod incertum sit voluntate an casu occiderit; si voluntate, post septem annos, si casu, post quinquennii tempora, acta legitima pœnitentia, ad communionem placuit admitti; quod si intra tempora constituta fuerint infirmata, accipiat communionem.

"If, in anger, a woman should strike her servant, so that the latter should die at the end of three days, the guilty woman shall undergo a seven years' penance if she struck so violently on purpose, and a five years' penance if she did not do so on purpose to kill: she shall not be received into communion till after this delay. If she should fall ill during the time of her penance, she may receive the communion."

This canon was inserted in the Corpus juris can.

CAN. 6. Si quicunque per maleficium hominem interfecerit

Si quis vero maleficio interficiat alteram, eo quod sine idololatria perficere scelus non potuit, nee in finem impertiendam illi esse communionem.

By maleficio is here to be understood the deceits of magic or sorcery, which they considered necessarily connected with idolatry.

The following canon needs no explanation.

CAN. 7. De pœnitentibus mœchiæ si rursus mœchaverint

Si quis forte fidelis post lapsum mœchiæ, post tempora constituta, acta pœnitentia, denuo fuerit fornicatus, placuit nec in finem habere eum communionem.

CAN. 8. De fœminis quæ relictis viris suis aliis nubunt

Item fœminæ, quæ nulla præcedente causa reliquerint viros suos et alteris se copulaverint, nec in finem accipiant communionem.

Some interpreters have thought that the question here was that only of a Christian woman leaving her husband, still a pagan, without any reason; for under no pretext could she leave a Christian husband to marry another. But the following canon proves conclusively that the eighth canon speaks of a Christian couple. If it adds without reason, that does not mean that there exist any cases in which a woman could leave her husband to marry another: the canon decrees only a more severe punishment if she should abandon her husband without reason; whilst the following canon prescribes what punishment to inflict in case she should leave her husband not entirely without a cause (if, for example, the husband is an adulterer).

The ninth canon, which has also been inserted in the Corpus juris canon, is thus worded:—

CAN. 9. De fœminis quæ adulteros maritos relinquunt et aliis nubunt

Item fœmina fidelis, quæ adulterum maritum reliquerit fidelem et alteram ducit, prohibeatur ne ducat; si duxerit, non prius accipiat communionem, nisi quem reliquit de sæculo exierit, nisi forsitan necessitas infirmitatis dare compulerit.

The following canons are much more difficult to explain.

CAN. 10. De relicta catechumeni si alterum duxerit

Si ea quam catechumenus relinquit duxerit maritum, potest ad fontem lavacri admitti: hoc et circa fœminas catechumenas erit observandum. Quodsi fuerit fidelis quæ ducitur ab eo qui uxorem inculpatam relinquit, et quum scierit illum habere uxorem, quam sine causa reliquit, placuit in finem hujusmodi dari communionem.

CAN. 11. De catechumena si graviter ægrotaverit

Intra quinquennii autem tempora catechumena si graviter fuerit infirmata, dandum ei baptismum placuit non denegari.

These two canons are difficult to explain, because the section between the two does not occupy its proper place. They treat, of two quite different cases, and each of these cases is subdivided into two others.

1. a. If a catechumen, without any cause, should leave his wife, who has not yet been baptized, and if the latter should marry another husband, she may be baptized.

b. In the same way, if a female catechumen should, without reason, leave her husband, still unbaptized, and that he should marry again, he may be baptized.

Such is the first case. It supposes that the party who is left without cause is not baptized. Here the tenth canon should stop. What follows treats of another question, viz. if the party who has unlawfully left the other can be married again. The canon does not mention whether the party to be married is baptized, or only a catechumen, and it establishes the following:—

2. a. If a Christian woman marries a man whom she knows to have illegally divorced his wife, she may communicate only on her deathbed. As a Christian, she ought to have known that, according to S. Paul, a Christian (and the catechumen is here considered as such) cannot put away his partner, though an unbeliever, if the latter wishes to continue to live with him.

b. If a female catechumen marries a man who has illegally divorced his wife, her baptism shall be put off five years longer (a further period of trial), and she can be baptized before that time only in case of a serious illness.

We think we have thus clearly and accurately explained the sense of these two canons, which have given so much trouble to commentators.

CAN. 12. De mulieribus quæ lenocinium fecerint

Mater vel parens vel quælibet fidelis, si lenocinium exercuerit eo quod, alienum vendiderit corpus vel potius suum, placuit eam nec in finem accipere communionem.

We might have remarked on the two preceding canons, that their titles are not quite adapted to their contents. It is the same with this one. It threatens with perpetual excommunication those fathers and mothers who should give up their children to prostitution, as well as all those who follow this shameful trade. The words vel potius suum corpus, etc., however, evidently apply only to the parents of the young prostitute: in fact, they sell their own flesh and blood in selling their daughter.

CAN. 13. De virginibus Deo sacratis si adulteraverint

Virgines quæ se Deo dicaverunt, si pactum perdiderint virginitatis atque eidem libidini servierint, non intelligentes quid admiserint, placuit nee in finem eis dandam esse communionem. Quod si semel persuasæ aut infirmi corporis lapsu vitiatæ omni tempore vitæ suæ hujusmodi fœminæ egerint pœnitentiam, ut abstineant se a coitu, eo quod lapsæ potius videantur, placuit eas in finem communionem accipere debere.

When virgins consecrated to God (whether nuns properly so called, or young girls who have consecrated their youth to God, still remaining in their families) have committed a carnal sin without acknowledging their offence, and so continuing obstinately in their blindness (for it is thus that we must understand non intelligentes quid admiserint), they must remain permanently excommunicated; but if they should acknowledge their sin, and do perpetual penance, without falling again, they may receive the communion at the end of their life. This canon was inserted in the Corpus juris can.

CAN. 14. De virginibus sæcularibus si mœchaverint

Virgines quæ virginitatem suam non custodierint, si eosdem qui eas violaverint duxerint et tenuerint maritos, eo quod solas nuptias violaverint, post annum sine pœnitentia reconciliari debebunt; vel si alios cognoverint viros, eo quod mœchatæ sunt, placuit per quinquennii tempora, acta legitima pœnitentia, admitti eas ad communionem oportere.

If a young girl who has made no vows has committed a carnal sin, and if she marries him with whom she has been led away, she shall be reconciled at the end of one year, without being condemned to penance; that is to say, that she may receive the communion at the end of one year, because she has violated only the marriage law, the rights of which she usurped before they were conferred upon her.

Some manuscripts read, post pœnitentiam unius anni reconcilientur; that is to say, that one year's penance should be imposed upon her. The difference between this reading and ours is not important, for our reading also imposes on the guilty one minor excommunication for a year; that is to say, privation of the communion, which we know was also a degree of penance, namely, the fourth. The canon only exempts her from the most severe degrees of excommunication, to which were attached positive works of penance. The other reading says nothing more. If this woman should marry any one except him with whom she had fallen, she would commit a sort of adultery, and ought to submit to five years of penance.

The three following canons forbid to marry pagans, Jews, or heretics, and require no explanation:—

CAN. 15. De conjugio eorum qui ex gentilitate veniunt

Propter copiam puellarum gentilibus minime in matrimonium dandæ sunt virgines Christianæ, ne ætas in flore tumens in adulterium animæ resolvatur.

CAN. 16. De puellis fidelibus ne infidelibus conjungantur

Hæretici si se transferre noluerint ad Ecclesiam catholicam, nec ipsis catholicas dandas esse puellas; sed neque Judæis neque hæreticis dare placuit, eo quod nulla possit esse societas fideli cum infideli: si contra interdictum fecerint parentes, abstineri per quinquennium placet.

CAN. 17. De his qui filias suas sacerdotibus gentilium conjungunt

Si qui forte sacerdotibus idolorum filias suas junxerint, placuit nec in finem iis dandam esse communionem.

CAN. 18. De sacerdotibus et ministris si mœchaverint

Episcopi, presbyteres (!) et diacones si in ministerio positi detecti fuerint quod sint mœchati, placuit propter scandalum et propter profanum crimen nec in finem eos communionem accipere debere.

We must here, as in other places, understand by mœchare, not only adultery in specie, but all fornication in general.

CAN. 19. De clericis negotia et mundinas sectantibus

Episcopi, presbyteres (!) et diacones de locis suis negotiandi causa non discedant, nec circumeuntes provincias quæstuosas nundinas sectentur: sane ad victum sibi conquirendum aut filium aut libertum aut mercenarium aut amicum aut quemlibet mittant, et si voluerint negotiari, intra provinciam negotientur.

S. Cyprian, in his work de Lapsis, also complains that many bishops left their churches and went into foreign provinces for the sake of merchandise, and to give themselves up to trade.

CAN. 20. De clericis et laicis usurariis

Si quis clericorum detectus fuerit usuras accipere, placuit eum degradari et abstineri. Si quis etiam laicus accepisse probatur usuras, et promiserit correptus jam se cassaturum nec ulterius exacturum, placuit ei veniam tribui: si vero in ea iniquitate duraverit, ab ecclesia esse projiciendum.

When we consider the seventeenth Nicene canon, which also forbids lending money at interest, we shall speak of the judgment of the ancient Church on this matter. The first part of our canon has been inserted by Gratian in the Corpus juris canon.

CAN. 21. De his qui tardius ad ecclesiam accedunt

Si quis in civitate positus tres dominicas ad ecclesiam non accesserit, pauco tempore abstineatur, ut correptus esse videatur.

As we have said before, Hosius proposed and had passed at the Council of Sardica a like statute against those who neglected to go to church. It is the eleventh canon of the Greek and the fourteenth of the Latin text of the decrees of Sardica.

CAN. 22. De catholicis in hæresim transeuntibus, si revertantur

Si quis de catholica Ecclesia ad hæresim transitum fecerit rursusque recurrerit, placuit huic pœnitentiam non esse denegandam, eo quod cognoverit peccatum suum; qui etiam decem annis agat pœnitentiam, cui post decem annos præstari communio debet; si vero infantes fuerint transducti, quod non suo vitio peccaverint incunctanter recipi debent.

CAN. 23. De temporibus jejuniorum

Jejunii superpositiones per singulos menses placuit celebrari, exceptis diebus duorum mensium Julii et Augusti propter quorumdam infirmitatem.

The superponere (ὑπερτίθεσθαι), or the superpositio (ὑπέρθεσις), was an extension or prolongation of the fast beyond the usual duration (until the evening). It consisted in eating absolutely nothing for a whole day.

CAN. 24. De his qui in peregre baptizantur, ut ad clerum non veniant

Omnes qui in peregre fuerint baptizati, eo quod eorum minime sit cognita vita, placuit ad clerum non esse promovendos in alienis provinciis.

None could be admitted into the ranks, of the clergy out of the province in which he had been baptized. This canon passed into the Corpus jur. can.

CAN. 25. De epistolis communicatoriis confessorum

Omnis qui attulerit literas confessorias, sublato nomine confessoris, eo quod omnes sub hac nominis gloria passim concutiant simplices, communicatoriæ ei dandæ sunt litteræ.

This canon has been interpreted in three ways. Mendoza, Baronius, and others, when commenting upon it, thought of the letters of peace (libelli pacis) which the martyrs and confessors gave to the lapsi, to procure for them a speedy reception into the Church. These libelli pacis, indeed, induced many a bishop to admit a lapsus too promptly; but our canon does not speak of this abuse: it does not complain that these letters deceived the bishops: it says, concutiant simplices. If the canon had been intended to warn the bishops against these libelli pacis, it would certainly not have said that they should give to the lapsis communicatorias literas; for this was what was wrong, that they were admitted too soon to communion. Aubespine and Herbst were of the opinion that the canon had reference to some Christians who, before going a journey, did not ask for letters of communion from their bishop, but preferred letters of recommendation given by their confessor, regarding these as more important, and that this practice was forbidden by one synod. This, again, is a mistake. The meaning of the canon is this: "If a Christian, wishing to take a journey, submits to his bishop the draught of a letter of recommendation, in which it is said that the bearer is a confessor, the bishop must erase the word confessor, sublato nomine confessoris, because many simple people are deceived by this title, and the bishop shall give common letters communicatorias."

CAN. 26. Ut omni sabbato jejunetur

Errorem placuit corrigi, ut omni sabbati die superpositiones celebremus.

The meaning of this canon also is equivocal. The title seems to imply that it orders a severe fast every Saturday, and the suppression of the contrary practice followed up to that time. It is thus explained by Garsias in Binius and Mendoza. However, as the sixty-fifth apostolic canon prescribes that, except Holy Saturday, no Saturday should be a fast-day, our canon may also mean, "The ancient error of fasting strictly every Saturday must be abolished:" that is to say, the superpositio is ordered only for Holy Saturday; and for other Saturdays, as for

Fridays, the statio only, that is to say, the half-fast is ordered. But in comparing this canon with the forty-third, where the same expressions are again found, we see that the ut determines what was to he henceforth observed, and not in what the error consisted. According to that, our decree would mean that the superpositio must be observed every Saturday, and we must adopt the explanation of Garsias.

CAN. 27. De clericis ut extraneas fœminas in domo non habeant

Episcopus vel quilibet alius clericus aut sororem aut filiam virginem dicatam Deo tantum secum habeat; extraneam nequaquam habere placuit.

This canon is more severe than the third similar canon of the Council of Nicæa. It allows the clergy to have with them in their house (a) only their sisters, or their own daughters; (b) and also that these must be virgins, and consecrated to God, that is, having vowed their virginity to God.

CAN. 28. De oblationibus eorum qui non communicant

Episcopum placuit ab eo, qui non communicat, munus accipere non debere.

In the same way as in the first canon, we must here understand by those qui non communicant,

Christians who, like penitents or catechumens, are not in the communio (community), and who therefore do not receive the holy Eucharist. The meaning of the canon is: "The bishop cannot accept at the altar the offerings (oblata) of those who do not communicate."

CAN. 29. De energumenis qualiter habeantur in ecclesia

Energumenus qui ab erratico spiritu exagitur, hujus nomen neque ad altare cum oblatione esse recitandum, nec permittendum ut sua manu in ecclesia ministret.

This canon, like the seventy-eighth apostolic canon, excludes demoniacs possessed by the evil spirit from active participation in divine service: they cannot present any offerings; their names cannot be read among those who are inscribed in the diptychs as offering the sacrifice (diptychis offerentium); and they must not be permitted to hold any office in the Church.

CAN. 30. De his qui post lavacrum mœchati sunt, ne subdiacones fiant

Subdiaconos eos ordinari non debere qui in adolescentia sua fuerint mœchati, eo quod postmodum per subreptionem ad altiorem gradum promoveantur: vel si qui sunt in præteritum ordinati, amoveantur.

CAN. 31. De adolescentibus qui post lavacrum mœchati sunt

Adolescentes qui post fidem lavacri salutaris fuerint mœchati, cum duxerint uxores, acta legitima pœnitentia placuit ad communionem eos admitti.

These two canons need no explanation.

CAN. 32. De excommunicatis presbyteris ut in nccessitate communionem dent

Apud presbyterum, si quis gravi lapsu in ruinam mortis inciderit, placuit agere pœnitentiam non debere, sed potius apud episcopum: cogente tamen infirmitate necesse est presbyterem (!) communionem præstare debere, et diaconem si ei jusserit sacerdos.

This canon is quite in conformity with the ancient custom, according to which the bishop only, and not a priest, could receive a penitent into the Church. It was only in a case of extreme necessity that a priest, or, according to the orders of a priest, a deacon, could give a penitent the communion, that is, could administer to him the eucharistic bread in sign of reconciliation: deacons often gave the communion in the ancient Church. The title of the canon is evidently wrong, and ought to be thus worded: De presbyteris ut excommunicatis in necessitate, etc. It is thus, indeed, that Mansi read it in several manuscripts.

CAN. 33. De episcopis et ministris ut ab uxoribus abstineant

Placuit in totum prohibere episcopis, presbyteris et diaconibus vel omnibus clericis positis in ministerio abstinere se a conjugibus suis et non generare filios: quicunque vero fecerit, ab honore clericatus exterminetur.

This celebrated canon contains the most ancient command of celibacy. The bishops, priests, and deacons, and in general all the clergy, qui in ministerio positi sunt, that is, who are specially employed in the service of the altar, ought no longer to have any conjugal intercourse with their wives, under pain of deposition, if they were married when they took orders. The history of the Council of Nicæa will give us the opportunity of considering the question of celibacy in the primitive Church. We will only add here, that the wording of our canon is defective: prohibere abstinere et non generare. The canon seems to order what, on the contrary, it would prohibit, viz.: "It is forbidden that the clergy should abstain from their wives." A similarly inexact expression is found in the eightieth canon.

CAN. 34. Ne cerei in cœmeteriis incendantur

Cereos per diem placuit in cœmeterio non incendi, inquietandi enim sanctorum spiritus non sunt. Qui hæc non observaverint arceantur ab Ecclesiæ communione.

It is forbidden to light wax candles during the day in cemeteries, for fear of troubling the spirits of the saints. Garsias thus explains this canon: "for fear of troubling and distracting the faithful, who pray in the cemeteries." He thus makes sancti the synonym of faithful. Binterim has taken it in the same sense: sanctorum with him is synonymous with sancta agentium; and he translates it, "so that the priests, who fulfil their holy offices, may not be distracted." Baronius, on the contrary, says: "Many neophytes brought the custom from paganism, of lighting many wax candles upon tombs. The Synod forbids this, because metaphorically it troubles the souls of the dead; that is to say, this superstition wounds them." Aubespine gives a fourth explanation. He begins with the supposition that the bishops of Elvira partook of the opinion, then very general, that the souls of the dead hovered over their tombs for some time. The Synod consequently forbade that wax candles should be lighted by day, perhaps to abolish a remnant of paganism, but also to prevent the repose of the souls of the dead from being troubled.

CAN. 35. Ne fæminœ in cœmeteriis pervigilent

Placuit prohiberi ne fœminæ in cœmeterio pervigilent, eo quod sæpe sub obtentu orationis latenter scelera committunt.

CAN. 36. Ne picturæ in ecclesia fiant

Placuit pictures in ecclesia esse non debere, ne quod colitur et adoratur in parietibus depingatur.

These canons are easy to understand: we have elsewhere explained why the ancient Church did not tolerate images. Binterim and Aubespine do not believe in a complete exclusion: they think that the Church in general, and the Synod of Elvira in particular, wished to proscribe only a certain kind of images. Binterim believes that this Synod forbade only one thing,—namely, that any one might hang images in the Church according to his fancy, and often therefore inadmissible ones. Aubespine thinks that our canon forbids only images representing God (because it says adoratur), and not other pictures, especially those of saints. But the canon also says colitur, and the prohibition is conceived in very general terms.

CAN. 37. De energumenis non baptizatis

Eos qui ab immundis spiritibus vexantur, si in fine mortis fuerint constituti, baptizari placet: si fideles fuerint, dandam esse communionem. Prohibendum etiam ne lucernas hi publice accendant; si facere contra interdictum voluerint, abstineatur a communione.

This canon, like the 29th, speaks of demoniacs. If they are catechumens, they may be baptized when at the point of death (in articulo mortis), but not before that. If they are baptized, the communion may be administered to them when at the point of death, but not before. However, as the 29th canon had before forbidden any ministry in the Church to demoniacs, ours particularly adds that they could not fulfil the least service in the Church, not even light the lamps. Perhaps it may have been the custom to have the lamps of the Church lighted by those who were to be baptized, or by those who were to communicate, on the day when they were to receive this sacrament; and the Synod forbids that demoniacs should do so, even if, in spite of their illness, they were able to receive a sacrament. The inscription of the canon does not correspond to its whole tenor.

CAN. 38. Ut in necessitate et fideles baptizent

Loco peregre navigantes aut si ecclesia proximo non fuerit, posse fidelem, qui lavacrum suum integrum habet nec sit bigamus, baptizare in necessitate infirmitatis positum, catechumenum, ita ut si supervixerit ad episcopum eum perducat, ut per manus impositionem perfici possit.

During a sea voyage, or in general, if no church is near, a layman who has not soiled his baptismal robe (by apostasy), and is not a bigamist, may baptize a catechumen who is at the point of death; the bishop ought afterwards to lay hands on the newly baptized, to confirm him.

CAN. 39. De gentilibus si in discrimine baptizari expetunt

Gentiles si in infirmitate desideraverint sibi manum imponi, si fuerit eorum ex aliqua parte honesta vita, placuit eis manum imponi et fieri Christianos.

This canon has been interpreted in two different ways. Binius, Katerkamp, and others, hold that the imposition of hands spoken of in this canon does not mean confirmation, but a ceremony by means of which any one was admitted into the lowest class of catechumens. These interpreters appeal principally to the pretended seventh canon of the second Œcumenical Council. We there read: "We admit them only as pagans: the first day we make them Christians (in the widest sense); the second, catechumens; the third, we exorcise them," etc. etc. According to that, our canon would say: "When a heathen, having a good name, desires during an illness that hands should be laid upon him, it ought to be done, that he may become a Christian." That is to say, he ought by the imposition of hands to be admitted among those who wish to be Christians, consequently among the Christians in the widest sense. The forty-fifth canon also takes the word catechumenus as synonymous with Christian. Besides, we find Constantine the Great received the imposition of hands at the baths of Helenopolis before his baptism: a ceremony of this kind then preceded the reception of the first sacrament. Relying upon these considerations, the commentators we mentioned say that the canon of Elvira does not speak of baptism, because this could not be administered until after much longer trial. The provost of the Cathedral at Köln, Dr. München, gives another explanation in his dissertation upon the first Synod of Arles. According to him,—

a. As the thirty-seventh canon allows the baptism of demoniacs, it is not probable that they would be more severe with respect to ordinary sick persons in the thirty-ninth canon. On the contrary, the Church has always been tender towards the sick: she has always hastened to confer baptism upon them, because it is necessary to salvation; and for that reason she introduced clinical baptism.

b. In the thirty-eighth canon the Church allows a layman to baptize one who should fall seriously ill during a sea voyage, but not to confirm him. She certainly, then, would allow this sick person to be confirmed if a bishop were present in the ship.

c. As for one who should fall ill upon land, he could easily call a bishop to him; and therefore the case foreseen by the thirty-eighth canon does not apply to him: it would be easy to confer baptism and confirmation on him.

d. The thirty-ninth canon, then, means: "Whoso shall fall ill upon land, and who can summon a bishop to him, may receive baptism and confirmation at the same time."

e. Understood in this way, the canon is more in unison with the two preceding, and with the practice of the ancient Church towards the sick.

CAN. 40. Ne id quod idolothytum est fideles accipiant

Prohibere placuit, ut quum rationes suas accipiunt possessores, quidquid ad idolum datum fuerit, accepto non ferant; si post interdictum fecerint, per quinquennii spatia temporum a communione esse arcendos.

That is to say: When the proprietors of lands and houses receive their rents (rationes),—for example, fruits from their farmers, who perhaps are still pagans,—they ought not to admit anything which had been sacrificed to the gods, under pain of five years' excommunication.

CAN. 41. Ut prohibeant domini idola colere servis suis

Admoneri placuit fideles, ut in quantum possunt prohibeant ne idola in domibus suis habeant; si vero vim metuunt servorem, vel se ipsos puros conservent; si non fecerint, alieni ab ecclesia habeantur.

The preceding canon had shown that many Christians had farmers who were pagans; the present canon supposes the case of a Christian having heathen slaves, and it enacts:

a. That he ought not, even in this case, to tolerate idols in his house.

b. That if he cannot conform to this rule, and must fear the slaves on account of their number, he may leave them their idols; but he must so much the more keep at a distance from them, and watch against every approach to idolatry.

CAN. 42. De his qui ad fidem veniunt quando baptizentur

Eos qui ad primam fidem credulitatis accedunt, si bonæ fuerint conversationis, intra biennium temporum placuit ad baptismi gratiam admitti debere, nisi infirmitate compellente coegerit ratio velocius subvenire periclitanti vel gratiam postulanti.

He who has a good name, and wishes to become a Christian, must be a catechumen for two years: then he may be baptized. If he should fall ill, and desire the grace of baptism, it may be granted to him before the expiration of two years.

CAN. 43. De celebratione Pentecostes

Pravam institutionem emendari placuit juxta auctoritatem Scripturarum, ut cuncti diem Pentecostes celebremus, ne si quis non fecerit, novam hæresim induxisse notetur.

Some parts of Spain had allowed the bad custom of celebrating the fortieth day after Easter, not the fiftieth; consequently the Ascension of Christ, and not Pentecost. Several ancient manuscripts, indeed, contain this addition: non quadragesimam. The same addition is found in an ancient abridgment of the canons of Elvira, with which Mansi makes us acquainted: post Pascha quinquagesima teneatur, non quadragesima. We learn also from Cassian, that in the primitive Church some Christians wished to close the paschal season with the feast of the Ascension, that is, at the fortieth day. They regarded all Easter-time only as a remembrance of Christ's sojourn among His disciples during the forty days which followed His resurrection; and therefore they wished to close this period with the feast of the Ascension. Herbst supposes that a Montanist party in Spain wished to suppress the feast of Pentecost altogether, because the Montanists believed that the Holy Spirit did not descend until He came in Montanus, who was regarded by his followers as the Comforter.

CAN. 44. De meretricibus paganis si convertantur

Meretrix quæ aliquando fuerit et postea habuerit maritum, si postmodum ad credulitatem venerit; incunctanter placuit esse recipiendam.

If a pagan courtezan has given up this abominable way of life, and is married, being still a pagan, there is no particular obstacle to her admission into the Church. She ought to be treated as other pagan women.

CAN. 45. De catechumenis qui ecclesiam non frequentant

Qui aliquando fuerit catechumenus et per infinita tempore, nunquam ad ecclesiam accesserit, si eum de clero quisque cognoverit esse Christianum, aut testes aliqui extiterint fideles, placuit ei baptismum non negari, eo quod veterem hominem dereliquisse videatur.

The case is here imagined of a catechumen who has not been to church for a long time, probably because he did not wish to be known as a Christian during a time of persecution; but afterwards his conscience awakes, and he asks to be baptized.

The canon ordains that if he is known to the clergy of the Church to which he belongs, and they know him to be a Christian, or if some of the faithful can attest this, he shall be admitted to baptism, because he appears to have put off the lukewarmness of the old man.

Aubespine gives another interpretation which appears forced, and shows that he most probably had not the text before him. According to him, the meaning of the canon would be: "When a catechumen has fallen away for a long time, and still after all desires baptism and to become a Christian, if he should suddenly lose speech, for example, from illness (the canon says not a word of all that), he may be baptized, provided a clergyman or several of the laity attest that he has desired baptism, and has become a real Christian." The Abbé Migne has placed this explanation in his Dictionary of the Councils.

CAN. 46. De fidclibus si apostaverint quamdiu pœniteant

Si quis fidelis apostata per infinita tempora ad ecclesiam non accesserit, si tamen aliquando fuerit reversus nec fuerit idolator, post decem annos placuit communionem accipere.

The sin of a Christian who should absent himself from church for a long time was naturally much greater than that of a catechumen. For this reason, the baptized Christian who has in fact apostatized is only received to the communion after a ten years' penance, and even then if he has not sacrificed to the gods. It appears to us that this canon alludes to the time of Diocletian's persecution; for during that terrible time more than one cowardly Christian did not go to church, gave no sign of Christian life, and thus apostatized in fact, without positively offering sacrifice to the idols.

CAN. 47. De eo qui uxorem habens sæpius mœchatur

Si quis fidelis habens uxorem non semel sed sæpe fuerit mœchatus in fine mortis est conveniendus: quod si se promiserit cessaturum, detur ei communio: si resuscitatus rursus fuerit mœchatus, placuit ulterius non ludere eum de communione pacis.

If a Christian who is married, and has been often guilty of adultery, is near death, they must go to see him (est conveniendus), and ask him whether, if he should recover, he promises to amend his ways. If he promises, the holy communion should be administered to him; if he should recover, and should again be guilty of adultery, the holy communion must not be allowed to be thus despised, it must henceforth be refused to him, even in articulo mortis. The sixty-ninth and seventy-eighth canons complete the meaning of this one.

CAN. 48. De baptizatis ut nihil accipiat clerus

Emendari placuit ut hi qui baptizantur, ut fieri solebat, numos in concha non mittant, ne sacerdos quod gratis accepit pretio distrahere videatur. Neque pedes eorum lavandi sunt a sacerdotibus vel clericis.

This canon forbids at the same time two things relative to baptism:

1. It was the custom in Spain for the neophytes, at the time of their baptism, to put an offering into the shell which had been used at the baptism. This offering, afterwards called the stole-rights, was to be suppressed.

2. The second part of the canon shows that there was the same custom in certain parts of Spain as at Milan and in Gaul, but which, from the testimony of St. Ambrose, did not exist at Rome, viz. that the bishop and clergy should wash the feet of the newly baptized when they left the baptismal font. Our Synod forbids this, and this canon has passed into the Corp. jur. can.

CAN. 49. De frugibus fidelium ne a Judæis benedicantur

Admoneri placuit possessores, ut non patiantur fructus suos, quos a Deo percipiunt cum gratiarum actione, a Judæis benedici, ne nostram irritam et infirmam faciant benedictionem: si quis post interdictum facere usurpaverit, penitus ab ecclesia abjiciatur.

The Jews were so numerous and so powerful in Spain during the first centuries of the Christian era, that they might at one time have hoped to be able to Judaize the whole country. According to the monuments—which, however, are of doubtful authority—they established themselves in Spain in the time of King Solomon. It is more likely that they crossed from Africa to the Spanish peninsula only about a hundred years before Christ. There they soon increased in number and importance, and could energetically carry on their work of proselytizing. This is the reason that the Synod of Elvira had to forbid to the priests and the laity all intimate intercourse with Jews (can. 50), and especially marriage (can. 16); for there is no doubt that at this period many Christians of high rank in Spain became Jews, as Jost shows in his work.

CAN. 50. De Christianis qui cum Judæis vescuntur

Si vero quis clericus vel fidelis cum Judæis cibum sumpserit, placuit eum a communione abstineri, ut debeat emendari.

CAN. 51. De hæreticis ut ad clerum non promoveantur

Ex omni hæresi fidelis si venerit, minime est ad clerum promovendus: vel si qui sunt in præteritum ordinati, sine dubio deponantur.

These canons are easy to understand.

CAN. 52. De his qui in ecclesia libellos famosos ponunt

Hi qui inventi fuerint libellos famosos in ecclesia ponere anathematizentur.

This canon forbids the affixing of satires (libellos famosos) in churches, or the reading of them. It has been inserted in the Corp. jur. can.

CAN. 53. De episcopis qui excommunicato alicno communicant

Placuit cunctis ut ab eo episcopo quis recipiat communionem a quo abstentus in crimine aliquo quis fuerit; quod si ælius episcopus præsumpserit eum admitti, illo adhuc minime faciente vel consentiente a quo fuerit communione privatus, sciat se hujusmodi causas inter fratres esse cum status sui periculo præstaturum.

One excommunicated by a bishop can only be restored by the bishop who condemned him.

Another bishop receiving him into communion, unless the first bishop acts at the same time, or approves of the reconciliation, must answer for it before his brethren, that is to say, before the provincial synod, and must run the danger of being deprived of his office (status).

CAN. 54. De parentibus qui fidem sponsaliorum frangunt

Si qui parentes fidem fregerint sponsaliorum, triennii tempore abstineantur; si tamen idem sponsus vel sponsa in gravi crimine fuerint deprehensi, erunt excusati parentes; si in iisdem fuerit vitium et polluerint se, superior sententia servetur.

If the parents of those who are betrothed fail to keep the promises made at the betrothal, these parents shall be excluded from the communion for three years, unless either of the betrothed persons be convicted of a very serious fault. In this case, the parents may break the engagement. If the betrothed have sinned together, the first arrangement continues; that is, the parents cannot then separate them. This canon is found in the Corp. juris can.

CAN. 55. De sacerdotibus gentilium qui jam non sacrificant

Sacerdotes qui tantum coronas portant, nec sacrificant nec de suis sumptibus aliquid ad idola præstant, placuit post biennium accipere communionem.

It may be asked whether the word sacerdotes is to be understood as referring to pagan priests who wished to be admitted as Christians, or to Christians who, as we have seen above (can. 2), still bore the office of flamines. Aubespine is of the latter opinion, and according to him the canon would have this meaning: "The Christian who bears the office of flamen, and wears the distinctive sign—that is, the crown—without having sacrificed himself, or having contributed money to pagan sacrifices, must be excluded from eucharistic communion for two years." Aubespine gives the two following reasons in support of his explanation: (a.) When a pagan priest wished to become a Christian, he was not kept longer or more strictly than others as a catechumen, even when he had himself offered sacrifice. (b.) If it had referred to a pagan priest wishing to become a Christian, the Synod would have said, placuit post biennium accepere lavacrum (baptism), and not accipere communionem. This latter expression is used only for those who have been excluded for some time from the Church, and are admitted afresh into her bosom.

For our part, we think that this fifty-fifth canon is nothing but a complement of the second and third canons, and that it forms with them the following gradation:—

Can. 2. Christians who, as flamincs, have sacrificed to idols, and given public pagan games, cannot receive the communion, even when at the point of death.

Can. 3. If they have not offered sacrifices, but have had the games celebrated, they may communicate at the close of their life, after a previous penance.

Can. 55. If they have not offered sacrifice, nor contributed by their fortune to pagan sacrifices (and to such public games), they may receive the communion after two years of penance.

This gradation is continued in the two following canons, the fifty-sixth and fifty-seventh: they refer to Christians who have not been flamines, but who have borne other offices in a heathen state, and so have been brought into relation with paganism.

The fifty-fifth canon evidently alludes to a former and not far distant time of persecution, during which Christians feared to refuse the office of flamines which fell to their lot, and by a half compliance wore the distinctive mark of their office, the crown, in order to pass uninjured through the time of persecution.

CAN. 56. De magistratibus et duumviris

Magistratus vero uno anno quo agit duumviratum, prohibendum placet ut se ab ecclesia cohibeat.

What the consuls were at Rome, the duumviri were, on a small scale, in the Roman municipalities: their office also lasted only a year. These duumviri were obliged, by virtue of their office, to watch over pagan priests personally, and the temples of the town; they had to preside at public solemnities, in processions, etc., which, like all the other national feasts of the Romans, had always more or less a semi-religious and pagan character. For this reason the Synod forbade the duumviri to enter the Church as long as they were in office. In limiting itself to this prohibition, it gave proof of great moderation and of wise consideration, which we ought to appreciate. An absolute prohibition to hold this office would have given up the charge of the most important towns to pagans. But the Council is much more severe in the following canon.

CAN. 57. De his qui vestimenta ad ornandam pompam dederunt

Matronæ vel earum mariti vestimenta sua ad ornandam sæculariter pompam non dent; et si fecerint, triennio abstineantur.

This canon is directed against Christians who should lend their garments for worldly shows, i.e. for public, half-heathenish religious processions. They are punished with three years of excommunication. But why are they treated so much more severely than the duumviri? Because these men and women were not obliged to lend their attire, whilst the duumviri were fulfilling their public duty as citizens. Perhaps also some gave their garments, that they might not be suspected during the persecutions.

CAN. 58. De his qui communicatorias litteras portant, ut de fide interrogentur

Placuit ubique et maxime in eo loco, in quo prima cathedra constituta est episcopatus, ut interrogentur hi qui communicatorias litteras tradunt an omnia recte habeant suo testimonio comprobata.

In Africa no metropolitan rights were attached to particular towns: they always belonged to the oldest bishop of the province, whose bishopric was then called prima sedes. Carthage only was the metropolitan see. It appears to have been the same in Spain before Constantine the Great divided that country into seven political provinces, which entailed the division into ecclesiastical provinces. This may explain why the Bishop of Acci presided at the Synod of Elvira: he was probably the oldest of all the bishops present. What is elsewhere called prima sedes in our canon is prima cathedra; and the bishops of the prima cathedra were to question Christian travellers about their respective dioceses, the latter were to present their recommendatory letters, and were to be asked if they could affirm that all was in a satisfactory state.

CAN. 59. De fidelibus ne ad Capitolium causa sacrificandi ascendant

Prohibendum ne quis Christianus ut gentilis ad idolum Capitolii causa sacrificandi ascendat et videat; quod si fecerit, pari crimine teneatur: si fuerit fidelis, post decem annos acta pœnitentia recipiatur.

Like Rome, many municipalities had a capitol, in the court of which sacrifices were offered to the gods, and many Christians were present at the ceremonies of the pagan worship. Was it from curiosity? was it in order to shelter themselves from inquiry, not to be known during the persecution, and to pass for heathen? This is what we are unable to decide. At any rate, the Synod declared that—

a. Any Christian, either baptized or a catechumen, who should be present at the sacrifices, should be considered as having offered sacrifice himself.

b. Consequently any Christian who has been present at these sacrifices shall be excommunicated and a penitent for ten years. The Synod says nothing about the punishment of guilty catechumens: in every case they were in general punished less severely than the faithful, and perhaps the fourth canon was applied to them by analogy.

CAN. 60. De his qui destruentes idola occiduntur

Si quis idola fregerit et ibidem fuerit occisus, quatenus in Evangelio scriptum non est neque invenietur sub apostolis unquam factum, placuit in numero eum non recipi martyrum.

It happened sometimes that too zealous Christians would destroy the idols, and have to pay for their boldness with their life. The Synod decrees that they must not be considered as martyrs, for the gospel does not require deeds of this kind, and the apostles did not act in this way; but they considered it praiseworthy if a Christian, whom they might wish to oblige to offer sacrifice to an idol, should overthrow the statue, and break it, as Prudentius Clemens relates with commendation of Eulalia, who suffered martyrdom in Spain in 304, and therefore a short time previous to this Synod.

CAN. 61. De his qui duabus sororibus copulantur

Si quis post obitum uxoris suæ sororem ejus duxerit et ipsa fuerit fidelis, quinquennium a communione placuit abstineri, nisi forte velocius dari pacem necessitas coegerit infirmitatis.

When S. Basil the Great ascended the archiepiscopal throne of Cæsarea, he forbade that a husband, after the death of his wife, should marry her sister; and when some one, of the name of Diodorus, reproached him upon this subject, Basil defended himself in a letter, which has been preserved, and proved that such marriages had always been prohibited at Cæsarea. The Spanish Fathers of Elvira shared S. Basil's opinions, as also did the Synod of Neocæsarea of 314, can. 2, as we shall see hereafter. It is well known that, according to canon law, these marriages are both forbidden and declared to be invalid.

CAN. 62. De aurigis et pantomimis si convertantur

Si auriga aut pantomimus credere voluerint, placuit ut prius artibus suis renuntient, et tunc demum suscipiantur, ita ut ulterius ad ea non revertantur, qui si facere contra interdictum tentaverint, projiciantur ab ecclesia.

The "Apostolical Constitutions" contain the same decree. On the subject of the repugnance of the ancient Church for all these pantomimic scenes, cf. Hefele, "Rigorismus in dem Leben und den Ansichten der alten Christen" (Severity in the Lives and Opinions of the early Christians), an essay published in the Tübinger Theol. Quartalschrift, 1841 (S. 396 ff.).

The following series of canons treats of carnal sins:—

CAN. 63. De uxoribus quæ filios ex adulterio necant

Si qua per adulterim absente marito suo conceperit, idque post facinus occiderit, placuit nec in finem dandam esse communionem, eo quod geminaverit scelus.

CAN. 64. De fœminis quæ usque ad mortem cum alienis viris adulterant

Si qua usque in finem mortis suæ cum alieno viro fuerit mœchata, placuit, nec in finem dandam ei esse communionem. Si vero eum reliquerit, post decem annos accipiat communionem acta legitima pœnitentia.

CAN. 65. De adulteris uxoribus clericorum

Si cujus clerici uxor fuerit mœchata et scierit eam maritus suus mœchari et non eam statim projecerit, nec in finem accipiat communionem, ne ab his qui exemplum bonæ conversationis esse debent, ab eis videantur scelerum magisteria procedere.

The Shepherd of Hermas had before, like this canon, stringently commanded not only the clergy, but all Christians, not to continue to live conjugally with an adulterous spouse, who would not amend his ways, but would persevere in sin. Dr. Herbst says, that what made the sixty-fifth canon necessary was probably the very frequent case of married men having taken orders, and not being able to have conjugal intercourse with their wives, who were therefore on that very account easily tempted to forget themselves.

The series of canons against carnal sins is continued in the following, which forbids marriage with a daughter-in-law:—

CAN. 66. De his qui privignas suas ducunt

Si quis privignam suam duxerit uxorem, eo quod sit incestus, placuit nec in finem dandam esse communionem.

CAN. 67. De conjugio catechumenœ fœminœ

Prohibendum ne qua fidelis vel catechumena aut comatos aut viros cinerarios habeant: quæcumque hoc fecerint, a communione arceantur.

If we attach any importance to the title of this canon, it must be thought to indicate that Christian women, whether catechumens or baptized, were forbidden to marry those designated by the name of cinerarios and comatos. In other manuscripts we read comicos and cenicos. If the latter reading is the true one, the meaning of the canon is very clear—"A Christian woman must not marry an actor;" and this prohibition would explain the aversion of the ancient Church to the theatre, which has been before mentioned. But it is probable that, not having been able to find out the meaning of the words comati and cinerarii, later copyists have altered them, and changed them into comici and scenici. Imagining that here was a prohibition of marriage, they could not understand why a Christian woman was not to marry a man having long hair, or even a hairdresser. We believe that Aubespine is right when he reminds us that many pagan women had foreign slaves, and especially hairdressers, in their service, who ministered not only to the needs of luxury, but to the secret satisfaction of their passions. Perhaps these effeminate slaves—these spadones—encouraging the licentiousness of their mistresses, wore long hair, or, coming from foreign countries—for instance, from Gallia comata—where long hair was always worn, they introduced this name of comati. Tertullian speaks of the cinerarii (peregrinæ proceritatis), and describes them as foreigners, with slight figures, and forming part of the suite of a woman of the world. He mentions them in connection with the spadones, who were ad licentiam secti, or, as S. Jerome says, in securam libidinem exsecti.

Juvenal has not forgotten to signalize these relations of Roman women with eunuchs: "Sunt, quas eunuchi imbelles et mollia semper Oscula delectent."

Martial denounces them, if possible, still more energetically. Perhaps these eunuchs wore long hair like women in order that they might be called comati. Let us finally remark, that in the Glossary cinerarius is translated by δοῦλος ἑταίρας.

If this second explanation of the sixty-seventh canon is accepted, it can be easily imagined why it should be placed in a series of canons treating of carnal sins.

CAN. 68. De catechumena adultera quæ filium necat

Catechumena, si per adulterium conceperit et præfocaverit, placuit eam in fine baptizari.

If a catechumen should conceive by an adulterer, and should procure the death of the child, she can be baptized only at the end of her life.

CAN. 69. De viris conjugatis postea in adulterium lapsis

Si quis forte habens uxorem semel fuerit lapsus, placuit eum quinquennium agere debere pœnitentiam et sic reconciliari, nisi necessitas infirmitatis coegerit ante tempus dari communionem: hoc et circa fœminas observandum.

Adultery committed once was punishable with five years of penance.

CAN. 70. De fœminis quæ consciis maritis adulterant

Si cum conscientia mariti uxor fuerit mœchata, placuit nec in finem dandam ei communionem; si vero eam reliquerit, post decem annos accipiat communionem, si eam cum sciret adulteram aliquo tempore in domo sua retinuit.

If a woman should violate conjugal fidelity with her husband's consent, the latter must not be admitted to communion, even at the end of his life. If he separated from his wife, after having lived with her at all since the sin was committed, he was excluded for ten years.

CAN. 71. De stupratoribus puerorum

Stupratoribus puerorum nec in finem dandam esse communionem.

Sodomites could not be admitted to communion, even on their deathbeds.

CAN. 72. De viduis mœchis si eumdem postea maritum duxerint

Si qua vidua fuerit mœchata et eumdem postea habuerit maritum, post quinquennii tempus acta legitima pœitentia, placuit eam communioni reconciliari: si alium duxerit relicto illo, nec in finem dandam esse communionem; vel si fuerit ille fidelis quem accepit, communionem non accipiet, nisi post decem annos acta legitima pœnitentia, vel si infirmitas coegerit velocius dari communionem.

When a widow had sinned, and had married her accomplice, she was condemned to five years of penance; if she should marry another man, she could never be admitted to communion, even on her deathbed; and if her husband were baptized, he was subject to a penance for ten years, for having married a woman who, properly speaking, was no longer free. This canon was inserted in the Corp. jur. can.

The following canons treat of informers and false witnesses.

CAN. 73. De delatoribus

Delator si quis extiterit fidelis, et per delationem ejus aliquis fuerit proscriptus vel interfectus, placuit eum nec in finem accipere communionem; si levior causa fuerit, intra quinquennium accipere poterit communionem; si catechumenus fuerit, post quinquennii tempora admittetur ad baptismum.

This canon has been inserted in the Corp. jur. can.

CAN. 74. De falsis testibus

Falsus testis prout est crimen abstinebitur; si tamen non fuerit mortale quod objecit, et probaverit quod non (other manuscripts have diu) tacuerit, biennii tempore abstinebitur: si autem non probaverit convento clero, placuit per quinquennium abstineri.

A false witness must be excluded from the communion for a time proportionate to the crime of which he has given false witness. Should the crime be one not punishable with death, and if the guilty one can demonstrate that he kept silence for a long time (diu), that is, that he did not willingly bear witness, he shall be condemned to two years of penance; if he cannot prove this, to five years. The canon is thus explained by Mendoza, Rémi Ceillier in Migne's Dictionary, etc., all preferring the reading diu. Burchard had previously read and quoted the canon with this variation, in his Collectio canonum. But Aubespine divides it into three quite distinct parts. The first, he says, treats of false witnesses; the second, of those who are too slow in denouncing a crime. They must be punished, but only by two years of penance, if they can prove that they have not (non) kept silence to the end. The third condemns those to five years of penance, who, without having borne false witness, still cannot prove what they affirm.

We confess that none of these explanations is quite satisfactory: the first would be the most easily admissible; but it is hardly possible to reconcile it with the reading non tacuerit, which, however, is that of the best manuscripts.

CAN. 75. De his qui sacerdotes vel ministros accusant nec probant

Si quis autem episcopum vel presbyterum vel diaconum falsis criminibus appetierit et probare non potuerit, nec in finem dandam ei esse communionem.

CAN. 76. De diaconibus si ante honorem peccasse probantur

Si quis diaconum se permiserit ordinari et postea fuerit detectus in crimine mortis quod aliquando commiserit, si sponte fuerit confessus, placuit eum acta legitima pœnitentia post triennium accipere communionem; quod si alius eum detexerit, post quinquennium acta pœnitentia accipere communionem laicam debere.

If any one should succeed in being ordained deacon, and it should be subsequently discovered that he had before that committed a mortal sin:

a. In case he was the first to make known his fault, he must be received into communion (as a layman) at the end of three years of penance.

b. In case his sin was discovered by another, at the end of five years. In both cases he was for ever suspended from his office of deacon.

CAN. 77. De baptizatis qui nondum confirmati moriuntur

Si quis diaconus regens plebem sine episcopo vel presbytero aliquos baptizaverit, episcopus eos per benedictionem perficere debebit: quod si ante de sæculo recesserint, sub fide qua quis credidit poterit esse justus.

When Christianity spread from the large towns, where it had been at first established, into the country, the rural churches at first formed only one parish with the cathedral church of the town. Either priests, or Chorepiscopi, or simple deacons, were sent to these rural assemblies, to exercise, within certain limits, the ministerial power. The solemnity of consecrating the Eucharist, and all that had reference to penance, was reserved for the bishop of the town.

The 77th canon refers to such deacons, and it ordains:

a. That baptism administered by the deacon ought to be completed, finished by the bishop's benediction (that is to say, by χειροτονία, or confirmation).

b. That if one who had been baptized by a deacon should die before having received this benediction from the bishop, he may notwithstanding be saved, by virtue of the faith which he professed on receiving baptism.

CAN. 78. De fidelibus conjugatis si cum Judæa vel gentili mœchatæ (i) fuerint

Si quis fidelis habens uxorem cum Judæa vel gentili fuerit mœchatus, a communione arceatur: quod si alius eum detexerit, post quinquennium acta legitima pœnitentia poterit dominicæ sociari communioni.

The 47th and 69th canons have already treated of adultery between Christians: the present canon speaks of a particular case of adultery committed with a Jewish or pagan woman, and decrees a penance of five years if the guilty one has not confessed himself. If he has made a spontaneous confession, the canon only gives this vague and general command, Arceatur, that is, that he should be excommunicated, but it does not say for how long a time: it might be supposed for three years, according to the analogy with the 76th canon. However, it would be strange that adultery with a Jewish or pagan woman should be punished only by three years of penance, while the 69th canon decrees, in a general way, five years' punishment to every adulterer. It is still more difficult to explain why real adultery should be less severely punished in the 78th canon than the evidently less criminal offence of a widow with a man whom she afterwards marries.

CAN. 79. De his qui tabulam ludunt

Si quis fidelis aleam, id est tabulam, luserit numis, placuit eum abstineri; et si emendatus cessaverit, post annum poterit communioni reconciliari.

The thimbles of the ancients had not any points or figures upon their sides (tabula), like ours, but drawings, pictures of idols; and whoever threw the picture of Venus, gained all, as Augustus says in Suetonius: quos tollebat universos, qui Venerem jecerat. It is on this account that the ancient Christians considered the game of thimbles to be not only immoral as a game of chance, but as having an essentially pagan character.

CAN. 80. De libertis

Prohibendum ut liberti, quorum patroni in sæculo fuerint, ad clerum non promoveantur.

He who should give a slave his freedom remained his patron; he had certain rights and a certain influence over him. The freedman continued to be dependent upon his former master; for this reason freedmen whose patrons were heathens could not take orders. This canon was placed in the Corp. jur. can.

CAN. 81. De fœminarum epistolis

Ne fœminæ suo potius absque maritorum nominibus laicis scribere audeant, quæ (qui) fideles sunt vel literas alicujus pacificas ad suum solum nomen scriptas accipiant.

If we should read qui instead of quæ, as Mendoza makes it, on the authority of several manuscripts, our canon is easy to understand. It then divides itself into two parts:

a. Women must not write in their own name to lay Christians, laicis qui fideles sunt; they may do so only in the name of their husbands.

b. They must not receive letters of friendship (pacificas) from any one, addressed only to themselves. Mendoza thinks that the canon means only private letters, and that it is forbidden in the interests of conjugal fidelity.

Aubespine gives quite another sense to the word litteras: he supposes that the Council wishes only to forbid the wives of bishops giving litteras communicatorias to Christian travellers in their own name, and that it also forbids them to receive such addressed to them instead of to their husbands.

If we read quæ, we must attach the words quæ fideles sunt to fœminæ, and the meaning continues on the whole the same.

Besides these eighty-one authentic canons, some others are attributed to the Council of Elvira: for instance, in the Corp. jur. can. (c. 17, causa xxii. q.

4; also c. 21, dist. ii. de consecrat., and c. 15, causa xxii. q. 5), there is evidently a mistake about some of these canons, which, as Mendoza and Cardinal d'Aguirre have remarked, belong to a Synodus Helibernensis or Hibernensis. We will remark finally, that whilst Baronius thinks little of the Synod of Elvira, which he wrongfully suspects of Novatian opinions, Mendoza and Natalis Alexander defend it eloquently.

SEC. 14. Origin of the Schism of the Donatists, and the first Synods held on this account in 312 and 313

The schism of the Donatists occasioned several synods at the beginning of the fourth century. Mensurius was bishop of Carthage during Diocletian's persecution. He was a worthy and serious man, who on the one side encouraged the faithful to courage and energy during the persecution, but on the other side strongly reproved any step which could increase the irritation of the heathen. He especially blamed certain Christians of Carthage, who had denounced themselves to the heathen authorities as possessors of sacred books (even when this was not really the case), in order to obtain martyrdom by their refusal to give up the Holy Scriptures. Nor would he grant the honours of martyrdom to those who, after a licentious life, should court martyrdom without being morally improved. We see, by a letter of Mensurius, how he himself behaved during the persecution. He relates, that when they required the sacred books from him, he hid them, leaving in the church only heretical books, which were taken away by the persecutors. The proconsul had soon discovered this cunning; but, however, did not wish to pursue Mensurius further. Many enemies of the bishop, especially Donatus Bishop of Casæ-Nigræ in Numidia, falsely interpreted what had passed: they pretended that Mensurius had, in fact, delivered up the Holy Scriptures; that, at any rate, he had told a sinful falsehood; and they began to excite disturbance in the Church of Carthage. However, these troubles did not take the form of a miserable schism till after the death of Mensurius. A deacon named Felix, being persecuted by the heathen, took refuge in the house of Bishop Mensurius. As the latter refused to give him up, he was taken to Rome, to answer in person for his resistance before Maxentius, who since Diocletian's abdication had possessed himself of the imperial power in Italy and in Africa. Mensurius succeeded in obtaining an acquittal; but he died on the way back to Carthage, and before arriving there, in 311. Two celebrated priests of Carthage, Botrus and Celestius, aspired to the vacant throne, and thought it their interest to invite to the election and ordination of the future bishop only the neighbouring prelates, and not those of Numidia. It is doubtful whether this was quite according to order. Inasmuch as Numidia formed a separate ecclesiastical province, distinct from the province of proconsular Africa, of which Carthage was the metropolis, the bishops of Numidia had no right to take part in the election of a Bishop of Carthage. But as the metropolitan (or, according to African language, the primate) of Carthage was in some sort the patriarch of the whole Latin Church of Africa; and as, on this account, Numidia was under his jurisdiction, the bishops of Numidia might take part in the appointment of a Bishop of Carthage. On the other side, the Donatists were completely in the wrong, when subsequently they pretended that the primate of Carthage ought to be consecrated by that metropolitan whose rank was the nearest to his own (primas, or primæ sedis episcopus or senex); consequently the new Bishop of Carthage ought to have been consecrated by Secundus Bishop of Tigisis, then metropolitan (Primas) of Numidia: and it is with reason that S. Augustine replied to them in the name of the whole African episcopate, during a conference held at Carthage in 411, that even the Bishop of Rome was not consecrated by the primate nearest to him in rank, but by the Bishop of Ostia. The two priests mentioned above found themselves deceived at the time of the election, which took place at Carthage: for the people, putting them on one side, elected Cecilian, who had been archdeacon under Mensurius; and Felix Bishop of Aptunga, suffragan of Carthage, consecrated him immediately. The consecration was hardly ended, when some priests and some of the laity of Carthage resolved to unite their efforts to ruin the new bishop. On his departure for Rome, Mensurius had confided the treasures of his church to the care of some Christians: at the same time he had given the list of everything entrusted to them into the hands of a pious woman, charging her, "in case he should not return, to remit this list to his successor." The woman fulfilled her commission; and the new bishop, Cecilian, claimed the property of the church from those with whom it had been left. This demand irritated them against him: they had hoped that no one would have known of this deposit, and that they might divide it amongst themselves.

Besides these laymen, the two priests mentioned above arrayed themselves against Cecilian. The soul of the opposition was a very rich lady, who had a great reputation for piety, named Lucilla, and who thought she was most grievously wronged by Cecilian. She had been in the habit, every time she communicated, of kissing the relics of a martyr not accounted such by the Church. Cecilian, who was at that time a deacon, had forbidden the worship of these relics not recognised by the Church, and the pharisaical pride of the woman could not pardon the injury.

Things were in this state when Secundus Bishop of Tigisis, in his office of episcopus primæ sedis of Numidia, sent a commission to Carthage to appoint a mediator (interventor) nominally for the reconciliation of the parties. But the commission was very partial from the beginning: they entered into no relation with Cecilian or his flock; but, on the contrary, took up their abode with Lucilla, and consulted with her on the plan to follow for the overthrow of Cecilian. The malcontents, says Optatus, then asked the Numidian bishops to come to Carthage to decide about the election and the consecration of Cecilian, and in fact Secundus of Tigisis soon appeared with his suffragans. They took up their abode with the avowed opponents of Cecilian, and refused to take part in the assembly or synod which he wished to call, according to custom, to hear the Numidian bishops; and, instead, they held a conciliabulum of their own, at which seventy met, and in a private house in Carthage, before which they summoned Cecilian to appear (312). Cecilian did not attend, but sent word "that if they had anything against him, the accuser had only to appear openly and prove it." No accusation was made; and besides, they could bring forward nothing against Cecilian, except having formerly, as archdeacon, forbidden the visiting of the martyrs in prison and the taking of food to them. Evidently, says Dupin, Cecilian had only followed the counsel of S. Cyprian, in forbidding the faithful to go in crowds to the prisons of the martyrs, for fear of inciting the pagans to renewed acts of violence. Although Cecilian was perfectly right in this respect, it is possible that in the application of the rule, right in itself, he may have acted with some harshness. This is at least what we must conclude if only the tenth part of the accusations raised against him by an anonymous Donatist have any foundation. He says, for instance, that Cecilian would not even allow parents to visit their captive sons and daughters, that he had taken away the food from those who wished to take it to the martyrs, and had given it to the dogs, and the like. His adversaries laid still greater stress on the invalidity of Cecilian's consecration, because his consecrator, Felix of Aptunga, had been a Traditor (i.e. had given up the sacred books) during the persecution of Diocletian. No council had heretofore ordained that the sacraments were valid, even when administered by heinous sinners; therefore Cecilian answered, with a sort of condescension towards his enemies, "that if they thought that Felix had not rightfully ordained him, they had only themselves to proceed to his ordination." But the bishops of Numidia did doubly wrong in thus setting themselves against Felix of Aptunga. First, the accusation of his having given up the sacred books was absolutely false, as was proved by a judicial inquiry made subsequently, in 314. The Roman officer who had been charged to collect the sacred books at Aptunga attested the innocence of Felix; whilst one Ingentius, who, in his hatred against Felix, had produced a false document to ruin him, confessed his guilt. But apart from this circumstance, Secundus and his friends, who had themselves given up the Holy Scriptures, as was proved in the Synod of Cirta, had hardly the right to judge Felix for the same offence. Besides, they had at this same Synod of Cirta consecrated Silvanus bishop of that place, who was also convicted of having been a Traditor. Without troubling themselves with all these matters, or caring for the legality of their proceeding, the Numidians proclaimed, in their unlawful Council, the deposition of Cecilian, whose consecration they said was invalid, and elected a friend and partisan of Lucilla's, the reader Majorinus, to be Bishop of Carthage. Lucilla had bribed the Numidian bishops, and promised to each of them 400 pieces of gold.

This done, the unlawful Numidian Council addressed a circular letter to all the churches of Africa, in which they related what had passed, and required that they should cease from all ecclesiastical communion with Cecilian. It followed from this, that Carthage, being in some sort the patriarchal throne of Africa, all the African provinces were implicated in this controversy. In almost every town two parties were formed; in many cities there were even two bishops—a Cecilian and a Majorinian. Thus began this unhappy schism. As Majorinus had been put forward by others, and besides as he died soon after his election, the schismatics did not take his name, but were called

Donatists, from the name of Donatus Bishop of
Casæ Nigræ, who had much more influence than
Majorinus, and also afterwards on account of
another Donatus, surnamed the Great, who became
the successor of Majorinus as schismatical Bishop
of Carthage. Out of Africa, Cecilian was everywhere
considered the rightful bishop, and it was to him
only that letters of communion (epistolæ
communicatoriæ) were addressed. Constantine the
Great, who meanwhile had conquered Maxentius in
the famous battle at the Milvian Bridge, also
recognised Cecilian, wrote to him, sent him a large
sum of money to distribute among his priests, and
added, "that he had heard that some unruly spirits
sought to trouble the Church; but that he had
already charged the magistrates to restore order,
and that Cecilian had only to apply to them for the
punishment of the agitators." In another letter,
addressed to the proconsul of Africa, Anulinus, he
exempted the clergy of the Catholic Church of
Carthage, "whose president was Cecilian," from all
public taxes.

Soon afterwards, the opponents of Cecilian, to
whom many of the laity joined themselves, remitted
two letters to the proconsul of Africa, begging him to
send them to the Emperor. Anulinus accordingly did
so. The title of the first letter, which S. Augustine
has preserved to us, viz. libellus Ecclesiæ
Catholicæ (that is to say, of the Donatist Church)

criminum Cæciliani, suffices to show its tenor; the second entreated the Emperor, on account of the divisions among the African bishops, to send judges from Gaul to decide between them and Cecilian. This latter letter, preserved by Optatus, is signed by Lucian, Dignus, Nasutius, Capito, Fidentius, et cæteris episcopis partis Donati. In his note upon this passage, Dupin has proved by quotations from this letter, as it is found in S. Augustine, that the original was partis Majorini, which Optatus changed into Donati, according to the expression commonly used in his time.

We see from the preceding that the Donatists deserved the reproach which was cast upon them, of being the first to call for the intervention of the civil power in a purely ecclesiastical case; and the Emperor Constantine himself, who was then in Gaul, openly expressed his displeasure on this subject, in a letter which he addressed to Pope Melchiades (Miltiades). However, to restore peace to Africa, he charged three bishops of Gaul—Maternus of Cöln, Reticius of Autun, and Marinus of Arles—to make arrangements with the Pope and fifteen other Italian bishops to assemble in a synod which was held at Rome in 313.

Synod at Rome (313)

Cecilian was invited to be present at this Synod, with ten bishops of his obedience. His adversaries were to send an equal number; and at their head stood Donatus of Casæ Nigræ. The conferences began at the Lateran Palace, belonging to the Empress Fausta, on October 2, 313, and lasted three days. The first day Donatus and his friends were first of all to prove their accusations against Cecilian; but they could produce neither witnesses nor documents: those whom Donatus himself had brought to witness against Cecilian, declared that they knew nothing against the bishop, and therefore were not brought forward by Donatus. On the contrary, it was proved that, when Cecilian was only a deacon, Donatus had excited divisions in Carthage; that he had re-baptized Christians who had been baptized before; and, contrary to the rules of the Church, had laid hands on fallen bishops to reinstate them in their offices. The second day the Donatists produced a second accusation against Cecilian; but they could no more prove their assertions than on the previous day. The continuation of an inquiry already begun concerning the unlawful Council of Carthage of 312, which had deposed Cecilian, was interrupted. As Donatus was totally unable on the third day, as on the two preceding, to produce a single witness, Cecilian was declared innocent, and Donatus condemned on his own confession. No judgment was pronounced on the other bishops of his party. The Synod, on the contrary, declared that if they would return to the unity of the Church, they might retain their thrones;

that in every place where there was a Cecilian and a Donatist bishop, the one who had been the longest ordained should remain at the head of the Church, whilst the younger should be set over another diocese. This decision of the Synod was proclaimed by its president the Bishop of Rome, and communicated to the Emperor.

After the close of the Synod, Donatus and Cecilian were both forbidden to return to Africa at once. Cecilian was detained at Brescia for a time. Some time afterwards, however, Donatus obtained permission to go to Africa, but not to Carthage. But the Pope, or perhaps the Synod before closing, sent two bishops, Eunomius and Olympius, to Africa, to proclaim that that was the catholic party for which the nineteen bishops assembled at Rome had pronounced. We see from this that the mission of the two bishops was to promulgate the decisions of the Synod; we also think, with Dupin, that their journey, the date of which is uncertain, took place immediately after the close of the Synod of Rome. The two bishops entered into communion with Cecilian's clergy at Carthage; but the Donatists endeavoured to prevent the bishops from accomplishing their mission; and some time after, as Donatus had returned to Carthage, Cecilian also returned to his flock.

New troubles soon agitated Africa, and the Donatists again brought complaints of Cecilian before the Emperor. Irritated with their obstinacy, Constantine at first simply referred them to the decision of the Synod of Rome; and when they replied by protesting that they had not been sufficiently listened to at Rome, Constantine decided, first, that a minute inquiry should be made as to whether Felix of Aptunga had really given up the Holy Scriptures (we have given above the result of this inquiry); next, that the whole controversy should be definitely settled by a great assembly of the bishops of Christendom; and consequently he called the bishops of his empire together for the 1st of August 314, to the Council of Arles in Gaul.

SEC. 15. Synod of Arles in Gaul (314)

Cecilian and some of his friends, as well as some deputies of the party of the Donatists, were invited to this Council, and the officials of the empire were charged to defray the expenses of the voyage of these bishops. Constantine specially invited several bishops, amongst others the Bishop of Syracuse. According to some traditions, there were no fewer than 600 bishops assembled at Arles. Baronius, relying on a false reading in S. Augustine, fixes the number at 200. Dupin thought there were only thirty-three bishops at Arles, because that is the number indicated by the title of the letter of the Synod addressed to Pope Silvester, and by the list of persons which is found in several MSS. Notwithstanding this comparatively small number, we may say that all the provinces of Constantine's empire were represented at the Council. Besides these thirty-three bishops, the list of persons also mentions a considerable number of priests and deacons, of whom some accompanied their bishops, and others represented their absent bishops as their proxies. Thus Pope Silvester was represented by two priests, Claudianus and Vitus, two deacons, Eugenius and Cyriacus. Marinus of Arles, one of the three judges (judices ex Gallia), who had been appointed beforehand by the Emperor, appears to have presided over the assembly: at least his name is found first in the letter of the Synod. With Marinus the letter mentions Agrœcius of Trier, Theodore of Aquileia, Proterius of Capua, Vocius of Lyons, Cecilian of Carthage, Reticius of Autun (one of the earlier judices ex Gallia), Ambitausus (Imbetausius) of Reims, Merokles of Milan, Adelfius of London, Maternus of Cöln, Liberius of Emerita in Spain, and others; the last named having already been present at the Synod of Elvira.

It is seen that a great part of Western Christendom was represented at Arles by some bishops; and the Emperor Constantine could truly say: "I have assembled a great number of bishops from different and almost innumerable parts of the empire." We may look on the assembly at Arles as a general council of the West (or of the Roman patriarchate).

It cannot, however, pass for an œcumenical council, for this reason, that the other patriarchs did not take any part in it, and indeed were not invited to it; and those of the East especially, according to S. Augustine, ignored almost entirely the Donatist controversy. But has not S. Augustine himself declared this Council to be œcumenical? In order to answer this question in the affirmative, an appeal has been made to the second book of his treatise, De Baptismo contra Donatistas, where he says: "The question relating to re-baptism was decided against Cyprian, in a full council of the whole Church" (plenarium concilium, concilium universæ Ecclesiæ). But it is doubtful whether S. Augustine meant by that the Council of Arles, or whether he did not rather refer to that of Nicæa, according to Pagi's view of the case. It cannot, however be denied that S. Augustine, in his forty-third letter (vii. No. 19), in speaking of the Council of Arles, calls it plenarium Ecclesiæ universæ concilium. Only it must not be forgotten that the expression concilium plenarium, or universale, is often employed in speaking of a national council; and that in the passage quoted S. Augustine refers to the Western Church (Ecclesia universa occidentalis), and not to the universal Church (universalis) in the fullest sense.

The deliberations of the Council of Arles were opened on the 1st of August 314. Cecilian and his accusers were present; but these were no more able than before to prove their accusations. We unfortunately have not in full the acts of the Council; but the synodical letter already quoted informs us that the accusers of Cecilian were aut damnati aut repulsi. From this information we infer that Cecilian was acquitted; and this we know to have been the actual result of the Donatist controversy. The Council, in its letter to the Pope, says, "that it would have greatly desired that the Pope (Silvester) had been able to assist in person at the sessions, and that the judgment given against Cecilian's accusers would in that case certainly have been more severe." The Council probably alluded to the favourable conditions that it had accorded to the Donatist bishops and priests, in case they should be reconciled to the Church.

The letter of the Council contains no other information relating to the affairs of the Donatists. At the time of the religious conference granted to the Donatists in 411, a letter of the African bishops was read, in which they said, that, "dating from the commencement of the schism (ab ipsius separationis exordio), consent had been given that every Donatist bishop who should become reconciled to the Church should alternately exercise the episcopal jurisdiction with the Catholic bishop: that if either of the two died, the survivor should be his sole successor; but in the case in which a church did not wish to have two bishops, both were to resign, and a new one was to be elected." From these words, ab ipsius separationis exordio, Tillemont concluded that it is to the Synod of Arles that this decision should be referred; for, as we have already seen, other proposals of reconciliation were made at Rome. It is not known whether the Synod of Arles decided anything else in the matter of the Donatists. But it is evident that two, perhaps three, of its twenty-two canons (Nos. 13, 14, and 8), refer to the schism of the African Church, which we shall show in examining them one by one.

The Synod of Arles was not satisfied, as their synodal letter tells us, merely to examine and judge the business of the Donatists: it wished to lend its assistance in other points relating to the necessities of the Church, especially to solve the paschal controversy, the question of the baptism of heretics, and to promulgate various rules for discipline. Convinced that it acted under the inspiration of the Holy Ghost, it used the formula, Placuit ergo, præsente Spiritu sancto et angelis ejus; and begged the Pope, who had the government of the larger diocese (majoris diœceseos gubernacula) under his control, to promulgate its decrees universally. The Synod also sent him the complete collection of its twenty-two canons, while in the letter previously quoted it had given only a short extract from them: consequently it may be maintained, with the brothers Ballerini, that the Synod addressed two letters to the Pope, of which the first, commencing with the enumeration of the bishops present, dwelt chiefly on the affairs of the Donatists, and gave but a short sketch of the other decisions; while the second included literally and exclusively all the decrees, and addressed itself to the Pope only in the words of introduction, and in the first canon. The Benedictines of S. Maur have published the best text of this second synodical letter, and of the canons of the Council of Arles, in the first volume of their Collectio conciliorum Galliæ of 1789, of which the sequel unfortunately has not appeared. We shall adopt this text:

Domino sanctissimo fratri Silvestro Marinus vel cœtus episcoporum qui adunati fuerunt in oppido Arelatensi. Quid decrevimus communi consilio caritati tuæ significamus, ut omnes sciant quid in futurum observare debeant.

CAN. 1. Ut uno die et tempore Pascha celebretur

Primo loco de observatione Paschæ Domini, ut uno die et uno tempore per omnem orbem a nobis observetur et juxta consuetudinem literas ad omnes tu dirigas.

By this canon the Council of Arles wished to make the Roman computation of time with regard to Easter the rule everywhere, and consequently to abolish that of Alexandria, and all others that might differ from it, taking for granted that the bishops of the Council knew the difference that existed between these and the Roman computation. We will not here give the details relating to the paschal controversy, but further on in the history of the Council of Nicæa, so as the better to grasp the whole meaning.

CAN. 2. Ut ubi quisque ordinatur ibi permaneat

De his qui in quibuscumque locis ordinati fuerint ministri, in ipsis locis perseverent.

The twenty-first canon contains the same decision, with this difference, that the former speaks only of the inferior ministers of the Church (ministri), while the latter speaks of the priests and deacons; and both express the view of the ancient Church, in accordance with which an ecclesiastic attached to one church ought not to change to another. We find the same prohibition even in the apostolic canons (Nos. 13 and 14, or 14 and 15); and in the fifteenth canon of Nicæa it is questioned whether this canon of Arles forbids only passing from one diocese to another, or if it forbade moving from one church to another in the same diocese. Dr. München understood the canon in the latter sense, founding his opinion on the seventy-seventh canon of the Synod of Elvira, which shows that each church in a diocese had its own minister. Of course the prohibition as to a change of churches in the same diocese, necessarily applies to moving from one diocese to another.

CAN. 3. Ut qui in pace arma projiciunt excommunicentur

De his qui arma projiciunt in pace, placuit abstineri eos a communione.

This canon has been interpreted in no less than four ways. Ivo of Chartres read, instead of in pace, in prælio; and an ancient manuscript, which was compared by Surius, read in bello. In this case the sense would be: "He who throws down his arms in war is excommunicated." Sirmond tried a second explanation, taking the view that arma projicere is not synonymous with arma abjicere, and signifies arma in alium conjicere. Thus, according to him, the canon forbids the use of arms except in case of war. Dr. München has developed this explanation, by applying the sentence arma projicere in pace to the fights of the gladiators, and he has considered this canon as a prohibition of these games. Constantine the Great, he says, forbade on the 1st October 325 the games of the gladiators in nearly the same terms: Cruenta spectacula in otio civili et domestica quiete non placent; quapropter omnino gladiatores esse prohibemus. Besides these, adds München, the two following canons are directed against the spectacula which were so odious to the early

Christians; and this connection also justifies the opinion that canon 3 refers to the spectacula, that is to say, to the fights of the gladiators. Aubespine has tried a fourth explanation. Many Christians, says he, under the pagan emperors, had religious scruples with regard to military service, and positively refused to take arms, or else deserted. The Synod, in considering the changes introduced by Constantine, set forth the obligation that Christians have to serve in war, and that because the Church is at peace (in pace) under a prince friendly to Christians. This explanation has been adopted, amongst others, by Rémi Ceillier, by Herbst, in the Dictionnaire des conciles of Abbé Migne, and in Abbé Guetté's recently published Histoire de l'église de France. We, however, prefer Dr. München's view of the matter.

CAN. 4. Ut aurigæ dum agitant excommunicentur

De agitatoribus qui fideles sunt, placuit eos quamdiu agitant a communione separari.

These agitators are the jockeys and grooms of the courses, identical with the aurigœ of the sixty-second canon of the Council of Elvira. In the same way that the preceding canon interdicted the games of the gladiators, which were celebrated at the amphitheatre, so this prohibits the racing of horses and chariots, which took place in the circus.

CAN. 5. Ut theatrici quamdiu agunt excommunicentur

De theatricis, et ipsos placuit quamdiu agunt a communione separari.

This canon excommunicates those who are employed in the theatres.

CAN. 6. Ut in infirmitate conversi manus impositionem accipiant

De his qui in infirmitate credere volunt, placuit iis debere manum imponi.

The thirty-ninth canon of Elvira expresses itself in the same manner; and in commenting upon it, we have said that the words manum imponi were understood by one party as a simple ceremony of admission to the order of catechumens without baptism; by others, especially by Dr. München, as expressing the administration of confirmation.

CAN. 7. De fidelibus qui præsides fiunt vel rem publicam agere volunt

De præsidibus qui fideles ad præsidatum prosiliunt, placuit ut cum promoti fuerint literas accipiant ecclesiasticas communicatorias, ita tamen ut in quibuscumque locis gesserint, ab episcopo ejusdem loci cura illis agatur, et cum cœperint contra disciplinam agere, tum demum a communione excludantur. Similiter et de his qui rempublicam agere volunt.

Like the preceding one, this canon repeats a similar statute of the Synod of Elvira. The fifty-sixth canon of Elvira had decreed that a Christian invested with a public office should abstain from appearing in church during the term of these duties, because these necessarily brought him into contact with paganism. But since the Council of Elvira an essential change had taken place. Constantine had himself gone over to Christianity; the Church had obtained full liberty; and if even before this time Christians had often been invested with public offices, this would henceforth be much more frequently the case. It was necessary that, under a Christian emperor and altered circumstances, the ancient rigour should be relaxed, and it is for this reason that the canon of Arles modified the decree of Elvira. If a Christian, it says, becomes præses, that is to say, governor, he is not, as heretofore, obliged to absent himself from church; on the contrary, letters of recommendation will be given him to the bishop of the country which is entrusted to his care (the governors were sent out of their native country, that they might rule more impartially). The bishop was bound to extend his care over him, that is to say, to watch over him, assist him with his advice, that he might commit no injustice in an office which included the jus gladii. If he did not listen to the warnings of the bishop, if he really violated Christian discipline, then only was he to be excluded from the Church. The same line of conduct was adhered to in regard of the municipal authorities as towards the imperial officers. Baronius has erroneously interpreted this canon, in making it exclude heretics and schismatics from holding public offices.

CAN. 8. De baptismo eorum qui ab hæresi convertuntur

De Afris quod propria lege sua utuntur ut rebaptizent, placuit ut si ad Ecclesiam aliquis de hæresi venerit, interrogent eum symbolum; et si perviderint eum in Patre et Filio et Spiritu sancto esse baptizatum, manus ei tantum imponatur ut accipiat Spiritum sanctum. Quod si interrogatus non responderit hanc Trinitatem, baptizetur.

We have already seen that several African synods, held under Agrippinus and Cyprian, ordered that whoever had been baptized by a heretic, was to be re-baptized on re-entering the Church. The Council of Arles abolished this law (lex) of the Africans, and decreed that those who had received baptism from heretics in the name of the holy Trinity were not to be again baptized, but simply to receive the imposition of hands, ut accipiat Spiritum sanctum. Thus, as we have already said, the imposition of hands on those converted was ad pænitentiam and ad confirmationem. The Council of Arles promulgated in this eighth canon the rule that has always been in force, and is still preserved in our time, with regard to baptism conferred by heretics: it was adopted and renewed by the nineteenth canon of the Œcumenical Council of Nicæa.

In several mss. Arianis is read instead of Afris; but it is known that at the time of the first Synod of Arles the sect of the Arians did not yet exist. Binius has thought, and perhaps with some reason, that this canon alluded to the Donatists, and was intended to refute their opinion on the ordination of Cecilian by Felix of Aptunga, by laying down this general principle: "That a sacrament is valid, even when it has been conferred by an unworthy minister." There is, however, no trace of an allusion to the Donatists: it is the thirteenth canon which clearly settles the particular case of the Donatists, as to whether a Traditor, one who has delivered up the Holy Scriptures, can validly ordain.

CAN. 9. Ut qui confessorum litteras afferuut, alias accipiant

De his qui confessorum literas afferunt, placuit ut sublatis iis literis alias accipiant communicatorias.

This canon is a repetition of the twenty-fifth canon of the Synod of Elvira.

CAN. 10. Ut is cujus uxor adulteraverit aliam illa vivente non accipiat

De his qui conjuges suas in adulterio deprehendunt, et iidem sunt adolescentes fideles et prohibentur nubere, placuit ut in quantum possit consilium iis detur, ne viventibus uxoribus suis licet adulteris alias accipiant.

In reference to the ninth canon of Elvira, the Synod of Arles has in view simply the case of a man putting away his adulterous wife; whilst, on the contrary, the Council of Elvira refers to the case of a woman leaving her adulterous husband. In both cases the two Councils alike depart from the existing civil law, by refusing to the innocent party the right of marrying again. But there is the noteworthy difference, that the right of re-marrying is forbidden to the woman, under penalty of permanent excommunication (can. 9 of Elvira); while the man is only strongly advised (in quantum possit consilium iis detur) not to marry again. Even in this case marriage is not allowed, as is shown by the expression et prohibentur nubere. This Synod will not allow that which has been forbidden, but only abstains from imposing ecclesiastical penance. Why is it more considerate to the man? Undoubtedly because the existing civil law gave greater liberty to the husband than to the wife, and did not regard the connection of a married man with an unmarried woman as adultery.

It may be observed that Petavius, instead of et prohibentur nubere, prefers to read et non prohibentur nubere, which would mean that, while they were not prohibited from marrying, they should be strongly recommended not to do so.

CAN. 11. De puellis quæ gentilibus junguntur

De puellis fidelibus quæ gentilibus junguntur placuit, ut aliquanto tempore a communione separentur.

This canon is evidently related to the fifteenth canon of Elvira, with, however, this difference, that the canon of Elvira chiefly relates to the parents, while that of Arles rather concerns daughters. This, too, enforces a penalty, which the other does not.

CAN. 12. Ut clerici fœneratores excommunicentur

De ministris qui fœnerant, placuit eos juxta formam divinitus datam a communione abstineri.

This canon is almost literally identical with the first part of the twentieth canon of Elvira.

CAN. 13. De iis qui Scripturas sacras, vasa dominica, vel nomina fratrum tradidisse dicuntur

De his qui Scripturas sanctas tradidisse dicuntur vel vasa dominica vel nomina fratrum suorum, placuit nobis ut quicumque eorum ex actis publicis fuerit detectus, non verbis nudis, ab ordine cleri amoveatur; nam si iidem aliquos ordinasse fuerint deprehensi, et hi quos ordinaverunt rationales subsistunt, non illis obsit ordinatio. Et quoniam multi sunt qui contra ecclesiasticam regulam pugnare videntur et per testes redemptos putant se ad accusationem admitti debere, omnino non admittantur, nisi, ut supra diximus, actis publicis docuerint.

The Emperor Diocletian had ordered, by his first edict for persecution in 303, first, that all the churches were to be destroyed; secondly, that all sacred books were to be burnt; thirdly, that Christians were to be deprived of all rights and all honours; and that when they were slaves, they were to be declared incapable of acquiring liberty. Consequently Christians were everywhere required to give up the holy books to be burnt, and the sacred vases to be confiscated by the treasury (ad fiscum). This canon mentions these two demands, and, besides these, the traditio nominum. It may be that, according to the first edict, some Christians, and especially the bishops, were required to remit the lists of the faithful belonging to their dioceses, in order to subject them to the decree which deprived them of all rights and honour. However, Dr. München thinks that the traditio nominum was first introduced in consequence of Diocletian's second edict. This edict ordered that all ecclesiastics should be imprisoned, and compelled to sacrifice. Many tried to escape the danger by flight; but it also happened that many were betrayed, and their names (nomina fratrum) given up to the heathen. The thirteenth canon orders the deposition of these Traditores, if they are ecclesiastics. But this penalty was only to be inflicted in case the offence of traditio was proved, not merely by private denunciations (verbis nudis), but by the public laws, by writings signed by officers of justice (ex actis publicis), which the Roman officers had to draw up in executing the Emperor's edict.

The Synod occupied itself with this question: "What must be done if a traditor bishop has ordained clergy?" This was precisely the principal question in the controversy with the Donatists; and the Synod decided "that the ordination should be valid, that is, that whoever should be ordained by such a bishop should not suffer from it" (non illis obsit ordinatio). This part of the passage is very plain, and clearly indicates the solution given by the Council; but the preceding words, et hi, quos ordinaverunt, rationales subsistunt, are difficult to explain. They may very well mean, "If those who have been ordained by them are worthy, and fit to receive holy orders;" but we read in a certain number of MSS., et de his, quos ordinaverint, ratio subsistit, that is to say, "If those are in question who have been ordained by them."

This canon has another conclusion which touches the Donatist controversy; namely: "Accusers who, contrary to all the Church's rules, procured paid witnesses to prove their accusations, as the adversaries of Felix of Aptunga have done, ought not at all to be heard if they cannot prove their complaints by the public acts."

CAN. 14. Ut qui falso accusant fratres suos usque ad exitum excommunicentur

De his qui falso accusant fratres suos, placuit eos usque ad exitum non communicare.

This canon is the sequel to the preceding: "If it is proved that any one has made a positively false and unwarrantable accusation against another (as a traditor), such a person will be excommunicated to the end of his life." This canon is worded in so general a manner, that it not only embraces the false denunciations on the particular case of the traditio, but all false denunciations in general, as the seventy-fifth canon of the Synod of Elvira had already done.

CAN. 15. Ut diacones non offerant

De diaconibus quos cognovimus multis locis offerre, placuit minime fieri debere.

During the persecution of Diocletian, a certain number of deacons seem to have assumed to themselves the right of offering the holy sacrifice, especially when there was no bishop or priest at hand. The Synod of Arles prohibited this. It will be seen that in this canon we translate offerre as "to offer the holy sacrifice," in the same sense as this word is used in the nineteenth canon. Binterim gives another interpretation. By offerre he understands the administration of the Eucharist to the faithful; and he explains the canon in this sense: "The deacons ought not to administer the communion to the faithful in various places, but only in the churches which are assigned to them." We must allow that offerre has sometimes this meaning; for example, in S. Cyprian, de Lapsis: Solemnibus adimpletis calicem diaconus offerre præsentibus cœpit; but,

a. It is difficult to suppose that the Synod of Arles should have employed the expression offerre in two senses so essentially different—in the fifteenth canon, where it would mean to administer the Eucharist, and in the nineteenth canon, where it would mean to offer the holy sacrifice—without having in either pointed out this difference more clearly.

b. The Synod evidently wished to put an end to a serious abuse, as it says, Minime fieri debere. Now it could not have been a very grave offence on the part of the deacons, if, in consequence of the want of clergy, they had administered the communion in several places: after all, they would only have done what they performed ex officio in their own churches.

CAN. 16. Ut ubi quisque fuit excommunicatus, ibi communionem consequatur

De his qui pro delicto suo a communione separantur, placuit ut in quibuscumque locis fuerint exclusi in iisdem communionem consequantur.

The fifty-third canon of the Synod of Elvira had already given the same order. This canon should be compared with the fifth canon of the Synod of Nicæa, the second and sixth of Antioch (in 341), and with the sixteenth of Sardica.

CAN. 17. Ut nullus episcopus alium conculcet episcopum

Ut nullus episcopus alium episcopum inculcet.

A bishop could in many ways inconvenience, molest (inculcare) a colleague; especially—

a. If he allowed himself to exercise various episcopal functions in any diocese other than his own; for example, to ordain clergy, which the Synod of Antioch forbade, in 341, by its thirteenth canon.

b. If he stayed a long time in a strange town, if he preached there, and so threw into the shade the bishop of the place, who might be less able, less learned than himself, for the sake of obtaining the other's see; which the eleventh canon (fourteenth in Latin) of Sardica also forbids.

CAN. 18. De diaconibus urbicis ut sine conscientia presbyterorum nihil agant

De diaconibus urbicis ut non sibi tantum præsumant, sed honorem presbyteris reservent, ut sine conscientia ipsorum nihil tale faciant.

The canon does not tell us in what these usurpations of the suburban deacons consisted (in opposition to the deacons of the country churches, who, being farther from the bishop, had less influence). The words honorem presbyteris reservent seem to imply that the Council of Arles referred to the deacons who, according to the evidence of the Council of Nicæa, forgot their inferiority to the priests, and took rank and place amongst them, which the Synod of Nicæa also forbade. The Synod of Laodicæa also found it necessary to order deacons to remain standing in the presence of priests, unless invited to sit down. The last words of our canon indicate that here also the allusion is to the functions that deacons were generally authorized to exercise in virtue of their charge, such as baptizing and preaching, but which they were not to discharge unless with the consent of the priests who were set over them.

CAN. 19. Ut peregrinis episcopis locus sacrificandi detur

De episcopis peregrinis qui in urbem solent venire, placuit iis locum dare ut offerant.

The seventeenth canon having forbidden bishops to exercise episcopal functions in a strange diocese, the nineteenth canon declares that the celebration of the holy sacrifice is not comprised in this prohibition, and consequently that a bishop should be allowed to offer the holy sacrifice in a strange diocese, or, as we should say, should be permitted to say Mass.

CAN. 20. Ut sine tribus episcopis nullus episcopus ordinetur

De his qui usurpant sibi quod soli debeant episcopos ordinare, placuit ut nullus hoc sibi præsumat nisi assumptis secum aliis septem episcopis. Si tamen non potuerit septem, infra tres non audeat ordinare.

The Synod of Nicæa, canon 4, made the same regulation, that all bishops should not singly ordain another bishop, and orders that there be at least three bishops for this purpose.

CAN. 21. Ut presbyteri aut diacones qui ad alia loca se transferunt deponantur

De presbyteris aut diaconibus qui solent dimittere loca sua in quibus ordinati sunt et ad alia loca se transferunt, placuit ut iis locis ministrent quibus præfixi sunt. Quod si relictis locis suis ad alium se locum transferre voluerint, deponantur.

Cf. the second canon, above, p. 185.

CAN. 22. De apostatis qui in infirmitate communionem pctunt

De his qui apostatant et nunquam se ad ecclesiam repræsentant, ne quidem pœnitentiam agere quærunt, et postea infirmitate accepti petunt communionem, placuit iis non dandam communionem nisi revaluerint et egerint dignos fructus pœnitentiæ.

The Council of Nicæa, in its thirteenth canon, softened this order, and allowed the holy communion to be administered to all sinners at the point of death who should desire it.

Besides, these twenty-two canons of the first Synod of Arles, which are certainly genuine, Mansi found six more in a MS. at Lucca. He thought, however, that these last must have been decreed by another Council of Arles. They are the following:—

CAN. 1 (24)

Placuit ut quantum potest inhibeatur viro, ne dimissa uxore vivente liceat ut aliam ducat super eam: quicumque autem fecerit alienus erit a catholica communione.

CAN. 2 (25)

Placuit ut mulierem corruptam clericus non ducat uxorem, vel is, qui laicus mulierem corruptam duxerit, non admittatur ad clerum.

CAN. 3 (26)

De aliena ecclesia clericum ordinare alibi nullus episcopus usurpet; quod si fecerit, sciat se esse judicandum cum inter fratres de hoc fuerit appetitus.

CAN. 4 (27)

Abstentum clericum alterius ecclesiæ alia non admittat; sed pacem in ecclesia inter fratres simplicem tenere cognoscat.

CAN. 5 (28)

Venientem de Donatistis vel de Montensibus per manus impositionis suscipiantur, ex eo quod contra ecclesiasticum ordinem baptizare videntur.

CAN. 6 (29)

Præterea, quod dignum, pudicum et honestum est, suademus fratribus ut sacerdotes et levitæ cum uxoribus suis non coeant, quia ministerio quotidiano occupantur. Quicumque contra hanc constitutionem fecerit, a clericatus honore deponatur.

If we consider, again, the occasion of this Synod— namely, the schism of the Donatists—we see that as soon as the Synod had pronounced its sentence upon them, they appealed anew to the Emperor, while the Catholic bishops asked permission of him to return to their homes. Constantine thereupon wrote a beautiful and touching letter to the bishops, thanking God for His goodness to him, and the bishops for the equitable and conciliatory judgment that they had pronounced. He complained of the perverseness, the pride, and obstinacy of the Donatists, who would not have peace, but appealed to him from the judgment of the Church, when the sentence of the priests ought to be regarded as that of the Lord Himself (sacerdotum judicium ita debet haberi, ac si ipse Dominus residens judicet). "What audacity, what madness, what folly!" he exclaims; "they have appealed from it like heathens." At the end of his letter he prays the bishops, after Christ's example, to have yet a little patience, and to stay some time longer at Arles, so as to try and reclaim these misguided men. If this last attempt failed, they might return to their dioceses; and he prayed them to remember him, that the Saviour might have mercy upon him. He said that he had ordered the officers of the empire to send the refractory from

Arles, and from Africa as well, to his court, where great severity awaited them.

These threats caused a great number of Donatists to return to the Church; others persevered in their obstinacy, and, according to Constantine's order, were brought to the imperial court. From that time there was no longer any occasion for the Catholic bishops to remain at Arles, and in all probability they returned to their dioceses. Arrived at court, the Donatists again prayed the Emperor to judge their cause himself. Constantine at first refused, but, for reasons with which we are not acquainted, ended by consenting to their demand. He summoned Cecilian, the Catholic Bishop of Carthage, as well as his Donatist adversaries, to appear before him at Rome, where he was staying, in August 315. Ingentius, the false accuser of Felix of Aptunga, was to be there to prove to the Donatists that they had improperly called in question the consecration of Cecilian; but Cecilian, for some unknown reason, did not appear. S. Augustine himself did not know why; and the Donatists profited by this circumstance, and urged the Emperor to condemn Cecilian for disobedience. Constantine, however, contented himself with granting him a delay, at the end of which Cecilian was to appear at Milan, which so exasperated many of the Donatists, that they fled from the court to Africa. The Emperor for some time thought of going himself into Africa to judge the cause of the Donatists in their own country. He accordingly sent back some Donatist bishops into Africa, and warned the others by letter of his project, adding, that if they could prove but one of their numerous accusations against Cecilian, he would consider such proof as a demonstration of all the rest.

The Emperor afterwards gave up this scheme, and returned to that which had been first proposed, and in November 316 caused the contending parties to appear before him at Milan. Cecilian presented himself before the Emperor, as well as his antagonists. The Emperor heard both sides, examined their depositions, and finally declared that Cecilian was innocent, that his adversaries were calumniators, and sent a copy of his decision to Eumalius, his vicar in Africa. The Donatists were thus condemned three times, by the two Synods of Rome and of Arles, and finally by the Emperor himself. In spite of this, to weaken the effect of the late sentence, they spread the rumour that the celebrated Hosius Bishop of Corduba, a friend of Cecilian, had prejudiced the Emperor against them.

The subsequent history of the schism of the Donatists does not belong to this place; and we have now to consider two other synods which were held in the East about the same time as that of Arles, and which merit all our attention. They are those of Ancyra and Neocæsarea.

SEC. 16. The Synod of Ancyra in 314

Maximilian having died during the summer of 313, the Church in the East began to breathe freely, says Eusebius. He says nothing further about these Synods; but one of the first, and certainly the most celebrated, of these Councils, was that of Ancyra, the capital of Galatia, which was held for the purpose of healing the wounds inflicted on the Church by the last persecution, and especially to see what could be done on the subject of the lapsi.

The best Greek MSS. of the canons of Ancyra contain a very ancient preface, which shows, without further specification, that the Council of Ancyra was held before that of Nicæa. The presence of Vitalis Bishop of Antioch at the Council of Ancyra proves that it was held before the year 319, which is the year of the death of that bishop. It is, then, between 313 and 319 that it was held. Binius believes he has discovered a still more exact date, in the fact of the presence of Basil Bishop of Amasia at our Synod. According to his opinion, this bishop suffered martyrdom in 316, under the Emperor Licinius; but Tillemont has proved that he was probably not martyred till 320.

It appears from the sixth canon of Ancyra that the Council was held, conformably to the apostolic canons, No. 38 (36), in the fourth week after Easter. Maximin having died during the summer of 313, the first Pentecost after his death fell in 314; and it is very probable that the Christians immediately availed themselves of the liberty which his death gave them to come to the aid of the Church.

This is also what the words of Eusebius clearly indicate. Baronius, Tillemont, Rémi Ceillier, and others, were therefore perfectly right in placing the Synod of Ancyra after the Easter which followed the death of Maximin; consequently in 314.

We have three lists of the bishops who were present at the Synod of Ancyra. They differ considerably from one another. That which, in addition to the bishops and the towns, names the provinces, is evidently, as the Ballerini have shown, of later origin: for (α) no Greek MS. contains this list; (β) it is wanting in the most ancient Latin translations; (γ) the lists of the provinces are frequently at variance with the civil division of the province at this time. For instance, the list speaks of a Galatia prima, of a Cappadocia prima, of a Cilicia prima and secunda, of a Phrygia Pacatiana, all divisions which did not then exist. Another list of the bishops who were present at Ancyra, but without showing the provinces, is found in the Prisca and in the Isidorian collection. Dionysius the Less does not give a list of the persons: one of this kind has not, until lately, been attached to his writings.

In this state of things, it is evident that none of these lists are of great value, as they vary so much from each other even as to the number of the bishops, which is left undecided, being put down between twelve and eighteen. In the longest list the following names are found: Vitalis of Antioch, Agricolaus of Cæsarea in Palestine, Marcellus of Ancyra, who had become so famous in the Arian controversy, Lupus of Tarsus, Basil of Amasia, Philadelphius of Juliopolis in Galatia, Eustolius of Nicomedia, Heraclius of Tela in Great Armenia, Peter of Iconium, Nunechius of Laodicea in Phrygia, Sergianus of Antioch in Pisidia, Epidaurus of Perga in Pamphilia, Narcissus of Neronias in Cilicia, Leontius of Cæsarea in Cappadocia, Longinus of Neocæsarea in Pontus, Amphion of Epiphania in Cilicia, Salamenus of Germanicia in Cœlesyria, and Germanus of Neapolis in Palestine. Several of these were present, eleven years after, at the first Œcumenical Council of Nicæa. They belonged, as we see, to such different provinces of Asia Minor and Syria, that the Synod of Ancyra may, in the same sense as that of Arles, be considered a concilium plenarium, that is, a general council of the Churches of Asia Minor and Syria. From the fact that Vitalis of Antioch is mentioned first (primo loco), and that Antioch was the most considerable seat of those who were represented at Ancyra, it is generally concluded that Vitalis presided over the Synod; and we admit this supposition, although the

Libellus synodicus assigns the presidency to Marcellus of Ancyra.

CAN. 1

Πρεσβυτέρους τοὺς ἐπιθύσαντας, εἶτα ἐπαναπαλαίσαντας μήτε ἐκ μεθόδου τινὸς ἀλλ' ἐξ ἀληθείας, μήτε προκατασκευάσαντας καὶ ἐπιτηδεύσαντας, καὶ πείσαντας ἵνα δόξωσι μὲν βασάνοις ὑποβάλλεσθαι, ταύτας δὲ τῷ δοκεῖν καὶ τῷ σχήματι προσαχθῆναι· τούτους ἔδιξε τῆς μὲν τιμῆς τῆς κατὰ τὴν καθέδραν μετέχειν, προσφέρειν δὲ αὐτοὺς ἢ ὁμιλεῖν ἢ ὅλως λειτουργεῖν τι τῶν ἱερατικῶν λειτουργιῶν μὴ ἐξεῖναι.

"Priests who sacrificed (during the persecution), but afterwards repenting, resumed the combat not only in appearance, but in reality, will continue to enjoy the honours of their office, but they may neither sacrifice or preach, nor fulfil any priestly office."

In this translation we have left out a great incidental proposition (from μήτε προκατασκευάσαντας to προσαχθῆναι), because to be understood it requires some previous explanations. Certain priests who had sacrificed to idols, wishing to be restored to favour, performed a sort of farce to deceive the bishop and the faithful. They bribed some officers and their subordinates, then presented themselves before them as Christians, and pretended to submit to all kinds of tortures, which were not really, but only apparently applied to them, according to the plan which had been previously arranged. The Council also says: "Without having made any arrangements, and without its being understood and agreed that they should appear to submit to tortures which were only to be apparently inflicted on them."

It was quite justifiable, and in accordance with the ancient and severe discipline of the Church, when this Synod no longer allowed priests, even when sincerely penitent, to discharge priestly functions. It was for this same reason that the two Spanish bishops Martial and Basilides were deposed, and that the judgment given against them was confirmed in 254 by an African synod held under S. Cyprian. The first canon, together with the second and third, was inserted in the Corpus juris can.

CAN. 2

Διακόνους ὁμοίως θύσαντας, μετὰ δὲ ταῦτα ἀναπαλαίσαντας τὴν μὲν ἄλλην τιμὴν ἔχειν, πεπαῦσθαι δὲ αὐτοὺς πάσης τῆς ἱερᾶς λειτουργίας, τῆς τε τοῦ ἄρτον ἢ ποτήριον ἀναφέρειν ἢ κηρύσσειν, εἰ μέντοι τινὲς τῶν ἐπισκόπων τούτοις συνίδοιεν κάματόν τινα ἢ ταπείνωσιν πράτητος καὶ ἐθέλοιεν πλεῖόν τι διδόναι ἢ ἀφαιρεῖν, ἐπ᾽ αὐτοῖς εἶναι τὴν ἐξουσίαν.

"In the same manner, the deacons who may have sacrificed, but have afterwards returned to the fight, shall keep the dignities of their office, but shall no longer fulfil any holy function, shall no longer offer the bread and wine (to the celebrant or to the communicants), shall no longer preach. But if any bishops, out of regard to their efforts (for their ardent penitence), and to their humiliation, wish to grant them more privileges, or to withdraw more from them, they have power to do so."

According to this, such deacons could no longer exercise their ministry in the Church, but they continued their offices as almoners to the poor, and administrators of the property of the Church, etc. etc. It is doubtful what is meant by "to offer the bread and the chalice." In the primitive Church, S. Justin testifies that the deacons distributed the holy communion to the laity. It is possible that the canon refers to this distribution. Van Espen, however, thinks that, at the time of the Synod, deacons no longer distributed the consecrated bread to the faithful, but only the chalice, according to a prescription of the Apostolic Constitutions, and an expression of Cyprian; so that ἀναφάτρειν ἄρτον ἤ ποτήριον (because there is mention of ἄρτον, bread) must here relate to the presentation of the bread and the chalice made by the deacon to the bishop or priest who celebrated at the time of the offertory. But it seems from the eighteenth canon of Nicæa, that this primitive custom, in virtue of which deacons also distributed the eucharistic bread as well as wine, had not entirely disappeared at the beginning of the fourth century, and consequently at the time of the Synod of Ancyra.

The word κηρύσσειν, to proclaim, needs explanation. It means in the first place the act of preaching; it is declared to be forbidden to diaconis lapsis. But deacons had, and still have, other things to proclaim (κηρύσσειν). They read the Gospel, they exclaimed: Flectamus genua, Procedamus in pace, Ne quis audientium, Ne quis infidelium; and these functions were also comprised in the κηρύσσειν.

Finally, the canon directs bishops to take into consideration the circumstances and the worth of the diaconi lapsi in adding to or deducting from the measures decreed against them.

CAN. 3

Τοὺς φεύγοντας καὶ συλληφθέντας ἢ ὑπὸ οἰκείων παραδοθέντας ἢ ἄλλως τὰ ὑπάρχοντα ἀφαιρεθέντας ἢ ὑπομείναντας βασάνους ἢ εἰς δεσμωτήριον ἐμβληθέντας βοῶντάς τε ὅτι εἰσὶ Χριστιανοὶ καὶ περισχισθέντας (περισχεθέυτας) ἤτοι εἰς τὰς χεῖρας πρὸς βίαν ἐμβαλλόντων τῶν βιαζομένων ἢ βρῶμά τιπρὸς ἀνάγκην δεξαμένους, ὁμολογοῦυτας δὲ διόλου ὅτι εἰσὶ Χριστιανοί, καὶ τὸ πένθος τοῦ συμβάυτος ἀεὶ ἐπιδεικνυμένους τῇ πάσῃ καταστολῇ καὶ τῷ σχήματι καὶ τῇ βίου ταπεινόητι· τούτους ὡς ἔξω ἁμαρτήματος ὄντας τῆς κοινωνίας μὴ κωλύεσθαι εἰ δὲ καὶ ἐκωλύθησαν ὑπό τινος, περισσοτέρας ἀκριβέας ἕνεκεν ἤ καί τινων ἀγνοίᾳ, εὐθὺς προσδεχθῆναι· τοῦτο δέ ὁμοίως ἐπί τε τῶν ἐκ τοῦ κλήρου καὶ τῶν ἄλλων λαϊκῶν, προσεξητάσθη δὲ κἀκεῖνο, εἰ δύνανται καὶ λαικοὶ τῇ αὐτῇ ἀνάγκῃ ὑποπεσόντες προσάγεθαι εἰς τάξιν· ἔδοξεν οὖν καὶ τούτους ὡς μηδὲν ἡμαρτηκότας, εἰ καὶ ἡ προλαβοῦσα εὑρίσκοιτο ὀρθὴ τοῦ βίου πολιτεία, προχειρίζεσθαι.

"Those who fled before persecution, but were caught, or were betrayed by those of their own houses, or in any other way, who have borne with resignation the confiscation of their property, tortures, and imprisonment, declaring themselves to be Christians, but who have subsequently been vanquished, whether their oppressors have by force put incense into their hands, or have compelled them to take in their mouth the meat offered to idols, and who, in spite of this, have persevered in avowing themselves Christians, and have evinced their sorrow for what had befallen them by their dejection and humility,—such, not having committed any fault, are not to be deprived of the communion of the Church; and if they have been so treated by the over-severity or ignorance of their bishop, they are immediately to be reinstated. This applies equally to the clergy and to the laity. In the same way it was to be inquired if the laity, to whom violence has been used (that is to say, who have been physically obliged to sacrifice), might be promoted to the ministry (τάξις, ordo); and it was decreed that, not having committed any fault (in the case of these sacrifices), they might be elected, provided their former life was found to be consistent."

The meaning of this canon is clear: "Physical constraint relieves from responsibility." That there had been physical constraint was proved in the following ways:—

(a.) By the previous endurance with which they had borne confiscation, tortures, and imprisonment.

(β.) By this, that during their sufferings they had always declared themselves Christians.

Among the expressions of this canon the word περισχισθέντας of the textus vulgatus presents the chief difficulties. Zonaras translates it thus: "If their clothes have been torn from their bodies:" for περισχίζω means to tear away, and with τινὰ to tear off the clothes from any one. But the true reading is περισχεθέντας, which Routh has found in three MSS. in the Bodleian Library, and which harmonizes the best with the versions of Dionysius the Less and of Isidore. We have used this reading (περισχεθέντας) in our translation of the canon; for περιέχω means to surround, to conquer, to subdue.

CAN. 4

Περὶ τῶν πρὸς βίαν θυσάντων, ἐπὶ δὲ τούτοις καὶ τῶν δειπνησάντων εἰς τὰ εἴδωλα, ὅσοι μὲν ἀπαγόμενοι καὶ σχήματι φαιδροτέρῳ ἀνῆλθον καὶ ἐσθῆτι ἐχρήσαντο πολυτεστέρᾳ καὶ μετέσχον τοῦ παρασκευασθέντος δείπνου ἀδιαφόρως, ἔδοξεν ἐνιαυτὸν ἀκροᾶσθαι, ὑποπεσεῖν δὲ τρία ἔτη, εὐχῆς δὲ μόνης κοινωνῆσαι ἔτη δύο, καὶ τότε ἐλθεῖν ἐπὶ τὸ τέλειον.

"As to those who have been forced to sacrifice, and who have besides eaten the meats consecrated to the gods (that is to say, who have been forced to take part in the feasts off the sacrifices), the Council decrees, that those who, being forced to go to the sacrifice, have gone cheerfully, dressed in their best, and without any sorrow (as if there was no difference between this and other meals), and shall there have eaten of it, shall remain one year amongst the audientes (second class of penitents), three years among the substrati (third class of penitents), shall take part in the prayers (fourth class) for two years, and then finally be admitted to the complete privileges of the Church (τὸ τέλειον), that is, to the communion."

CAN. 5

Ὅσοι δὲ ἀνῆλθον μετὰ ἐσθῆτος πενθικῆς καὶ ἀναπεσόντες ἔφαγον μεταξὺ δι' ὅλης τῆς

ἀνακλίσεως δακρύοντες, εἰ ἐπλήρωσαν τὸν τῆς
ὑποπτώσεως τριετῆ χρόνον χωρὶς προσφορᾶς
δεχθήτωσαν· εἰ δὲ μὴ ἔφαγον, δύο ὑποπεσόντες ἔτη
τῷ τρίτῳ κοινωνησάτωσαν χωρὶς προσφορᾶς, ἵνα
τὸ τέλειον τῇ τετραετίᾳ λάβωσι, τοὺ δὲ ἐπισκόπους
ἐξουσίαν ἔχειν τὸν τρόπον τῆς ἐπιστροφῆς
δοκιμάσαντας φιλανθρωπεύεσθαι ἢ πλείονα
προστιθέναι χρόνον· πρὸ πάντων δὲ καὶ ὁ προάγων
βίος καὶ ὁ μετὰταῦτα ἐξεταζέσθω, καὶ οὕτως ἡ
φιλανθρωπία ἐπιμετρείσθω.

"Nevertheless, those who have appeared there (that
is, at the feast of the sacrifices) in mourning habits,
who have been full of grief during the repast, and
have wept during the whole time of the feast, shall
be three years amongst the substrati, and then be
admitted, without taking part in the offering; but if
they have not eaten (and have merely been present
at the feast), they are to be substrati for two years,
and the third year they shall take part in the offering
(in the degree of the consistentes, σύστασις), so as
to receive the complement (the holy communion) in
the fourth year. The bishops will have the power,
after having tried the conduct of each, to mitigate
the penalties, or to extend the time of penitence; but
they must take care to inquire what has passed
before and after their fall, and their clemency must
be exercised accordingly."

We may see that this canon is closely allied to the
preceding one, and that the one explains the other:

there only remains some obscurity arising from the expression χωρὶς προσφορᾶς. Aubespine thought that there is here a reference to the offerings which were presented by penitents, in the hope of obtaining mercy; but Suicer remarks that it is not so, and that the reference here is certainly to those offerings which are presented by the faithful during the sacrifice (at the offertory). According to Suicer, the meaning of the canon would be: "They may take part in divine worship, but not actively;" that is, "they may mingle their offerings with those of the faithful:" which corresponds with the fourth or last degree of penitence. But as those who cannot present their offerings during the sacrifice are excluded from the communion, the complete meaning of this canon is: "They may be present at divine service, but may neither offer nor communicate with the faithful." Consequently χωρὶς προσφορᾶς also comprises the exclusion from the communion; but it does not follow from this that προσφορὰ means the sacrament of the altar, as Herbst and Routh have erroneously supposed. The eucharistic service has, we know, two parts: it is, in the first place, a sacrifice; and then, as a reception of the eucharistic bread, it is a sacrament. And the whole act may be called προσφορά; but the mere reception of the communion cannot be called προσφορά. The canon does not clearly point out the time during which penitents were to remain in the fourth degree of penitence, except in the case of those who had not actually eaten of the sacrificed meats. It says, that at the end of a year they could be received in full, that is to say, at the eucharistic table. The time of penitence is not fixed for those who had actually eaten the sacrificed meats: perhaps it was also a year; or it may be they were treated according to the fourth canon, that is to say, reduced for two years to the fourth degree of penitence. The penitents of the fifth canon, less culpable than those of the fourth, are not, as the latter, condemned to the second degree of penitence.

CAN. 6

Περὶ τῶν ἀπειλῇ μόνον εἰξάνρων κολάσεως καὶ ἀφαιρέσεως ὑπαρχόντων ἢ μετοικίας καὶ θυσάντων καὶ μέχρι τοῦ παρόντος καιροῦ μὴ μετανοησάντων μηδὲ ἐπιστρεψάντων, νῦν δὲ παρὰ τὸν καιρὸν τῆς συνόδου προσελθόντων καὶ εἰς διάνοιαν τῆς ἐπιστροφῆς γενομένων, ἔδοξε μέχρι τῆς μεγάλης ἡμέρας εἰς ἀκρόασιν δεχθῆναι, καὶ μετὰ τὴν μεγάλην ἡμέραν ὑποπεσεῖν ταία ἔτη καὶ μετὰ ἄλλα δύο ἔτη κοινωνῆσαι χωρὶς προσφορᾶς, καὶ οὕτως ἐλθεῖν ἐπὶ τὸ τέλειον, ὥστε τὴν πᾶσαν ἐξαετίαν πληρῶσαι· εἰ δέ τινες πρὸ τῆς συνόδου ταύτης ἐδέχθησαυ εἰς μετάνοιαν, ἀπ᾽ ἐκείνου τοῦ χρόνου λελογίσθαι αὐτοῖς τὴν ἀρχὴν τῆς ἐξαετίας· εἰ μέντοι κίνδυνς καὶ θανάτου προσδοκία ἐκ νόσου ἢ ἄλλης τινὸς προφάσεως συμβαίη, τούτους ἐπὶ ὅρῳ δεχθῆναι.

"As to those who yielded on the first threat of punishment and of the confiscation of their property, or of exile, and who have sacrificed, and to this day have not repented or returned, but who on the occasion of this Synod have repented, and shall resolve to return, it is decreed, that until the great feast (Easter) they shall be admitted to the degree of audientes; that they shall after the great feast be substrati for three years; then that they shall be admitted, but without taking part in the sacrifice for two years, and that then only they shall be admitted to the full service (to the communion), so that the whole time will be six years. For those who have been admitted to a course of penitence previous to this Synod, the six years will be allowed to date from the moment of its commencement. If they were exposed to any danger, or threatened with death following any illness, or if there was any other important reason, they would be admitted, conformably to the present prescription (ὅρος)."

The meaning of the last phrase of the canon is, that if the sick regain their health, they will perform their penance, according to what is prescribed. Zonaras thus very clearly explains this passage. This canon is made intelligible by the two preceding. A similar decision is given in the eleventh Nicene canon.

As we have previously remarked (sec. 16), there is a chronological signification in the expression "till the next Easter," compared with that of "the six years shall be accomplished." According to the thirty-sixth (thirty-eighth) apostolic canon, a synod was to be held annually in the fourth week after Easter. If, then, a penitent repented at the time of the synod, and remained among the audientes till the next Easter, he had done penance for nearly a year. And adding three years for the degree of the substratio, and two for the last degree, the six years were completed. It is then with good reason that we have deduced from the sixth canon that the Council of Ancyra was held shortly after Easter, and very probably in the fourth week after this feast, that is, in the time prescribed by the apostolic canons.

CAN. 7

Περὶ τῶν συνεστιαθέντων ἐν ἑορτῇ ἐθνικῇ ἐν τόπῳ ἀφωροσμένῳ τοῖς ἐθνικοῖ, ἴδια βρώματα ἐπικομισαμένων καὶ φαγντων, ἔδοξε διετίαν ὑποπεσόντας δεχθῆναν Τὸ δὲ εἰ χρὴ μετὰ τῆς προσφορᾶς ἕκαστον τῶν ἐπιακόπων δοκιμάσαι καὶ τὸν ἄλλον βίον ἐφ᾽ ἑκάστου ἀξιῶσαι.

"As to those who, during a heathen festival, have seated themselves in the locality appointed for that festival, and have brought and eaten their food there, they shall be two years substrati, and then admitted. As to the question of their admission to the offering, each bishop shall decide thereon, taking into consideration the whole life of each person."

Several Christians tried, with worldly prudence, to take a middle course. On the one hand, hoping to escape persecution, they were present at the feasts of the heathen sacrifices, which were held in the buildings adjoining the temples; and on the other, in order to appease their consciences, they took their own food, and touched nothing that had been offered to the gods. These Christians forgot that S. Paul had ordered that meats sacrificed to the gods should be avoided, not because they were tainted in themselves, as the idols were nothing, but from another, and in fact a twofold reason: 1st, Because, in partaking of them, some had still the idols in their hearts, that is to say, were still attached to the worship of idols, and thereby sinned; and 2dly, Because others scandalized their brethren, and sinned in that way. To these two reasons a third may be added, namely, the hypocrisy and the duplicity of those Christians who wished to appear heathens, and nevertheless to remain Christians. The Synod punished them with two years of penance in the third degree, and gave to each bishop the right, either at the expiration of this time to admit them to communion, or to make them remain some time longer in the fourth degree.

CAN. 8

Οἱ δὲ δεύτερον καὶ τρίτον θύσαντες μετὰ βίας, τετραρτίαν ὑοπεσέτωσαν, δύο δὲ ἔτη χωρὶς

προσφορᾶς κοινωνησάτωσαν, καὶ τῷ ἑβδόμῳ
τελείως δεχθήτωσαν.

"Those who, being compelled, have sacrificed two
or three times, shall remain substrati for four years;
they shall take part in the worship, without
presenting any offering, for two years (as
consistentes of the fourth degree); the seventh they
shall be admitted to the communion."

CAN. 9

Ὅσοι δὲ μὴ μόνον ἀπέστησαν ἀλλὰ καὶ
ἐπανέστησαν καὶ ἠσάγκασαν ἀδελφοὺς καὶ αἴτιοι
ἐγένοντο τοῦ ἀναγκασθῆναι, οὗτοι ἔτη μὲν τρία τὸν
τῆς ἀκρόσεως δεξάσθωσαν τόπον, ἐν δὲ ἄλλη
ἐξαετίᾳ τὸν τῆς ὑποπτώσεως, ἄλλον δὲ ἐνιαυτὸν
κοινωνησάτωσαν χωρὶς προσφορᾶς, ἵνα τὴν
δεκαετίαν πληρώσαντες τοῦ τελείου μετάσχωσιν· ἐν
μέντοι τούτῳ χρόνῳ καὶ τὸν ἄλλον αὐτῶν
ἐπιτηρεῖαθαι βίον.

"Those who have not only apostatized, but have
become the enemies of their brethren, and have
compelled them (to apostasy), or have been the
cause of the constraint put upon them, shall remain
for three years among the audientes (second
degree), then six years with the substrati; they shall
then take part in the worship, without offering (in
quality of consistentes), for one year; and not until
the expiration of ten years shall they receive full

communion (the holy Eucharist). Their conduct during all this time shall also be watched."

CAN. 10

Διάκονοι ὅσοι καθίστανται, παρ' αὐτὴν τὴν κατάστασιν εἰ ἐμαρτύραντο καὶ ἔφασαν χρῆναι γαμῆσαι, μὴ δυνάμενοι οὕτως μένειν, οὗτοι μετὰ ταῦτα γαμήσαντες ἔστωσαν ἐν τῇ ὑπηρεσίᾳ διὰ τὸ ἐπιτραπῆναι αὐτοὺς ὑπὸ τοῦ ἐπισκόπου· τοῦτο δὲ εἴ τινες σιωπήσαντες καὶ καταδεξάμενοι ἐν τῇ χειροτονίᾳ μένειν οὕτως μετὰ ταῦτα ἦλθον ἐπὶ γάμον, πεαῦσθαι αὐτοὺς τῆς διακονίας.

"If deacons, at the time of their appointment (election), declare that they must marry, and that they cannot lead a celibate life, and if accordingly they marry, they may continue their offices, because the bishop (at the time of their institution) gave them leave to marry; but if at the time of their election they have not spoken, and have agreed in taking holy orders to lead a celibate life, and if later they marry, they shall lose their diaconate."

This canon has been inserted in the Corpus juris canonici.

CAN. 11

Τὰς μνηστευθείσας κόρας καὶ μετὰ ταῦτα ὑπ' ἄλλων ἁρπαγείσας ἔδοξεν ἀποδίδοσθαι τοῖς προμνηστευσαμένοις, εἰ καὶ βίανὑπ' αὐτῶν πάθοιεν.

"Damsels who are betrothed, who are afterwards carried off by others, shall be given back to those to whom they are betrothed, even when they have been treated with violence."

This canon treats only of betrothed women (by the sponsalia de futuro), not of those who are married (by the sponsalia de præsenti). In the case of the latter there would be no doubt as to the duty of restitution. The man who was betrothed was, moreover, at liberty to receive his affianced bride who had been carried off, or not. It was thus that S. Basil had already decided in canon 22 of his canonical letter to Amphilochius.

CAN. 12

Τοὺς πρὸ τοῦ βαπτίσματος τεθυκότας καὶ μετὰ ταῦτα βαπτισθέντας ἔδοξεν εἰς τάξιν προάγεσθαι ὡς ἀπολουσαμένους.

"Those who have sacrificed to the gods before their baptism, and who have afterwards been baptized, may be promoted to holy orders, as (by baptism) they are purified from all their former sins."

This canon does not speak generally of all those who sacrificed before baptism; for if a heathen sacrificed before having embraced Christianity, he certainly could not be reproached for it after his admission. It was quite a different case with a

catechumen, who had already declared for
Christianity, but who during the persecution had lost
courage, and sacrificed. In this case it might be
asked whether he could still be admitted to the
priesthood. The Council decided that a baptized
catechumen could afterwards be promoted to holy
orders.

The fourteenth canon of Nicæa also speaks of the
catechumens who have committed the same fault.

CAN. 13

Χωρεπισκόπους μὴ ἐξεῖναι πρεσβυτέρους ἤ
διακόνους ξειροτονεῖν, ἀλλὰ μηδὲ πρεσβυτέρους
χωρὶς τοῦ ἐπιτραπῆναι ὑπὸ τοῦ ἐπισκόπου μετὰ
γραμμάτων ἐν ἑτέρᾳ παροικίᾳ.

The literal translation of the Greek text is as
follows:—

"It is not permitted to the chorepiscopi to ordain
priests and deacons; neither is this permitted to the
priests of the towns in other parishes (dioceses)
without the written authority of the bishop of the
place."

In our remarks on the fifty-seventh canon of the
Council of Laodicea, where it is forbidden to appoint
chorepiscopi (or country bishops) for the future, we
shall explain what must be understood by this office,
which is here mentioned for the first time. Compare

also the eighth and tenth canons of the Synod of Antioch in 341, and the second proposition of the sixth canon of the Council of Sardica. If the first part of the thirteenth canon is easy to understand, the second, on the contrary, presents a great difficulty; for a priest of a town could not in any case have the power of consecrating priests and deacons, least of all in a strange diocese. Many of the most learned men have, for this reason, supposed that the Greek text of the second half of the canon, as we have read it, is incorrect or defective. It wants, say they, ποιεῖν τι, or aliquid agere, i.e. to complete a religious function. To confirm this supposition, they have appealed to several ancient versions, especially to that of Isidore: sed nec presbyteris civitatis sine episcopi præcepto amplius aliquid imperare, vel sine auctoritate literarum ejus in unaquaque (some read ἐν ἑκάστῃ instead of ἐν ἑτέρᾳ) parochia aliquid agere. The ancient Roman MS. of the canons, Codex canonum, has the same reading, only that it has provincia instead of parochia. Fulgentius Ferrandus, deacon of Carthage, who long ago made a collection of canons, translates in the same way in his Brcviatio canonum: Ut presbyteri civitatis sine jussu episcopi nihil jubeant, nec in unaquaque parochia aliquid agant. Van Espen has explained this canon in the same way.

Routh has given another interpretation. He maintained that there was not a word missing in this canon, but that at the commencement one ought to read, according to several MSS., χωρεπισκόποις in the dative, and further down ἀλλὰ μὴν μηδὲ instead of ἀλλὰ μηδὲ, then πρεσβυτέρους (in the accusative) πόλεως, and finally ἑκάστῃ instead of ἑτέρᾳ; and that we must therefore translate, "Chorepiscopi are not permitted to consecrate priests and deacons (for the country), still less (ἀλλὰ μὴν μηδὲ) can they consecrate priests for the town without the consent of the bishop of the place." The Greek text, thus modified according to some mss., especially those in the Bodleian Library, certainly gives a good meaning. Still ἀλλὰ μὴν μηδὲ does not mean, but still less: it means, but certainly not, which makes a considerable difference.

Besides this, it can very seldom have happened that the chorepiscopi ordained priests and deacons for a town; and if so, they were already forbidden (implicite) in the first part of the canon.

CAN. 14

Τοὺς ἐν κλήρῳ πρεσβυτέρους ἢ διακόνους ὄντας καὶ ἀπεχομένους κρεῶν ἔδοξεν ἐφάπτεσθαι, καὶ οὕτως, εἰ βούλοιντο, κρατεῖν ἑαντῶν εἰ δὲ βούλοιντο (βδελύσσοιντο), ὡς μηδὲ τὰ μετὰ κρεῶν βαλλόμενα λάχανα ἐσθίειν, καὶ εἰ μὴ ὑπείκοιεν τῷ κανόνι, πεπαῦσθαι αὐτοὺς τῆς τάξεως.

"Those priests and clerks who abstain from eating meat ought (during the love-feasts) to eat it (taste it); but they may, if they will, abstain from it (that is to say, not eat it). If they disdain it (βδελύσσοιντο), so that they will not eat even vegetables cooked with meat, and if they do not obey the present canon, they are to be excluded from the ranks of the clergy."

The fifty-second apostolic canon had already promulgated the same law with reference to the false Gnostic or Manichean asceticism, which declared that matter was satanic, and especially flesh and wine. Zonaras has perceived and pointed out that our canon treated of the agapæ, or love-feasts, of the primitive Christians. He shows, besides, that ἐφάπτεσθαι means, to touch the meats, in the same sense as ἀπογεύεσθαι, to taste. Matthæus Blastares agrees with Zonaras. Finally, Routh has had the credit of contributing to the explanation of this canon, inasmuch as, relying on three MSS., the Collectio of John of Antioch and the Latin versions, he has read εἰ δὲ βδελύσσοιντο instead of εἰ δὲ βούλοιντο, which has no meaning here. If βούλοιντο is to be preserved, we must, with Beveridge, insert the negation μὴ. But the reading βδελύσσοιντο has still in its favour that the fifty-second apostolic canon, just quoted, and which treats of the same question, has the expression βδελυσσόμενος in the same sense as our canon.

Let us add that κρατεῖν ἑαυτῶν ought to be taken in the sense of ἐγκρατεῖν, that is, to abstain.

CAN. 15

Περὶ τῶν διαφερόντων τῷ κυριακῷ, ὅσα ἐπισκόπου μὴ ὄντος πρεσβύτεροι ἐπώλησαν, ἀναβαλεῖσθαι (ἀνακαλεῖσθαι) τὸ κυριακὸν, ἐν δὲ τῇ κρίσει τοῦ ἐπισκόπου εἶναι, εἴπερ προσήκει ἀπολαβεῖν τὴν τιμὴν εὔτε καὶ μὴ, διὰ τὸ πολλάκις τὴν εἴσοδον (πρόσοδον) τῶν πεπραμένων ἀποδεδωκέναι αὐτοῖς τούτοις πλείονα τὴν τιμήν.

"If the priests, during the vacancy of an episcopal see, have sold anything belonging to the Church, she (the Church) has the right to reclaim it (ἀνακαλεῖσθαι); and it is for the bishop to decide whether they (the buyers) are to receive the price given for the purchase, seeing that often the temporary use of the article sold to them has been worth more than the price paid for it."

If the purchaser of ecclesiastical properties has realized more by the temporary revenue of such properties than the price of the purchase, the Synod thinks there is no occasion to restore him this price, as he has already received a sufficient indemnity from the revenue, and that, according to the rules then in force, interest drawn from the purchase money was not permitted. Besides, the purchaser hall done wrong in buying ecclesiastical property during the vacancy of a see (sede vacante). Beveridge and Routh have shown that in the text ἀνακαλεῖσθαι and πρόσοδον must be read.

CAN. 16

Περὶ τῶν ἀλογευσαμένων ἢ καὶ ἀλογευομένων, ὅσοι πρὶν εἰκοσαετεῖς γενέσθαι ἥμαρτον, πέντε καὶ δέκα ἔτεσιν ὑποπεσόντες κοινωνίας τυγχανέτωσαν τῆς εἰς τὰς προσευχάς, εἶτα ἐν τῇ κοινωνίᾳ διατελέσαντες ἔτη πέντε, τότε καὶ τῆς προδφορᾶς ἐφαπτέσθωσαν ἐξεταζέσθω δὲ αὐτῶν καὶ ὁ ἐν τῇ ὑποπτώσει βίος, καὶ οὕτως τυγχανέτωσαν τῆς φιλανθρωπίας εἰ δέ τινες κατακόρως ἐν τοῖς ἁμαρτήμασι γεγόνασι, τὴν μακρὰν ἐχέτωσαν ὑπόπτωσιν ὅσοι δὲ ὑπερβάντες τὴν ἡλικίαν ταύτην γυναῖκας ἔχοντες περιπεπτώκασι τῷ ἁμαρτήματι, πέντε καὶ εἴκοσι ἔτη ὑποπεσέτωσαν καὶ κοινωνίας τυγχανέτωσαν τῆς εἰς τὰς προσευχάς, εἶτα ἐκτελέσαντες πέντε ἔτη ἐν τῇ κοινωνίᾳ τῶν εὐχῶν τυγχανέτωσαν τῆς προσφορᾶς εἰ δέ τινες καὶ γυναῖκας ἔχοντες καὶ ὑπερβάντες τὸν πεντηκονταετῆ χρόνον ἥμαρτον, ἐπὶ τῇ ἐξόδῳ τοῦ βίου τυγχανέτωσαν τῆς κοινωίας.

"Those who have been or are. now guilty of lying with beasts, supposing they are not twenty years old when they commit this sin, ought to be substrati for five years; they should then be allowed to join in the prayers, without offering the sacrifice (and would consequently live in the fourth degree of penitence);

and after that time they might assist at the holy sacrifice. An examination must also be made of their conduct while they were substrati, and also notice taken of the lives they led. As for those who have sinned immoderately in this way (i.e. who have for a long time committed this sin), they must undergo a long substratio (no allowance will be made in their case). Those who are more than twenty, and have been married, and have nevertheless fallen into this sin, ought to be allowed to share in the prayers only after a substratio of twenty-five years; and after five years' sharing in the prayers, they should be allowed to assist at the holy sacrifice. If married men more than fifty years old fall into this sin, they shall receive the communion only at the end of their lives."

On the expressions substrati, participation in prayers and in the sacrifice, cf. the remarks above on canons 4 and 5.

CAN. 17

Τοὺς ἀλογευσαμένους καὶ λεπροὺς ὄντας ἤτοι λεπρώσαντας, τούτους προσέταξεν ἡ ἁγία σύνοδος εἰς τοὺς χειμαζομένους εὔχεσθαι.

It is not easy to give the real meaning of this canon. It may perhaps mean: "Those who have committed acts of bestiality, and, being lepers themselves, have now (ἤτοι) made others so, must pray among the χειμαζομένοις." Others translate it: "Those who have committed acts of bestiality, and are or have been lepers (λεπρώσαντας, i.e. having been leprous), shall pray among the χειμαζομένοις." This last translation seems to us inexact; for λεπρώσαντας does not come from λεπράω, but from λεπρόω, which has a transitive meaning, and signifies "to make leprous." But even if we adopt the former translation without hesitation, it is still asked if the leprosy of which the canon speaks is the malady known by that name, and which lepers could communicate to others especially by cohabitation; or if it means spiritual leprosy, sin, and especially the sin of bestiality, and its wider extension by bad example. Van Espen thinks that the canon unites the two ideas, and that it speaks of the real leprosy caused precisely by this bestial depravity. By the word χειμαζόμενοι some understand those possessed. This is the view of Beveridge and Routh. Others, particularly Suicer, think that the Council means by it penitents of the lowest degree, the flentes, who had no right to enter the church, but remained in the porch, in the open air, exposed to all inclemencies (χειμών), and who must ask those who entered the church to intercede for them.

As, however, the possessed also remained in the porch, the generic name of χειμαζόμενοι was given to all who were there, i.e. who could not enter the church. We may therefore accept Suicer's explanation, with whom agree Van Espen, Herbst, etc. Having settled this point, let us return to the explanation of λέπρα. It is clear that λεπρώσαντας cannot possibly mean "those who have been lepers;" for there is no reason to be seen why those who were cured of that malady should have to remain outside the church among the flentes. Secondly, it is clear that the words λεπροὺς ὄντας, etc., are added to give force to the expression ἀλογευσάμενοι. The preceding canon had decreed different penalties for different kinds of ἀλογευσάμενοι. But that pronounced by canon 17 being much severer than the preceding ones, the ἀλογευσάμενοι of this canon must be greater sinners than those of the former one. This greater guilt cannot consist in the fact of a literal leprosy; for this malady was not a consequence of bestiality. But their sin was evidently greater when they tempted others to commit it. It is therefore λέπρα in the figurative sense that we are to understand; and our canon thus means: "Those who were spiritually leprous through this sin, and tempting others to commit it made them leprous."

CAN. 18

Εἴ τινες ἐπίσκοποι κατασταθέντες καὶ μὴ δεχθέντες ὑπὸ τῆς παροικίας ἐκείνης, εἰς ἣν ὠνομάσθησαν, ἑτέραις βούλοιντο παροικίαις ἐπιέναι καὶ βιάξεσθαι τοὺς καθεστεῶτας καὶ στάσεις κινεῖν κατ' αὐτῶν, τούτους ἀφορίζεσθαι ἐὰν μέντοι βούλοιντο εἰς τὸ πρεσβυτέριον καθέξεσθαι, ἔνθα ἦσαν πρότερον πρεσβύτεροι, μὴ ἀποβάλλεσθαι αὐτοὺς τῆς τιμῆς· ἐὰν δὲ διαστασιάζωσι πρὸς τοὺς καθεστῶτας ἐκεῖ ἐπισκόπους, ἀφαιρεῖσθαι αὐτοὺς καὶ τὴν τιμὴν τοῦ πρεσβυτερίου καὶ γίνεσθα αὐτοὺς ἐκκηύκτους.

"If bishops, when elected, but not accepted by the parish for which they are nominated, introduce themselves into other parishes, and stir up strife against the bishops who are there instituted, they must be excommunicated. But if they (who are elected and not accepted) wish to live as priests in those places where they had hitherto served as priests, they need not lose that dignity. But if they stir up discord against the bishop of the place, they shall be deprived of their presbyterate, and be shut out from the Church."

As long as the people collectively had a share in the election of bishops, it often happened in the primitive Church that a bishop, regularly elected, was either expelled or rejected by a rising of the people. Even although, at the time of his election, the majority were in his favour, yet the minority often put a stop to it; just as we saw in 1848 and 1849, how a very small minority tyrannized over whole towns and countries, and even drove out persons who displeased them. The thirty-fifth apostolical canon (thirty-sixth or thirty-seventh according to other reckonings) and the eighteenth of Antioch

(A.D. 341) spoke also of such bishops driven from their dioceses.

When one of these bishops tried by violence or by treachery to drive a colleague from his see, and to seize upon it, he was to incur the penalty of ἀφορίζεσθαι. Van Espen understood by that, the deprivation of his episcopal dignity; but the ἀφορισμὸς of the ancient Church signified more than that: it signified excommunication, at least the minor excommunication, or exclusion from the communion of the Church.

But the canon adds, if a bishop not accepted by his Church does not make these criminal attempts, but will live modestly among the priests of his former congregation, he can do so, and "he shall not lose his dignity." Is it here a question of the title and dignity of a bishop, but without jurisdiction; or does the word τιμὴ signify here only the rank of a priest? Dionysius the Less (Exiguus) has taken it in the latter sense, and translated it, "If they will, as presbyters, continue in the order of the priesthood" (si voluerint in presbyterii ordine ut presbyteri residere). The Greek commentators Zonaras and others have taken it in the same sense. This canon was added to the Corp. jur. can. (c. 6, dist. 92).

CAN. 19

Ὅσοι παρθενίαν ἐπαγγελλόμενοι ἀθετοῦσι τὴν ἐπαγγελίαν, τὸν τῶν διγάμων ὅρον ἐκπληρούτωσαν. Τὰς μέντοι συνερχομένας παρθένους τισὶν ὡς ἀδελφὰς ἐκωλύσαμεν.

"All who have taken a vow of virginity, and have broken that vow, are to be considered as bigamists (literally, must submit to the decrees and prescriptions concerning bigamists). We also forbid virgins to live as sisters with men."

The first part of the canon regards all young persons—men as well as women—who have taken a vow of virginity, and who, having thus, so to speak, betrothed themselves to God, are guilty of a quasi bigamy in violating that promise. They must therefore incur the punishment of bigamy (successiva), which, according to S. Basil the Great, consisted in one year's seclusion. This canon, which Gratian adopted (c. 24, causa 27, quæst. 1), speaks only of the violation of the vow by a lawful marriage, whilst the thirteenth canon of Elvira speaks of those who break their vow by incontinence. In the second part the canon treats of the συνείσακτοι. On this point we refer to our remarks on the third canon of Nicæa, and on the twenty-seventh of Elvira.

CAN. 20

Ἐάν τινος γυνὴ μοιχευθῇ ἢ μοιχεύσῃ τις, ἐν ἑπτὰ ἔτεσι δοκεῖ (δεῖ) αὐτὸν τοῦ τελείου τυχεῖν κατὰ τοὺς βαθμοὺς τοὺς προάγοντας.

"If any one has violated a married woman, or has broken the marriage bond, he must for seven years undergo the different degrees of penance, at the end of which he will be admitted into the communion of the Church."

The simplest explanation of this canon is, "that the man or woman who has violated the marriage bond shall undergo a seven years' penance;" but many reject this explanation, because the text says αὐτὸν τύχειν, and consequently can refer only to the husband. Fleury and Routh think the canon speaks, as does the seventieth of Elvira, of a woman who has broken the marriage tie with the knowledge and consent of her husband. The husband would therefore in this case be punished for this permission, just as if he had himself committed adultery. Van Espen has given another explanation: "That he who marries a woman already divorced for adultery is as criminal as if he had himself committed adultery." But this explanation appears to us more forced than that already given; and we think that the Greek commentators Balsamon and Zonaras were right in giving the explanation we have offered first as the most natural. They think that the Synod punished every adulterer, whether man or woman, by a seven years penance. There is no reason for making a mistake because only the word αὐτὸν occurs in the passage in which the penalty is fixed; for αὐτὸν here means the guilty party, and applies equally to the woman and the man: besides, in the preceding canon the masculine ὅσοι ἐπαγγελόμενοι includes young men and young women also. It is probable that the Trullan Synod of 692, in forming its eighty-seventh canon, had in view the twentieth of Ancyra. The sixty-ninth canon of Elvira condemned to a lighter punishment—only five years of penance—him who had been only once guilty of adultery.

CAN. 21

Περὶ τῶν γυναικῶν τῶν ἐκπορνευουσῶν καὶ ἀναιρουσῶν τὰ γεννώμενα καὶ σπουδαζουσῶν φθόρια ποιεῖν ὁ μὲν πρότερος ὅρος μέχρις ἐξόδου ἐκώλυσεν, καὶ τούτῳ συντίθενται φιλανθρωπότερον δὲ τι εὑρόντες ὡρίσαμεν δεκαετῆ χρόνον κατὰ τοὺς βαθμοὺς τοὺς ὡρισμένους (adde πληρῶσαι).

"Women who prostitute themselves, and who kill the children thus begotten, or who try to destroy them when in their wombs, are by ancient law excommunicated to the end of their lives. We, however, have softened their punishment, and condemned them to the various appointed degrees of penance for ten years."

The sixty-third canon of Elvira had forbidden the communion to be administered to such women even on their death-beds; and this was the canon which the Synod of Ancyra had probably here in view. The expression καὶ τούτῳ συντίθενται is vague: τινὲς may be understood, and it might be translated, "and some approve of this severity;" or we might understand αἱ, and translate with Routh, "The same punishment will be inflicted on those who assist in causing miscarriages:" the words then mean, "and those who assist them." We think, however, the first explanation is the easier and the more natural. Gentianus Hervetus and Van Espen have adopted it, translating thus: et ei quidam assentientur.

CAN. 22

Περὶ ἑκουσίων φόνων, ὑποπιπτέτωσαν μὲν, τοῦ δὲ τελείου ἐν τῷ τέλει τοῦ βίου καταξιούσθωσαν.

"As to wilful murderers, they must be substrati, and not allowed to receive the communion as long as they live."

CAN. 23

Ἐπὶ ἀκουσίων φόνων, ὁ μὲν πρότερος ὅρος ἐν ἑπταετίᾳ κελεύει τοῦ τελείου μετασχεῖν κατὰ τοὺς ὡρισμένους βαθμούς· ὁ δὲ δεύτερος τὸν πενταετῆ χρόνον πληρῶσαι.

"As to unpremeditated murder, the earlier ordinance allowed communion (to the homicide) at the end of a seven years' penance; the second required only five years."

Of the first and second ordinances referred to in this canon nothing further is known; as to the terms ὅρος, τέλειον, and βαθμοὶ, see the canons of Ancyra already explained.

CAN. 24

Οἱ καταμαντευόμενοι καὶ ταῖς συνηθείαις τῶν χρόνων (ἐθνεῶν) ἐξακολουθοῦντες ἤ εἰσάγοντές τινας εἰς τοὺς ἑαυτῶν οἴκους ἐπὶ ἀνευρέσει φαρμακειῶν ἤ καὶ καθάρσει, ὑπὸ τὸν κανόνα πιπτέτωσαν τῆς πενταετίας κατὰ τοὺς βαθμοὺς ὡρισμένους, τρία ἔτη ὑποπτώσεως καὶ δύο ἔτη εὐχῆς χωρὶς προσφορᾶς.

"Those who foretell the future, and follow pagan customs, or admit into their houses people (magicians) in order to discover magical remedies, or to perform expiations, must be sentenced to a five years' penance, to three years of substratio, and to two years of attendance at prayers without the sacrifice (non-communicating attendance)."

We must refer to the explanations we have given under canon 4 on the different degrees of penance. It has long been known (as witnesses we have the old Greek commentators Balsamon and Zonaras, and the old Latin interpreters Dionysius the Less and Isidore, confirmed by Routh) that the correct reading is ἐθνῶν instead of χρονῶν. The canon threatens equally diviners and those who consult them and summon them to their houses to prepare magical remedies and perform expiations.

CAN. 25

Μνηστευσάμενός τις κόρην προσεφθάρη τῇ ἀδελφῇ αὐτῆς, ὡς καὶ ἐπιφορέσαι αὐτήν ἔγημε δὲ τὴν μνηστὴν μετὰ ταῦτα, ἡ δὲ φθαρεῖσα ἀπήγξατο οἱ συνειδότες ἐκελεύσθησαν ἐν δεκαετίᾳ δεχθῆναι εἰς τοὺς συνεστῶτας κατὰ τοὺς ὡρισμένος βαθμούς.

"A certain person who had betrothed himself to a girl, had connection with her sister, so that she became pregnant: he then married his betrothed, and his sister-in-law hanged herself. It was determined that all his accomplices should be admitted among the sistentes (i.e. to the fourth degree of penance), after passing through the appointed degrees for ten years."

The Council here decides, as we see, a particular case which was submitted to it; and it condemned not only the particular offender, but all the accomplices who had assisted him to commit the crime, who had advised him to leave her he had seduced, and to marry her sister, or the like. The punishment inflicted was very severe, for it was only at the end of ten years (passed in the three first degrees of penance) that the offenders were admitted to the fourth degree. It is not stated how long they were to remain in that degree before admission to the communion. The Greek verb προσφθείρομαι generally means, "to do anything to one's hurt:" joined to γυναικὶ or some other similar word, it has the meaning we have given it. We have rendered ἀπήγξατο by "hanged herself;" we ought, however, to note that ἀπάγχω signifies every kind of suicide.

SEC. 17. Synod of Neocæsarea (314–325)

According to the title which the ancient Greek MSS. give to the canons of the Synod of Neocæsarea in Cappadocia, this Synod was held a little later than that of Ancyra, but before that of Nicæa. The names of the bishops who assisted at it seem to furnish a second chronological support to this view. They are for the most part the same as those who are named at the Council of Ancyra, Vitalis of Antioch at their head (the Libellus Synodicus reckons twenty-four of them); but neither the Greek MSS. nor Dionysius the Less have these names. Tillemont and other writers have for this reason raised doubts as to the historical value of these lists, and the brothers Ballerini have not hesitated to disallow their authenticity. It remains, however, an incontestable fact, that the Synod of Neocæsarea took place at about the same time as that of Ancyra, after the death of Maximin the persecutor of the Christians (313), and before the Synod of Nicæa (325). Ordinarily the same date is assigned to it as to that of Ancyra, 314 or 315; but to me it seems more probable that it took place several years later, because there is no longer any question about the lapsed. The Synod of Ancyra had devoted no fewer than ten canons (1–9 and 12) to this subject, as a persecution had then just ceased; the Synod of Neocæsarea did not touch on these matters, probably because at the time when it assembled the lapsed had already received their sentence, and there were no more measures necessary to be taken on that subject. The Libellus Synodicus, it is true, states that the Synod of (Neo) Cæsarea occupied itself with those who had sacrificed to the gods or abjured their religion, or had eaten of sacrifices offered to idols, and during the persecution; but the canons of the Council say not a word of them. It is probable that the late and very inaccurate Libellus Synodicus confounded, on this point, the Synod of Neocæsarea with that of Ancyra. It has, without any grounds, been alleged that the canons of Neocæsarea which spoke of the lapsi have been destroyed.

CAN. 1

Πρεσβύτερος ἐὰν γήμῃ, τῆς τάξεως αὐτὸν μετατίθεσθαι, ἐὰν δέ πορνεύσῃ ἤ μοιχεύσῃ, ἐξωθεῖσθαι αὐτὸν τέλεον καὶ ἄγεσθαι αὐτὸν εἰς μετάνοιαν.

"If a priest marry, he shall be removed from the ranks of the clergy; if he commit fornication or adultery, he shall be excommunicated, and shall submit to penance."

The meaning is as follows: "If a priest marry after ordination, he shall be deposed from his priestly order, and reduced to the communio laicalis; if he is guilty of fornication or adultery, he must be excommunicated, and must pass through all the degrees of penance in order to regain communion with the Church." We have seen above, in canon 10 of Ancyra, that in one case deacons were allowed to marry after ordination,—namely, when they had announced their intention of doing so at the time of their election. In the case of priests neither the Council of Ancyra nor that of Neocæsarea made any exception. This first canon has been inserted in the Corp. jur. can.

CAN. 2

Γυνὴ ἐὰν γήμηται δύο ἀδελφοῖς, ἐξωθείσθω μέχρι θανάτου, πλὴν ἐν τῷ θανάτῳ, διὰ τὴν φιλανθρεπίαν, εἰποῦσα ὡς ὑλιάνασα λύσει τὸν γάμον, ἕξει τὴν μετάνοιαν· ἐὰν δὲ τελευτήσῃ ἡ γυνὴ ἐν τοιούτῳ γάμῳ οὖσα ἤτοι ὁ ἀνήρ, δυσχερὴς τῷ μείναντι ἡ μετάνοια.

"If a woman has married two brothers, she shall be excommunicated till her death; if she is in danger of death, and promises in case of recovery to break off this illegitimate union, she may, as an act of mercy, be admitted to penance. If the woman or husband die in this union, the penance for the survivor will be very strict."

This is a question of marriage of the first degree of affinity, which is still forbidden by the present law. The canon punishes such marriages with absolute excommunication; so that he who had entered into such should not obtain communion even in articulo mortis, unless he promised in case of recovery to break this union. This promise being given, he can be admitted to penance (ἕξει τὴν μετάνοιαν). Zonaras thus correctly explains these words: "In this case he shall receive the holy communion in articulo mortis, provided he promises that, if he recovers, he will submit to penance." Canon 6 of Ancyra was explained in the same way.

CAN. 3

Περὶ τῶν πλείστοις γάμοις περιπιπτόντων ὁ μὲν χρόνος σαφής ὁ ὡρισμένος, ἡ δέ ἀναστροφὴ καὶ ἡ πίστις αὐτῶν συντέμνει τὸν χρόνον.

"As for those who have been often married, the duration of their penance is well known; but their good conduct and faith may shorten that period."

As the Greek commentators have remarked, this canon speaks of those who have been married more than twice. It is not known what were the ancient ordinances of penitence which the Synod here refers to. In later times, bigamists were condemned to one year's penance, and trigamists from two to five years. S. Basil places the trigamists for three years among the audientes, then for some time among the consistentes. Gratian has inserted this third canon of Neocæsarea in the c. 8, causa 31, quæst. 1, in connection with canon 7 of the same Synod.

CAN. 4

Ἐὰν πρόθηταί τις ἐπιθυμῆσαι (ἐπιθυμήσας) γυναικὸς συγκαθευδῆσαι μετ' αὐτῆς (αὐτῇ), μή ἔλθη δὲ εἰς ἔργον αὐτοῦ ἡ ἐνθύμησις, φαίνεται ὅτι ὑπὸ τῆς χάριτος ἐρρύσθη.

"If a man who burns with love for a woman proposes to live with her, but does not perform his intention, it is to be believed that he was restrained by grace."

Instead of ἐπιθυμῆσαι we must read, with Beveridge and Routh, who rely upon several MSS., ἐπιθυμήσας. They also replace μετ' αὐτῆς by αὐτῇ. The meaning of this canon is, that "he who has sinned only in thought must not undergo a public penance."

CAN. 5

Κατηχούμενος, ἐὰν εἰσερχόμενος εἰς (τὸ) κυριακὸν
ἐν τῇ τῶν κατηχουμένων τάξει στήκη, οὗτος δὲ
(φανῇ) ἁμαρτάνων, ἐὰν μὲν γόνυ κλίνων, ἀκροάσθω
μηκέτι ἁμαρτάνων• Ἐὰν δὲ καὶ ἀκροώμενος ἔτι
ἁμαρτάνῃ, ἐξωθείσθε.

"If a catechumen, after being introduced into the
Church, and admitted into the ranks of the
catechumens, acts as a sinner, he must, if he is
genuflectens (i.e. to say, in the second degree of
penance), become audiens (the lowest degree),
until he sins no more. If, after being audiens, he
continues to sin, he shall be entirely excluded from
the Church."

Routh, on good critical grounds, recommends the
introduction into the text of τὸ and φανῇ. The form
στήκη and the verb στήκω, to stand up, do not occur
in classical Greek, but are often found in the New
Testament, e.g. in S. Mark 11:25, and are formed
from the regular perfect ἕστηκα. Hardouin thinks the
canon has in view the carnal sins of catechumens;
and ἁμάρτημα has elsewhere this meaning, e.g. in
canons 2, 9, and 14 of Nicæa.

CAN. 6

Περὶ κυοφορούσης, ὅτι δεῖ φωτίζεσθαι ὁπότε
βούλεται• οὐδὲν γὰρ ἐν τούτῳ κοινωνεῖ ἡ τίκτουσα

τῷ τικτομένῳ, διὰ τὸ ἑκάστου ἰδίαν τὴν προαίρεσιν τὴν ἐπὶ τῇ ὁμολογίᾳ δείκνυσθαι.

"A woman with child may be illuminated (i.e. to say, baptized) whenever she demands it; for she who bears has nothing on this account in common with him who is borne, since each party must profess his own willingness (to be baptized) by his confession of faith."

Some thought that when a woman with child is baptized, the grace of the sacrament is given to the fruit of her womb, and so to baptize this child again after its birth is in a manner to administer a second baptism; and they conclude that they ought not to baptize a pregnant woman, but that they must wait till her delivery.

CAN. 7

Πρεσβύτερον εἰς γάμους διγαμούντων (διγαμοῦντος) μὴ ἑστιᾶσθαι, ἐπεὶ μετάνοιαν αἰτοῦντος τοῦ διγάμου, τίς ἔσται ὁ πρεσβύτερος, ὁ διὰ τῆς ἑστιάσεως συγκατατιθέμενος τοῖς γάμοις;

"No priest shall eat at the marriage feast of those who are married for the second time; for if such a bigamist should (afterwards) ask leave to do penance, how stands the priest who, by his presence at the feast, had given his approval to the marriage?"

We have already seen by canon 3, that in the East that successive bigamy (bigamia successiva) which is here in question, as Beveridge thinks, and not bigamy properly so called, was punished in the East by a year's penance. The meaning of the canon is as follows: "If the bigamist, after contracting his second marriage, comes to the priest to be told the punishment he has to undergo, how stands the priest himself, who for the sake of the feast has become his accomplice in the offence?"

CAN. 8

Γυνή τινος μοιχευθεῖσα λαϊκοῦ ὄντος, ἐὰν ἐλεγχθῇ φανερῶς, ὁ τοιοῦτος εἰς ὑπηρεσίαν ἐλθεῖν οὐ δύναται· ἐὰν δέ καὶ μετὰ τὴν χειροτονίαν μοιχευθῇ, ὀφείλει ἀπολῦσαι αὐτήν· ἐὰν δέ συζῇ, οὐ δέναται ἔχεσθαι τῆς ἐγχειρισθείσης αὐτῷ ὑπηρεσίας.

"If the wife of a layman has been unfaithful to her husband, and she is convicted of the sin, her (innocent) husband cannot be admitted to the service of the Church; but if she has violated the law of marriage after her husband's ordination, he must leave her. If, in spite of this, he continues to live with her, he must resign the sacred functions which have been entrusted to him."

The Corp. jur. can. has adopted this canon. The reason for this ordinance evidently consists in this, that through the close connection between a man

342

and his wife, a husband is dishonoured by an adulterous wife, and a dishonoured man cannot become an ecclesiastic. The Pastor of Hermas had already shown that a husband must leave his adulterous wife.

CAN. 9

Πρεσβύτερος, ἐὰν προημαρτηκώς σώματι προαχθῇ καὶ ὁμολογήσῃ ὅτι ἥμαρτε πρὸ τῆς χειροτονίας, μὴ προσφερέτω, μένων ἐν τοῖς λοιποῖς διά τὴν ἄλλην σπουδήν• τὰ γὰρ λοιπὰ ἁμαρτήματα 'φασαν οἱ πολλοὶ καὶ τὴν χειροθεσίαν ἀφιέναι• ἐὰν δὲ αὐτὸς μὴ ὁμολογῇ, ἐλεγχθῆναι δέ φανερῶς μὴ δυνηθῇ, ἐπ' αὐτῷ ἐκείνῳ ποιεῖσθαι τὴν ἐξουσίαν.

"A priest who has committed a carnal sin before being ordained, and who of his own accord confesses that he has sinned before ordination, must not offer the holy sacrifice; but he may continue his other functions if he is zealous, for many think that other sins (except that of incontinence) were blotted out by his ordination as priest. But if he does not confess it, and he cannot clearly be convicted, it shall be in his own power to act (as he will, i.e. to offer the sacrifice, or to refrain from offering)."

Cf. can. 22 of the Council in Trullo, and can. 1, causa 15, quæst. 8, in the Corp. jur. can.

CAN. 10

Ὁμοίως καὶ διάκονος, ἐὰν ἐν τῷ αὐτῷ ἁμαρτήματι περιπέσῃ, τὴν τοῦ ὑπηρέτου τάξιν ἐχέτω.

"In the same way, the deacon who has committed the same sin must only have the office of an inferior minister."

The preposition ἐν before τῷ αὐτῷ is struck out by Routh, on the authority of several MSS. By ministri (ὑπήρεται) are meant the inferior officers of the Church—the so-called minor orders, often including the sub-deacons. This canon, completely distorted by false translations (of the Prisca and Isidore), was made into one canon with the preceding in the Corp. jur. can.

CAN. 11

Πρεσβύτερος πρὸ τῶν τριάκοντα ἐτῶν μὴ χειροτονείσθω, ἐὰν καὶ πάνυ ᾖ ὁ ἄνθρωπος ἄξιος, ἀλλὰ ἀποτηρείσθω· ὁ γὰρ Κύριος Ἰησοῦς Χριστὸς ἐν τῷ τρισκοστῷ ἔτει ἐφωτίσθη καὶ ἤρξατο διδάσκειν.

"No one is to be ordained priest before he is thirty years old. Even although he be in every respect worthy, he must wait; for our Lord Jesus Christ, when thirty years old, was baptized, and began (at that age) to teach."

We know that, in the primitive Church, φωτίζεσθαι, to be illuminated, means to be baptized. We find this canon in the Corp. jur. can.

CAN. 12

Ἐὰν νοσῶν τις φωτισθῇ, εἰς πρεσβύτερον ἄγεσθαι οὐ δύναται,—οὐκ ἐκ προαιρέσεως γάρ ἡ πίδτις αὐτοῦ, ἀλλ' ἐξ ἀνάγκης,—εἰ μὴ τάχα διὰ τὴν μετὰ ταῦτα αὐτοῦ σπουδὴν καὶ πίστιν καὶ διὰ σπάνιν ἀνθρώπων.

"If a man is baptized when he is ill, he cannot be ordained priest; for it was not spontaneously, but of necessity (through fear of death), that he made profession of the faith—unless, perhaps, he has displayed great zeal and faith, or if the supply of candidates fails."

All commentators, except Aubespine, say that this canon, which was received into the Corp. jur. can., speaks of those who, by their own fault, have deferred the reception of baptism till their deathbed. Aubespine thinks that it refers to catechumens who have not received baptism earlier through no fault of their own, but who, finding themselves smitten by a severe sickness, are baptized before the usual time, i.e. before receiving all the necessary instruction. It was, he added, on account of this want of instruction that they were forbidden to enter the priesthood if they regained their health. But the forty-seventh canon of Laodicea tells us that in the primitive Church it was the duty of such catechumens to receive instruction even after baptism, and this alone overthrows Aubespine's conjecture.

CAN. 13

Ἐπιχώριοι πρεσβύτεροι ἐν τῷ κυριακῷ τῆς πόλεως προσφέρειν οὐ δύνανται παρόντος ἐπισκόπου ἢ πρεσβυτέρων πόλεως, οὔτε μὴν ἄρτον διδόναι ἐν εὐχῇ οὐδὲ ποτήριον· ἐὰν δέ ἀπῶσι καὶ εἰς εὐχὴν κληθῇ μόνος, δίδωσιν.

"Country priests must not offer the holy sacrifice in the town church (the cathedral) when the bishop or the town priests are present: they must not do more than distribute, with prayer, the bread and the chalice. But if the bishop and his priests are absent, and if the country priest be invited to celebrate, he may administer holy communion."

Instead of κληθῇ μόνος, the old Latin translators of the canons, Dionysius the Less and Isidore, read κληθῶσι, μόνοι; that is to say, "If they are asked, then only can they administer the Lord's Supper;" and Routh recommends this reading. This canon is contained in the Corp. jur. can.

CAN. 14

346

Οἱ δέ χωρεπίσκοποι εἰσὶ μέν εἰς τύπον τῶν ἑβδομήκοντα· ὡς δὲ συλλειτουργοὶ διὰ τὴν σπουδὴν (τὴν) εἰς τοὺς πτωχοὺς προσφέρουσι τιμώμενοι.

"The chorepiscopi represent the seventy disciples of Christ as fellow-workers; and on account of their zeal for the poor, they have the honour of offering the sacrifice."

A function is here assigned to the chorepiscopi which is denied to country priests, namely, the offering of the holy sacrifice in the cathedral, in the presence of the bishop and the town priests. On the chorepiscopi, compare c. 13 of Ancyra, and our remarks below on canon 57 of Laodicea. Many MSS. and editions have canons 13 and 14 in one.

CAN. 15

Διάκονοι ἑπτὰ ὀφείλουσιν εἶναι κατὰ τὸν κανόνα, κἄν πάνυ μεγάλη ἔη ἡ πόλις· πεισθήσῃ δέ ἀπὸ τῆς βίβλου τῶν Πράξεων.

"In even the largest towns there must be, as a rule, no more than seven deacons. This may be proved from the Acts of the Apostles."

This canon was given in the Corp. jur. can.

348